Biolaw, Economics and Sustainable Governance

This book offers an accurate and updated approach to the main contributions of cosmopolitan biolaw in relation to sustainability, global governance, organizational health care economics and COVID-19.

Bringing together different robust and dense biojuridical epistemologies to analyze key bioethical problems as well as the health care, management, economics and sustainability issues of our time, it constitutes a paradigmatic text in its field. In addition to exploring different epistemologies and jurisdictional scopes of biolaw, including the relationships between this new field and the challenges that have arisen in the current globalized and technologized world, the book addresses controversial issues straight from today's headlines: For example, the basics for health care, finance and organizational economics, global biojuridical principles for governance, globalization, bioscientific empowerment, global and existential risk and sustainability challenges for a post-pandemic world.

The book encourages readers to think impartially in order to know and understand the bioethical and biojuridical dilemmas that stem from current economics and sustainability issues. Accordingly, it will be a valuable resource for courses in the fields of biolaw, law, bioethics, global sustainability, organizational health care economics and global governance at different professional levels.

Erick Valdés is the president and founding member of The International Network of Biolaw.

Jacob Dahl Rendtorff is professor at Roskilde University, Denmark.

Finance, Governance and Sustainability: Challenges to Theory and Practice Series

Series Editor: Professor Güler Aras
Yildiz Technical University, Turkey;
Georgetown University, Washington DC, USA

Focusing on the studies of academicians, researchers, entrepreneurs, policy makers and government officers, this international series aims to contribute to the progress in matters of finance, good governance and sustainability. These multidisciplinary books combine strong conceptual analysis with a wide range of empirical data and a wealth of case materials. They will be of interest to those working in a multitude of fields, across finance, governance, corporate behavior, regulations, ethics and sustainability.

Stakeholder Engagement and Sustainability Reporting
Marco Bellucci and Giacomo Manetti

Management Scholarship and Organisational Change
Representing Burns and Stalker
Miriam Green

Ethics, Misconduct and the Financial Services Industry
Towards a Theory of Moral Business
Barbara Fryzel

Foundations of a Sustainable Economy
Moral, Ethical and Religious Perspectives
Edited by Umar Burki, Toseef Azid and Robert Francis Dahlstrom

Biolaw, Economics and Sustainable Governance
Addressing the Challenges of a Post-Pandemic World
Erick Valdés and Jacob Dahl Rendtorff

For more information about this series, please visit www.routledge.com/Finance-Governance-and-Sustainability/book-series/FINGOVSUST

Biolaw, Economics and Sustainable Governance

Addressing the Challenges of a Post-Pandemic World

Erick Valdés and Jacob Dahl Rendtorff

Routledge
Taylor & Francis Group
LONDON AND NEW YORK

First published 2022
by Routledge
2 Park Square, Milton Park, Abingdon, Oxon OX14 4RN

and by Routledge
605 Third Avenue, New York, NY 10158

Routledge is an imprint of the Taylor & Francis Group, an informa business

British Library Cataloguing-in-Publication Data
A catalogue record for this book is available from the British Library

Library of Congress Cataloguing-in-Publication Data
Names: Valdés, Erick, author. | Dahl Rendtorff, Jacob, author.
Title: Biolaw, economics and sustainable governance: addressing the challenges of a post-pandemic world / Erick Valdés and Jacob Dahl Rendtorff.
Description: Abingdon, Oxon; New York, NY: Routledge, 2022 | Series: Finance, governance and sustainability: challenges to theory and practice | Includes bibliographical references and index.
Identifiers: LCCN 2021023710 (print) | LCCN 2021023711 (ebook) | ISBN 9780367707576 (hbk) | ISBN 9780367707590 (pbk) | ISBN 9781003147848 (ebk)
Subjects: LCSH: Sustainability--Government policy. | Sustainable development--Government policy. | Finance--Government policy. | COVID-19 (Disease)
Classification: LCC HC79.E5 V243 2022 (print) | LCC HC79.E5 (ebook) | DDC 338.9/27--dc23
LC record available at https://lccn.loc.gov/2021023710
LC ebook record available at https://lccn.loc.gov/2021023711

ISBN: 978-0-367-70757-6 (hbk)
ISBN: 978-0-367-70759-0 (pbk)
ISBN: 978-1-003-14784-8 (ebk)

DOI: 10.4324/9781003147848

Typeset in Bembo
by MPS Limited, Dehradun

We dedicate this book to the many active, devoted and bright participants of the International Network of Biolaw, established in 2015, without whom this project of developing cosmopolitan biolaw would never have been possible.

Contents

Notes on Authors ix
Preface x
Acknowledgments xvi

Introduction: Biolaw, economics and sustainability in pandemic times 1

PART I
History, scopes and epistemologies of biolaw 11

1 From bioethics to biolaw 13

2 Biolaw in different parts of the world 26

3 Biolaw and society 44

PART II
The philosophy of biolaw 59

4 Philosophical foundations of ethics of biolaw 61

5 The legal history of biolaw 77

6 Toward Homo sapiens 2.0: Bioethical challenges to biolaw in the twenty-first century 95

PART III
Biolaw, organizational economics and health care 117

7 Corporate governance, social responsibility and stakeholder management 119

8 Health care organization ethics and ethical values in hospital management 145

PART IV
Biolaw, governance and sustainability 167

9 Universal principles for governance in an ever-changing world 169

10 Global sustainability and cosmopolitan biolaw 196

Conclusions: Toward a cosmopolitan biolaw in post-pandemic times 214

References 221

Index 233

Notes on Authors

Erick Valdés, Ph.D., is the president and founding member of The International Network of Biolaw. He has been Visiting Research Scholar at Princeton University, United States; Adjunct Research Scholar at the Kennedy Institute of Ethics at Georgetown University, United States; and Adjunct Professor of Bioethics and Theories of Democracy at American University and George Mason University, United States. Currently, Valdés' main research interests include biolaw, bioethics, public policy, sustainability and existential risks. He has written and published internationally on issues of biolaw, bioethics, policy and globalization (ORCID: 0000-0002-7320-9265).

Jacob Dahl Rendtorff, Ph.D. and Dr. Scient. Adm., is professor at Roskilde University, Denmark. Rendtorff has written and edited on issues of existentialism and hermeneutics, French philosophy, ethics, bioethics and biolaw, business ethics and philosophy of management as well as philosophy of law. Rendtorff is a founding member of The International Network of Biolaw and member of the Steering Committee of FISP (International Federation of Philosophical Societies). Rendtorff is editor of the Springer Series Ethical Economy. Presently, Rendtorff's main research interests include bioethics and biolaw, sustainability, social responsibility and cosmopolitan business ethics (ORCID: 0000-0001-9021-4720).

Preface

There is no good book without a long history of debate, publication and network of people who have contributed to it. Indeed, the development of a cosmopolitan biolaw for governance, finance and sustainability is based on many years of research and discussions. It began with the work of Jacob together with Peter Kemp on bioethics and biolaw at the Center for Ethics and Law in Nature and Society, Copenhagen, Denmark, which was established in 1993. The aim of the Center for Ethics and Law was to initiate cooperation and research on ethics and law in particular, with focus on bioethics and biolaw, societal ethics and social law and environmental ethics and environmental law. The initial research aim of the Center was to do research on the specification and clarification of fundamental bioethical principles, particularly in relation to law. The focus was on two different levels: On the empirical and social level, information was collected on legislation and legal practice involving bioethics; and on the theoretical and philosophical level, the goal was to clarify fundamental questions concerning bioethics and biolaw, including biorights and their relationships. The objectives of the Center's research in relation to biolaw involved analysis of the connections among ethical conceptions, juridical practices and legislative procedures; documentation and enlargement of knowledge relating to basic concepts of ethics and law employed in the scientific and public debate concerning health care, medical treatment, social welfare, the environment, agriculture and genetic information; understanding the roles played by gender, religion and philosophical traditions in bioethics and biolaw; clarification and restructuring of basic concepts of bioethics and biolaw, social ethics and social law; environmental ethics and environmental law; and developing a formulation competency in ethics in order to validate and elevate public debate.

During the first years of the Center, Peter Kemp and Jacob formulated the European Biomed-II research project on Basic Ethical Principles in European Bioethics and Biolaw (1995–1998) with 22 research groups in more than 14 countries from institutions in different European countries. The project was supported by the European Commission. The aim of the project was to analyze and discuss the ongoing European discussion of the basic ethical principles of autonomy, dignity, integrity and vulnerability in ethics and law in Europe, with focus on examination of the similarities and differences between European nations in bioethics and biolaw. As a result of this research project, researchers formulated in 1998 the Barcelona Declaration, which was a list of policy proposal, based on the three-year research program on bioethics and biolaw. Moreover, Jacob and Peter Kemp published the book *Basic Ethical Principles in European Bioethics and Biolaw* I-II (Copenhagen and Barcelona 2000), where the first volume presented the basic ethical principles in bioethics and biolaw and the second volume presented the partners' research in relation to the research project on the basic ethical principles in Europe. The book provided a general analysis of autonomy, dignity, integrity and vulnerability in bioethics and biolaw, as well as it demonstrated the conceptions of the principles in different philosophical and ethical traditions in different countries, based on input from the different research groups in the different European countries. The methodology of the research was based on critical hermeneutics where principles were related to the empirical reality of bioethics and biolaw. The report was an interpretation of the basic ethical principles in relation to the European ethical and legal traditions. The core of the ethical principles in bioethics and biolaw was the protection of the human person and the human body in relation to the progress of biomedicine and biotechnology. In particular, the importance of the basic ethical principles was considered in relation to the human body between person and thing so that human dimension of the human body was protected in the different fields of biomedicine. Thus, after presenting the principles of autonomy, dignity, integrity and vulnerability, the role and function of the principles in the different subfields of biomedicine were analyzed.

In the decades following the publication of *Basic Ethical Principles in European Bioethics and Biolaw I-II*, there was widespread debate in Europe about the role and function of basic ethical principles in bioethics and biolaw. Indeed, during the 1990s and 2000s, there was a strong conceptual debate about the foundations of bioethics and biolaw in Europe. Moreover, Jacob developed the basic concepts of bioethics and biolaw as a general framework for sustainability, governance and corporate social responsibility in private business and public administration. The idea was that the four ethical principles of autonomy, dignity, integrity and vulnerability have important significance as guiding principles of governance and business ethics. Although the principles were proposed for bioethics and biolaw, the research agenda was now to develop them as principles for organizational governance not only in the health care sector but more generally in different surroundings and industries in society. The basic structure of this research was to show that bioethics and biolaw are important ideas that do not only apply at the individual level but also get their basic significance at the organizational level. In this way, it was argued that the ideas of autonomy, dignity, integrity and vulnerability are very important ethical notions in order to propose an ethical framework for the ethics and law of governance, management and social responsibility of organizations. This research culminated with Jacob's book *Cosmopolitan Business Ethics: Towards a Global Ethos of Management* from 2017.

About 2009, Erick started to work at Georgetown University, first at the Pellegrino Center for Clinical Bioethics and later at the Kennedy Institute of

Ethics, on the possibility of juridifying bioethics. This endeavor led him to get involved in biolaw to analyze its relationships to bioethics and discriminate both fields' epistemological scopes. Later on, he began to address the origins of biolaw, placing its birth on theoretical and procedural expansions of American bioethics and showing how this field influenced European law's jurisprudence and instruments. His efforts have been very useful for further deepening of the field. He also analyzed historical events that caused the emergence of American bioethics as well as connected important international texts that identified principles to govern biomedical research with human subjects and the seminal book *Principles of Biomedical Ethics*, which indirectly influenced European bioethics and biolaw. Erick's work implied to recognize different biolaw epistemologies emerged along the time, by showing that those theories understood biolaw from bioethics, by fostering different kinds of wrong relationships called juridification, complementation, subjection, overlap, substitution, colonization and intersection. Through these significant distinctions, Erick reformulated and juridified European biolaw's principles, the development that we use in this book to configure our conception of cosmopolitan biolaw. His investigation succeeded in configuring a new conception of biolaw as a new legal epistemology, a new deliberative model for legal science and a new hermeneutical approach in line with current demands and interpellations of biomedical sciences, insofar as biolaw also is understood now as a new branch of law that enhances traditional law.

Furthermore, Erick's work implied to reach very relevant conclusions for the development of biolaw. He was able to prove that biolaw represents a comprehensive and nonfragmented approach to legal conflicts arising from bioscientific surroundings as it does not offer deliberative phases, separated from each other. In this way, biolaw does not address legal problems from fossilized legal theories or from existing norms of traditional law, but it creates original normative universes able to peruse unprecedented legal problems that new bioscientific practices imply. Also, biolaw has an extrinsic normative content (along with its intrinsic one), which perfects other branches of law, recategorizing institutions of traditional law. Erick also could demonstrate that the strength of the biojuridical perspective compared with the traditional one relies on the capacity of biolaw to provide more certainty and legal security for governance and oversight of biomedicine, by contributing to the categorical expansion of other branches of law, as well as building impartial criteria to analyze legal conflicts provoked by new applications of biosciences.

At the same time of this opening up of a new conception of biolaw toward governance and organization, there was also an increasing global focus in order to develop biolaw's cosmopolitan and international dimension. This debate was related to the global deliberation on global bioethics and biolaw with the different declarations, conventions and policies from the United Nations, including the problems of global governance, sustainability and legal regulations. Thus, with the foundation of The International Network of Biolaw in Santiago, Chile, as an international academic organization focused on epistemological and philosophical aspects of biolaw, the debate about this new field and its relationships to bioethics found a global and universal basis for discussion. The International Network of Biolaw includes participation of world-renowned scholars and specialists on biolaw and bioethics from the United States, United Kingdom, France, Australia, Denmark, New Zealand, Spain, Belgium, Italy, Greece, Mexico, Colombia, Argentina, Uruguay and Chile. Indeed, the initiative for the establishment of the Network was led by Erick whose presidency was agreed by unanimity in the framework of the First International Seminar of Biolaw, which was held at Universidad del Desarrollo, in Santiago, Chile, on 12 and 13 March 2015. Since then, The International Network of Biolaw has met annually in countries like Chile, Colombia, Mexico, Argentina and Spain.

The aim of The International Network of Biolaw is to establish and maintain effective channels of communication in relation to research on practice on biolaw in the world, in order to promote and deepen the epistemological and methodological study and development of the field, promoting congresses, the creation of new journals, strategic academic plans, academic exchange, cooperation agreements and the projection and extension of important international activities as Global Seminars, which have counted on the participation of world-renowned keynote speakers. The framework for the understanding of biolaw promoted by the Network is that, in the absence of a general, regulatory and binding legal framework, this new field represents an attempt to provide the basis for sustainable governance of legislation on biomedical practices and genetic techniques, and thus, it promotes its consequent application in doctrinal and jurisprudential terms. Especially because biolaw represents an interdisciplinary and transdisciplinary epistemological field, it addresses legally controversial aspects of biomedical practices that impact not only the scientific field but also ethical, legal, social and political settings. Therefore, as formulated in the mission statement of the Network, biolaw represents a valid theoretical and procedural framework to deliberate about the legal viability of the scope of biomedicine and biotechnology, as well as to regulate those biotechnological techniques that go beyond therapy and, as such, display a reductionist and deterministic understanding of the human being: On the one hand, they reduce it to a set of genetic codes that must be deciphered and enhanced; on the other, they seek to predetermine human biology, modifying its genetic makeup. As a matter of fact, the legally controversial issues of biomedicine continue to be approached from the too general perspective of traditional law, ignoring the specificity of genetic techniques and their eventual consequences. In this sense, the absolute novelty of the problems raised by biotechnological development requires, by force of its own implications, specificity and originality in the analysis, namely, a biolaw applied to legal disputes arising by virtue of biomedical empowerment. In this way, the Network has been an epistemological platform to transmit and project the main theoretical and practical facets of biolaw at an international level.

This book can be considered to be built of these different research traditions following the work on the relation among ethics and law, basic ethical principles in European bioethics and biolaw, developing basic ethical principles for business ethics, corporate social responsibility, sustainability, governance and philosophy, configuring biolaw as an epistemologically independent field and establishing The International Network of Biolaw to formulate a cosmopolitan approach to biolaw. We consider the book as a contribution to the ongoing international discussion in the fields of sustainability and governance as biolaw enters as central topic on the scene of global organization and decision-making. As a contribution to the topics of finance, governance and sustainability, the book seeks to integrate the discussions of bioethics and biolaw with the debates of organizational governance and management. The idea is that policy makers and government officers, organizational employees, entrepreneurs and other decision-makers, as well as academics and researchers need a comprehensive understanding of biolaw in order to really access the implication of sustainability for governance. Indeed, this has been highlighted by the contemporary challenges of COVID-19 pandemic for governance and sustainability in the global context. Thus, the book combines reflections on bioethics and biolaw with an analysis of problems of finance, economics, governance and sustainability. We have focused on biolaw, but we provide an outlook to finance, governance and sustainability in order to demonstrate the importance of this field at all levels of global institutions.

This is the background for our definition of biolaw and its different epistemologies with the international and cosmopolitan focus in the first part of the book. Moreover, the second part presenting the philosophical foundation for the ethics of biolaw gives the necessary understanding of the ethics and political philosophy of biolaw as an important foundation for reflected judgment and decision-making in different organizational contexts with regard to sustainability and sustainable development. In the same perspective, our legal history of biolaw's conception of the body can help to understand the challenges of sustainability in the twenty-first century. New biomedical and biotechnological developments can imply huge challenges to global sustainable development. In the third section of the book, we make the explicit link between corporate governance social responsibility and stakeholder management with topics of finance sustainability and governance in business and business organizations. Indeed, with the discussion of ethics committees, organization ethics and hospital management, the book contributes to situate discussions of governance and sustainability within the practical organization of hospitals and health care organizations and institutions. Finally, in the fourth part, we propose universal principles of biolaw as cosmopolitan standards for governance in an ever-changing world. Here we can see how the ideas of social responsibility and solidarity become universal and cosmopolitan principles that function as a biojuridical framework for global governance, economy and sustainability.

Accordingly, the universal principles that we propose in this book provide important ethical and legal limitations of globalization of economic markets and contribution to ensure global equality and combat global poverty. In this sense, those principles are proposed as guidelines and instruments of cosmopolitan biolaw for global governance. This is indeed an important framework for global environmental protection in times of the Anthropocene and COVID-19. Moreover, the principles are important ethical and legal conditions for the United Nations' Sustainable Development Goals (SDGs). Therefore, in times of COVID-19 and in the movement toward a post-pandemic world, it is essential to establish universal principles as solid foundations for a cosmopolitan biolaw understood as the basis for finance, governance and sustainability.

E.V.
J.D.R.
April 2021

Acknowledgments

This book is a result of many years of research on basic ethical principles in bioethics and biolaw as well as on the epistemology of biolaw. The founding work on the concepts at the Center for Ethics and Law in Nature and Society from 1993 by Peter Kemp and his colleagues provided the initial definition of European bioethics and biolaw, founded on the basic ethical principles of autonomy, dignity, integrity and vulnerability in the framework of responsibility and solidarity. Later, the European Biomed-II research project with 22 research groups in 14 countries about "Basic Ethical Principles in European Bioethics and Biolaw" provided with the Barcelona Declaration from 1998, the first international formulation of basic ethical principles in European bioethics and biolaw. With his work on cosmopolitanism at the Danish University of Education, Peter Kemp consolidated the international dimension of European bioethics and biolaw. The research groups from the Department of Social Sciences and Business at Roskilde University contributed from 1999 to help Jacob apply the basic ethical principles of bioethics and biolaw to finance, governance and sustainability, as the basic ethical principles were formulated as essential for business ethics and corporate social responsibility. With the establishment of The International Network of Biolaw at the First International Seminar on Biolaw held at the Universidad del Desarrollo, in Santiago, Chile, in 2015, this perspective on sustainability and cosmopolitanism received an international focus with the efforts of Erick and Juan Alberto Lecaros to promote international dialog between philosophies of ethical principles in the United States and Europe, a work that was further developed on subsequent seminars on biolaw in Colombia, Mexico, Argentina and Spain.

In the meantime, Erick worked on configuring a more compelling and denser epistemology for biolaw. His developments were very relevant for the field as he was able to identify several distinctive features of biolaw regarding traditional law, other branches of law and bioethics. For the first time, the normative content of biolaw, as well as its epistemological scopes, was defined as aimed at modeling it as an independent and compelling branch of law, with a legally binding scope, which boosts the effectiveness of new deliberative models for law, as well as utterly reinforces hermeneutical approaches, in tune with the juridical intricacy of troubling legal scenarios created by biomedical sciences' latest applications.

Important milestones published on this journey toward cosmopolitan bioethics and biolaw are the following:

Rendtorff Jacob Dahl & Peter Kemp: *Basic Ethical Principles in European Bioethics and Biolaw, Autonomy, Dignity, Integrity and Vulnerability, Vol. I–II*, Barcelona & Copenhagen 2000.

Kemp, Peter, Jacob Rendtorff & Niels Mattsson Johansen (eds): *Bioethics and Biolaw, Vol I–II*, Rhodos international Publishers, Copenhagen 2000.

Rendtorff, Jacob Dahl: "Basic Ethical Principles in European Bioethics and Biolaw: Autonomy, Dignity, Integrity and Vulnerability – Towards a foundation of Bioethics and Biolaw" in *Medicine, Health Care and Philosophy* 5: 235–244, 2002, Kluwer Academic Publishers, 2002.

Rendtorff, Jacob Dahl: "Basic Ethical Principles Applied to Service Industries", Service Industries Journal, vol. 29, no 1. 2009.

Kemp, Peter & Jacob Dahl Rendtorff: "The Barcelona Declaration. Towards an Integrated Approach to Basic Ethical Principles", *Synthesis Philosophica*, vol. 46, no. 2, pp. 239–251. 2009.

Erick Valdés, "Biolaw, Genetics and Human Rights. Analysis of European Biolaw' Scopes and Their Possible Application in the United States as Source of Fourth Generation Human Rights," *Universitas. Journal of Philosophy, Law and Politics,* 17.

Rendtorff, Jacob Dahl: "European Perspectives". *Handbook of Global Bioethics*. Ed. Henk A.M.J. ten Have.

Bert Gordijn. Dordrecht, Heidelberg, New York, London: Springer Science+Business Media B.V., 2014.

Rendtorff, Jacob Dahl 2015, "Update of European bioethics: basic ethical principles in European bioethics and biolaw" BIOETHICS UPdate, vol 1, no. 2, pp. 113–129.

Erick Valdés, "Making Principlism More Practical", *Journal of Bioethics and Law* 35, 2015.

Erick Valdés, "Biolaw, Genetic Harm and Fourth Generation Human Rights", *Mexican Journal of Comparative Law,* 144, 2015.

Erick Valdés, "Biolaw and Subjects of Rights", *Law and the Human Genome Review* 43, 2015.

Rendtorff, Jacob Dahl 2016, "Basic Ethical Principles as Symbolic Foundations and Core Values of European Biolaw", *Ethics, Medicine and Public Health*, vol 2, no. 2, pp. 205–212.

Rendtorff, Jacob Dahl, 2017, *Cosmopolitan Business Ethics: Towards a Global Ethos of Management.* Routledge, Abingdon. Finance, Governance and Sustainability: Challenges to Theory and Practice Series.

Erick Valdés, "Biolaw and its Contribution to Colombian and Ibero American Legal Systems", *Mexican Journal of Comparative Law,* 151, 2018.

Erick Valdés, "Biolaw, Genotype and Ibero American Criminal Law," *Law and the Human Genome Review* 49, 2018.

Erick Valdés and Juan Alberto Lecaros (eds), *Biolaw and Policy in the 21st Century: Building Answers for New Questions*, Switzerland, Springer, 2019.

Erick Valdés, "Towards a New Conception of Biolaw," in: Erick Valdés and Juan Alberto Lecaros (eds), *Biolaw and Policy in the 21st Century: Building Answers for New Questions*, Switzerland, Springer, 2019.

Erick Valdés, "Dysgenic Biomedical Practices and Their International Regulation," in: Erick Valdés and Juan Alberto Lecaros (eds), *Biolaw and Policy in the 21st Century: Building Answers for New Questions*, Switzerland, Springer, 2019.

Erick Valdés and Ingrid Brena (eds), *Biolaw and Human Rights: Contemporary Biojuridical Perspectives*, Mexico City, Institute of Juridical Research, UNAM, 2020.
Erick Valdés, *Biolaw: Origins, Doctrine and Juridical Applications on the Biosciences*, Switzerland, Springer, 2021.

Therefore, we have written this book on a strong research tradition of bioethics and biolaw. Indeed, our present work on cosmopolitan biolaw in relation to economics and sustainable governance is based on more than twenty-five years of research, carried out by Jacob first and then conducted and deepened by Erick. We would like to thank all the involved researchers, research centers and research groups as well as national and international networks for their contribution to our formulation in this book of universal principles in cosmopolitan biolaw, related to finance, global governance and sustainability.

Introduction: Biolaw, economics and sustainability in pandemic times

1 Toward biolaw in a post-pandemic world

This is a book on implications and applications of cosmopolitan biolaw to economics and sustainable governance in pandemic and post-pandemic times. In this fashion, we discuss legal and political foundations of economic organization, global governance and sustainability in order to improve deliberation and action in those relevant settings. We display arguments by integrating them into a vision of biolaw related to finance and political economics that current ideas of sustainability and governance are grounded upon. Thus, our idea of cosmopolitan biolaw applied to those issues encompasses a holistic and futuristic vision of a whole global society strongly molded by murky economic paradigms, which erode justice and human and nonhuman vulnerability. Apathy and inaction before those archetypes can significantly dwindle the odds of getting over global inequalities, especially in times we live in nowadays. By facing such state of things, we argue that a cosmopolitan biolaw may be able to adeptly address disturbing contemporary issues and scenarios that otherwise could provoke ravaging aftermaths for life as a whole.

We know that epistemologies of sustainability and governance appeal to a growing audience in several aspects. However, while there are many studies on governance and finance, the focus to include sustainability is often missed. Therefore, making biolaw converge with finance, governance and sustainability implies an elevated potential to understand and solve current global problems as it provides a compelling perspective to peruse those relevant issues. In this way, cosmopolitan biolaw can fill ideological, political, ethical and juridical gaps presented in governance and sustainability by bringing together original approaches to the intersection of those fields.

A contemporary challenge to biolaw is the emergence of the pandemic society with the rise of the COVID-19 virus epidemic all over the world. With regard to globalization, the virus has been very efficient, and in some sense, the pandemic was possible only because of globalization, because travel and global transportation of the virus have been extremely quick, and it has turned out to be impossible to prevent it from moving from country to country despite strong efforts to do so. With the massive infections, this has

DOI: 10.4324/9781003147848-101

been the worst pandemic since the Spanish Flue of 1918. Worldwide societies have been marked by lockdowns and other strong precautions as initiatives to deal with the contagion. At the same time, there have been many social, political and economic changes in the society with COVID-19. We can witness a break in growth and acceleration in the society, as economic development in many societies has been delayed by the lockdowns and other measures to stop the pandemic (Jensen & Schultz, 2020). This has also challenged the basic structures of culture and everyday life in many countries as social life was replaced by isolationism and requirements to stay at home in order to ensure safety and stop the disease from spreading out.

The new epidemic world becoming a global pandemic one has been characterized by the emergence of biopolitics where states globally have been strong interventionists in order to face the virus in their countries (Jensen & Schultz, 2020). In this context, the new global pandemic society can be considered as more than just a public scenario with increased disease. It is rather a social environment with fundamental changes that requires us to discuss our basic concepts of biopolitics, bioethics and biolaw. Following the German sociologist Ulrich Beck (1994), we can say that it is a global community that needs reflective self-monitoring of basic concepts and self-understandings. Therefore, we need to develop bioethics and biolaw on the basis of the global changes that emerged from the new developments of risk and cosmopolitan societies (Jensen & Schultz, 2020). Thus, to understand the new challenges of biolaw in the pandemic world, we must look at the social, economic and political transformations that characterize contemporary developments of the contemporary civilization.

On this basis, and assuming that humanity will be able to overcome this current state of things, in this book we explore the main contributions of biolaw to global health care economy and sustainable governance for a post-pandemic world. We elaborate a framework of universal principles that can represent an epistemological and methodological platform to identify new hermeneutical keys for a new interpretation of the objectives and scope that new organizational health care economy and global governance should display in an ever-changing world. The first theme and objective of the book are to address the different epistemologies and jurisdictional scopes of biolaw as well as the relationships this field builds with new societal challenges arisen in the current globalized and technologized world. Then, we present the ethical foundations of biolaw in the ethics of the body and explore principlist basis for health care and organizational values by highlighting the biolegal dimensions of management and corporate social responsibility. Further, the book identifies, defines and justifies universal principles for governance by relating and applying them to controversial scenarios, such as inter-species policy, public responsibility, the raise of bioscientific power, the future of life and resource allocation in pandemics. Moreover, we can mention how and why biolaw contributes to shape a new framework for global sustainability, understood from a nonanthropocentric perspective. Finally, the work approaches to governance and sustainability challenges for a post-COVID-19 world, by addressing how biolaw comes into play in this problematic context.

2 The challenges of the pandemic in contemporary society

Accordingly, the background of the book is the need to rethink biolaw after the challenges of the COVID-19 pandemic. In this context, it is important to discuss to which extent the pandemic society represents a new condition of community, where the social, economic and political transformations have changed the circumstances of health care, law and ethics radically (Jensen & Schultz, 2020). As different states display different national strategies to combat the disease that have influence on the structure and formation of society, we see how these different policies change its biopolitical structure. Here it is important to discuss the long-term principles and values following from the fundamental change of social structure during the pandemic. This is not trivial because risk society has changed into a catastrophic one where biopolitical interventions and the lockdown have demonstrated the vulnerabilities of modern communities and have shown the close relation among medicine, politics and biopolitical governance.

While postmodern sociologists like Paul Virilio and Hartmut Rosa have characterized complex societies as based on collective and economic acceleration and high speed as the foundation of multiple social changes, the emergence of the pandemic society has slowed down these processes of modernization. Nevertheless, the increase of biopolitics and strong governance demonstrates that we combine elements of disciplinary community, as suggested by Foucault, with a new powerful form of monitoring and social command, which characterizes the pandemic society of control. Shoshana Zuboff's concept of surveillance capitalism has become increasingly relevant in relation to our lives – in general, in relation to our increased use of the internet, and in particular, in the use of information technology to control COVID-19 with like disease apps or similar digital instruments (Jensen & Schultz, 2020). Combined with surveillance capitalism, there is an intensification of social monitoring in the pandemic society where the speed and acceleration of social change have been replaced by the reflexivity of the lockdown. However, the lockdown did not really stop social change, but it has rather accelerated the speed of digitalization of society and increased its structural change by moving from physical to digital communication.

Thus, in terms of social change, the virus has led to fundamental variations that may even persist after the pandemic. It seems that the fundamental social organization has been strongly influenced by the pandemic, which has created new societal infrastructures. In this context, the threats of the virus have produced more insecurity, and at the same time, biopolitical strategies have been used to struggle against the pandemic by significantly impacting the structure of the public sphere (Jensen & Schultz, 2020). The re-emergence of topics like quarantine requirements, hand spirits, vaccine as a strategy to avoid the disease and the general emphasis on the individual responsibility for health are biopolitical instruments that have manifested the comeback of a strong institutional administration implying a limitation of liberalism within the space of the state's biopolitical control.

The virus's challenges have led nations to a biopolitical configuration of dominance where authorities have taken over the power of society in order to manage the global risks of the disease. In these biopolitical times, medical experts gained power and supplemented politicians in decision-making. The figure of the medical expert as a "God in White" has regained a lot of social authority (Jensen & Schultz, 2020). As suggested by Foucault and Agamben, biopolitical power masters risk society in the attempt to govern threats, health and biopolitical challenges in globalization. The pandemic is, however, complicated from a social perspective because it can be considered as an expression of the challenges of the era of the Anthropocene, where the virus is both natural and a part of mankind and its structures as it essentially spreads among and contaminates human beings.

Global inequality between social classes boosted as COVID-19 evolved. While poor people were more exposed to the disease and, in many cases, also suffered economically from the pandemic crisis, the richest in the society became even richer because of the catastrophe. Moreover, housing prices and stocks were rising during the crisis. There has been a bias of class difference between those who died and those who survived. People's exposure to the virus and degree of seriousness of illness and potential for survival were largely dependent on their social level and fortune. In this context, the global pandemic reproduces social inequalities between different countries on the planet. COVID-19 has been destructive for the elderly, poor and most vulnerable all over the world. In particular, original populations in Brazil and other nations who did not have access to health care and ventilators have tolerated great suffering by the disease.

Furthermore, global migration has changed by COVID-19. The vision of open borders and free travel all over the globe has become an illusion. It has been more difficult to migrate, and some exodus have, on the contrary, been forced ones. The dream of migration has been challenged by COVID-19 as it is dangerous to move from the developing to the developed world. Thus, COVID-19 has increased the vulnerability of migrants and formulated a new agenda of migration for the international community.

Another example of increased vulnerability caused by the crisis related to COVID-19 is the oppression of women globally (Jensen & Schultz, 2020). Men are more vulnerable to the disease, but females have suffered from the crisis due to the reproduction of inequalities between the sexes in terms of more housework and augmented unemployment of women. Even though female leaders like Angela Merkel have been much more efficient than, for example, Donald Trump or Boris Johnson, because of stronger concern for the vulnerable, many women have suffered from the crisis and experienced increased inequality.

Indeed, the crisis has made humanity more aware of its bodily existence and not only the individual body but the collective body of humanity as well. There has been increased focus on the relation between individual and collective bodily dependence on the social intersubjectivity of the embodied community. In this context, dying and death have been a critical concern during the pandemic, which has expressed the deepest fears and anguish of dying by humanity (Jensen & Schultz, 2020). The challenge of death was provoking during the pandemic, and society faced the presence of death as a very concrete possibility in the context of the disease. At the same time, the media accentuated a kind of striptease and pornography of death being following the catastrophic developments of the disease very closely. The pandemic augmented the focus on death in society and made us aware of the risks of death in daily life.

This presence of death is behind the attempts to create a normal life after the pandemic. This raises questions like: Will there be a new normal of daily life after the corona epidemic? Will our habits of daily life change with the lockdown, and will the new habits be repeated after it? How has the pandemic changed our lives fundamentally? Or, has humanity been able to overcome the pandemic due to our creativity and capacity to endure in strong crisis? And, how can we regain the power of humanity in society by developing bioethics and biolaw in a post-pandemic world?

3 Governance and sustainability challenges for a post-COVID-19 world: How biolaw comes into play

We dedicate some pages to explore, expose and suggest distributive criteria for resource allocation in the context of the current pandemic. We can see four types of moral disagreement (clash of principles and meta-principles), which engender relativism in deliberation and need to be procedurally overcome to guarantee reasoning success in resource allocation. Thus, resource distribution may be a source of disagreement on multiple levels, which shows the insufficiency of common morality to achieve plausible consensus regarding (i) fact disagreements, (ii) disagreement due to lack of information or data, (iii) disagreement about norms and their applicability and (iv) conceptual disagreements about crucial moral notions. Common morality principles are prima facie, and these vague and general norms must be specified to narrow their scope and add content to them. If there are competitive specifications, we can then apply moral balance and deliberately determine which one is more plausible and which norms should prevail over others. Weighing situations and courses of action within a process of moral deliberation is not related to common sense or to prima facie principles as these are usually only formally shared. Rather, any deliberative process is related to the relative weight and binding force of norms. Furthermore, as an eventual balance could also be intuitive, partial or arbitrary, we must determine other criteria to reduce intuition, partiality and arbitrariness in moral and legal balancing of substantial and procedural rules for resource allocation.

Another problem is how far the state can go in promoting the population's health while severely limiting citizens' freedom. This question is pertinent in the current scenario of the global pandemic the world is going through, because governments have been practically forced to enact curfews and states of exception to prevent the free movement of people in public space, imposing the principle of public health over individual autonomy. In this context, many dissonant voices have risen criticizing this measure and requesting the immediate restitution of their right to self-determination. However, what is the right thing to do in this case, and why?

To reach greater clarity in this matter, we can discuss the possibility of juridifying a classic and still original John Stuart Mill's argument. According to his harm principle, Mill could justify the limitation of acts that can cause harm to others. In this sense, he could approve state and government campaigns to dissuade people from going out, meeting and even from working. However, Mill would not have agreed to a legally binding ban, especially if the work ban could involve even more critical and larger-scale harm than illness. Is today's society mature enough to trust the individual as the best judge of his acts and interests? Are states and governments wrongly imposing unwanted paternalism on their citizens? Is it legally acceptable to leave millions of people out of work by predicting a global health disaster? It seems that public policies have not considered this element in the equation.

Furthermore, we also argue that the pandemic has given rise to various conspiracy theories about the origin of the virus and its eventual deliberate introduction to the natural and human environment. For this reason, the terms "biosecurity" and "bioterrorism" have become popular again. The term "biosecurity" refers to the measures that are implemented to stop the spread and introduction into life's environment of harmful organisms to humans, animals and plants. Biosecurity's main goal is to protect human health and to increase and optimize the protection of agricultural products through the prevention, control and management of biological risk factors. It is also intended to protect humans, animals and natural life against bioterrorism and to prevent its hostile aftermaths, as well as to offer advice on the most efficient measures or institutional, social and individual actions that must be taken accordingly. In this fashion, biosecurity issues represent one of the most important societal challenges for biolaw.

At the same time, the design, development and implementation of an effective constellation of measures that have the capacity to protect and guarantee the population's health, from a wide range of natural threats or bioterrorist attacks, must be a new focus of interest for biolaw, which requires a specific approach, precisely determined by the specificity of the legal facets that bioterrorism contains. In this way, biosecurity issues connect to the possibility of facing severe global and even existential risks, matter that we also address later on.

On the other hand, concerned about how human rights may be affected by the coronavirus crisis, the United Nations called for countries to tackle the pandemic with a more cooperative, global and human rights–based approach. Since the beginning of the COVID-19 outbreak, United Nations human rights officials and independent experts have stressed the importance of protecting individuals' rights. In an informal statement, addressed to the Human Rights Council on 9 April 2020, Michelle Bachelet, High Commissioner for Human Rights, called for urgent and detailed measures to prevent COVID-19 from creating "greater inequalities" in all this suffering. Bachelet stated that many countries, particularly in Europe, have taken unprecedented measures to protect workers' rights and minimize the number of unemployed as a result of the crisis and encouraged "all states with sufficient resources to do the same." She also noted that the African Development Bank issued the world's most ambitious social bond – a $3 billion fund – to help African governments expand access to health care and other essential goods and services. "This is exactly the kind of innovative thinking that we need," she stressed. She stated that her office is developing a series of good economic and social practices, used by many countries around the world – many of them are developing countries – and that they will present them to the members of the Human Rights Council. She will also work to integrate human rights into the United Nations' economic and social programs (United Nations COVID-19 Response).

In this way, the Office of the High Commissioner recommends that we must be aware of the current statute of new fundamental rights in the pandemic's context, by reflecting on different topics of interest. (i) While everyone has the right to lifesaving interventions, this responsibility falls into governments' action. The resources' scarcity or the use of public or private insurance plans should never justify discrimination against certain groups of people. (ii) Cases of widespread domestic violence are very likely to increase, as already suggested by police and reports. Home can be a place of fear and abuse for many women and children. The situation worsens considerably in isolation cases such as the quarantines imposed during the pandemic. All states must take steps to combat COVID-19 but must not abandon women and children who experience domestic violence. (iii) Reports of abandoned elderly people or corpses found in residences are alarming and appear to be unacceptable. (iv) Internally displaced persons suffer a greater risk of exposure to COVID-19 due to their limited access to health, running water, sanitation, food and decent housing.

Therefore, COVID-19 is not only a health problem but it can also be a virus that aggravates xenophobia, hatred and exclusion. There are reports of physical violence suffered by Chinese and Asian people; hate speech that blames minorities, such as Romanians and Hispanics, for the virus spread; and politicians who ask that immigrants not be allowed access to medical services. Everything shows that states must urgently emphasize that the human rights of most vulnerable and marginalized ones must be especially protected.

The book also addresses synoptically the raise of new individual subjective rights (biorights) in the context of human challenge trials. It is important to explore the ethical and legal plausibility of subjecting humans, in cases of extreme necessity, to human challenge trials. For this reason, it is necessary to move toward a configuration of criteria for the selection of subjects, incentives for participation and even coercion, which tolerate a legally binding content in political and social universes of democratic and pluralistic nature. Competing arguments and positions need to be analyzed. The conclusion will be that, in the midst of a predictive scenario, the consequentialist content is the densest one for the moral and legal calculation about human challenge trials.

4 Contents and structure of our argument about biolaw in cosmopolitan society

The aim of this book is to show the importance of universal and cosmopolitan biolaw as the basis for international governance and sustainability in a post-COVID-19 world. Indeed, the virus has demonstrated the need for such a biolaw to deal with global governance and create good transition toward more sustainable international legal and economic structure. In this context, universal biolaw can also be considered as a contribution to the realization of the United Nation's Sustainable Development Goals (SDGs). Here, biolaw is an instrument for creating a better relation between protection of the environment and the social and cultural development of society toward sustainability. Against this background, we have structured the book in the following main sections and chapters.

The book has four main parts with ten chapters, this introduction and a conclusion. In Part I, we present the history, scopes and epistemologies of biolaw. This includes in Chapter 1 a presentation of the movement from bioethics to biolaw and a discussion of the idea of global bioethics seen in relation to biomedical ethics and the different theories and approaches to biolaw from the point of view of theory of knowledge and perspectives on legal and ethical research. In Chapter 2 we present the development of biolaw in the different parts of the world in order to discuss the possibility of a cosmopolitan approach to biolaw as the basis for a universal governance model. We present the European, Mediterranean, American and international conceptions on this journey toward a cosmopolitan biolaw. Finally, in Chapter 3 we discuss the concept of biolaw in terms of jurisdiction and in relation to its societal challenges.

In Part II we present the philosophy of biolaw related to the discussion of the connections between bioethics and biolaw. We begin by discussing the relation between biolaw and ethics. The philosophical foundations of the ethics of biolaw demonstrate how biolaw emerges out of a democratic political discussion of deliberative biopolitics. Chapter 4 discusses the threat of biopower in relation to the legal status of the body in law and legislation. Moreover, we present the foundations of international biolaw as based on the ethics of the good life seen from the perspective of universal norms and law. Moreover, it is the function of judgment to find the right balance in legislation about the human body and life. Chapter 5 presents the legal history of biolaw related to the human body between person and thing. The chapter presents the body in the perspective of cultural anthropology with focus on the relation to the body in different perspectives as, for example, theology and medicine. Moreover, we explore how the relation to the body has changed in the governance of modern legal systems. In Chapter 6 we present the changed relations to the body with the bioethical challenges to biolaw in the twenty-first century. With the dreams of enhancement and eternal life, biomedicine is marked by the intention to move beyond the condition of vulnerable existence and finitude, which remains, however, the anthropological condition of human life in technocosmos.

In Part III we discuss the governance of biolaw from the point of view of business ethics, corporate social responsibility and stakeholder management. In health care organization, it is important to work with values and stakeholder management. In this context, business ethics contributes to sustainable development of society with focus on the selection and prioritization of stakeholders as essential for corporate social responsibility and corporate governance of health care organizations. Thus, Chapter 7 proposes a vision of fairness of governance in health care organizations and economics. In Chapter 8 we relate this discussion to the role of ethics in organization ethics and hospital management. Here, we emphasize that it is important to establish a system of bioethics and biolaw in hospital organizations because this supports the integration of ethics in professional development and organizational learning. Moreover, integration of bioethics and biolaw into hospital organizations contributes to legitimacy of decision-making in health care systems, and this can be seen as realization of bioethics and biolaw in practice.

In Part IV we elaborate on the relation among biolaw, governance and sustainability in cosmopolitan society. This part moves from the meso-level of hospital organizations to the macrolevel of international law in order to propose universal principles for governance in an ever-changing world. In Chapter 9 we discuss the problems and challenges of proposing biolaw for governance in a globalized world. We relate the concept of social responsibility to the biojuridical framework for global governance with emphasis on the integration of the responsibility for animals and nature in the formulation of global governance principles. Here we highlight the role of the principles of autonomy, dignity, integrity, vulnerability and justice for dealing with sustainable development with focus on important problems of protection of human and nonhuman entities, solution to the global environmental crisis and future health risks like the COVID-19 emergency. This development of principles and instruments for international global governance can be seen as contribution to understanding the legal framework of the United Nation's SDGs. This focus is also the framework for Chapter 10, where we ask deeper ethical and biojuridical questions about economy and sustainability, effective altruism as individual and cosmopolitan action for sustainability, animal sustainability and the relations between biotechnology, pandemic and existential risks.

Finally, in the conclusion, we summarize our position on biolaw based on universal principles. Here, we emphasize how our vision of cosmopolitan biolaw in times of COVID-19 can be proposed as the basis for the United Nation's SDGs. Thus, we present the universal and cosmopolitan biolaw as an important framework for interjurisdictional governance integrating basic principles into the purposes for global sustainability.

Part I

History, scopes and epistemologies of biolaw

1 From bioethics to biolaw

1.1 The idea of a global bioethics

There exists a connection between bioethics and biolaw. Even though that relationship has been rather epistemologically promiscuous, it is difficult to deny the fact that bioethics eventually impacted the development of biolaw in Europe, especially regarding the deliberative model that this new field adopted to address a whole new constellation of juridical problems arisen from biomedical settings. As bioethics colonized Europe, incipient biolaw was acquiring a principlist configuration aimed at understanding and governing disturbing bioscientific practices able to challenge juridical atmospheres as never before.

Principles of American bioethics represented a sort of theoretical and procedural horizon for European biolaw to gain more density and effectivity to analyze new biojuridical problems and seek to provide original and compelling solutions for them. The need for creating new frameworks to respond to harsh questions and rule complex scenarios adeptly encompassed new interpellations for law. New life sciences law, which emerged in the arena of international law, started to work with a cluster of principles as guidelines to deliberate on and rule biosciences and new technologies in general.

European biolaw's principlism took from American bioethics various relevant conceptual and procedural categories. This justifies dedicating some pages to explore important features of bioethics. However, bioethics also evolved throughout the twentieth century because it was not always based upon a principlist structure. In fact, its first conception was a global one, meaning an ethics of life as a whole. As this primigenial intellection contributed to epistemologically nourish American bioethics, we think it deserves some attention now.

1.1.1 Fritz Jahr

The term "bioethics" was not ushered in with Van Rensselaer Potter's 1970 paper, "Bioethics: The Science of Survival," as many bioethics experts used to think. In 1927, Fritz Jahr, a German protestant pastor, philosopher and

DOI: 10.4324/9781003147848-1

educator published an editorial entitled "Bio-Ethik. Eine Umschau über die ethischen Beziehungen des Menschen zu Tier und Pflanze" ("Bio-Ethics. Reviewing the Ethical Relations of Humans toward Animals and Plants") in the leading German natural science journal *Kosmos*. The origin of the term and concept "bioethics" occurred 43 years before Potter published his famous work. This means that we should consider Potter's ideas a continuation of Jahr's seminal contribution.

It is true that Jahr's ideas are rather naive. However, his thought encompasses a rare sensitivity regarding the main ontological categories of contemporaneity, especially to its overwhelming technological development. Jahr coined the term "bioethics," but he also proposed an incipient epistemological content to it long before the Nuremberg Trials. His conceptual configuration was not dense enough, but it undoubtedly represented an inspiring intellection destined to become a fundamental disciplinary atmosphere to understand ethical scopes of biotechnological empowerment that hatched in the 1980s.

As Potter's bioethics is quite similar to Jahr's original conception, we will synoptically expose the main intuitions, concepts and categories that both Jahr and Potter contributed to the disciplinary configuration of bioethics. It is not clear if the National Commission took these ideas into consideration to elaborate the Belmont Report; however, both Jahr's and Potter's pivotal notions are, at least, tacitly present in whole bioethics developed in the 1970s.

Between 1927 and 1938, Jahr published an impressive array of papers on bioethics and other related topics, such as animal ethics, ecology, public health and education, so as this book is devoted to analyze several aspects of corporative ethics, governance, sustainability and organizational economics in health care, it seems not to be trivial to address the most remarkable facets of Jahr's thoughts. Even though his work did not enjoy popularity, he displayed an interesting constellation of acute intuitions on what bioethics should be as well as the environments this new field must conquer at that moment. He characterizes bioethics as a fundamental attitude, meaning an *êthos* or way of living. In this sense, bioethics should be part of human character, an ethical virtue turning into a unique discipline. Hence, Jahr's bioethics points to an independent field of knowledge endowed with specific epistemological features and exclusive procedural scopes.

Jahr also redefines traditional moral obligations by extending them to animals and nature, so in his thought, the concept of human responsibility abandons classical anthropocentrism of all previous ethics, which entails a radical reconfiguration of conventional criteria of moral correction known until then. This sort of premonitory trait in his understanding of bioethics work constituted a theoretical precedent for remarkable ideas developed long after, such as Jonas' imperative of responsibility and Singer's animal ethics, among others.

Moreover, Jahr implicitly defines bioethics as a secular and pluralistic field as it requires a new form of deliberation to address new moral problems that scientific and technological power encompasses. In this fashion, bioethics is, according to the German thinker, a new normative universe to govern the use of technoscientific advances through democratic and public participation and oversight. He imagines global bioethics aimed at engendering sufficient and necessary conditions for human beings to respect life as a whole, based upon a bioethical imperative stating, "Respect every living being, in principle, as an end in itself, and treat it, if possible, as such!" (Jahr, 1934). This formulation implies a post-metaphysical extension of Kantian one as Jahr's imperative includes animals and nature as subjects of moral consideration. Thus, the overriding criterion to determine which entities ought to be respected as ends in themselves is not rationality but life.

The scope of Jahr's ideas is not trivial because it represents the starting point of an applied ethics concerned about life, health care and environment. This new ethics is focused on the idea that scientific and technological development needs new keys for moral deliberation, new rules and procedures as well as a new terminology to get over traditional semantic anachronism and deal with harsh moral controversies with more accuracy and objectivity.

Therefore, Jahr's imperative entails one of the first modern formulations of the principle of nonmaleficence, encompassing the duty to self-preservation and not to harm others under any circumstance. According to him, we have a key duty: To respect all living beings as ends in themselves and treat them as such. However, carrying out this task is something complex.

The potential realization of such moral duties toward all living beings may seem to be utopian. But we cannot ignore that moral obligations toward a living being refer to its needs and, respectively, to its destiny. Therefore, Jahr's bioethics represents a combination of deontology and teleology, as the achievement of ends is mediated by the observance of certain categorical duties. In this way, he proposes neither a tyranny of unshakable principles nor an abuse of casuistry in moral deliberation.

Moreover, Jahr introduces a concept of responsibility as a criterion of deliberation for any ethics. According to him, bioethics is a moral attitude that implies respect and responsibility toward all living entities. Thus, he thinks that it is no longer possible to understand existence, if people ignore the possible and unpredictable consequences of human action, modified by new science and technologies. Therefore, he introduces the concept of responsibility into the ethical discussion long before Hans Jonas. Furthermore, he prophetically advises precaution with regard to scientific progress, especially in experimental physiology and psychology, as well as he identifies the need to ethically regulate technoscientific power in order to avoid human tyranny over other living entities (Jahr, 1927).

Jahr's bioethics is not the same as we know today. However, his ideas point to the first categories that would make up current bioethics. Indeed, Jahr tacitly includes in his conception of bioethics important insights about autonomy, social justice and nonmaleficence. Therefore, beyond being the creator of the term and concept "bioethics," he engendered the intellectual and theoretical bases for its epistemological and disciplinary development. Also, his seminal ideas tuned with crucial concepts we address in this book, such as global governance, health care ethics, organizational ethics and sustainability, among others. For all these reasons, Jahr certainly deserves a prominent place in the history of bioethics.

1.1.2 Van Rensselaer Potter

In 1970, Van Rensselaer Potter published his article "Bioethics: A Science of Survival." In this work, the American oncologist proposed the term "bioethics" to define a new epistemological field, through which human beings could be able to acquire "the knowledge of how to use knowledge" (Potter, 1971). This new wisdom could also be called "the science of survival" as one of the primary objectives of Potter's bioethics was to improve quality of life, conceived as a whole, by promoting, at the same time, a convergence between science and humanities. For this reason, the American physician used to say that the term "bioethics" emphasized "the two most important ingredients to achieve a new wisdom: Biological knowledge and human values."

As Potter understood bioethics as a bridge between sciences and humanities, the task of this new discipline was shown to be vast and, therefore, vague. However, and despite the fact that his conception indicated a complementation between ethics and biology, Potter's bioethics should not be understood as a mere conjunction or methodological meeting of both disciplines.

According to this understanding, Potter (1971) did not suggest abandoning traditional science or irrationally embracing a new idea or conception of it. Rather, he proposed to cross the borders between scientific and humanistic disciplines to obtain a broader vision of proper human problems emerging as a result of technological empowerment and, thus, to reach an objective consensus in terms of a future survival of mankind by improving the future generations' quality of life. In other words, Potter was looking for better ways to re-examine traditional scientific premises in order to establish adequate conditions of existence (and survival, in particular), including individual, social and environmental categories.

Later on, in 1971, Potter published his famous book *Bioethics. Bridge to the Future*, in which he insisted on his idea of bioethics as a new interdisciplinary knowledge. However, the book is essentially a compilation of articles already published in academic journals. Most of them do not refer directly to bioethics and do not even mention the name of the emerging discipline. Only two of them address the topic directly: The first article, "Bioethics: A Science of Survival," and the last one, "Survival as a Goal for Wisdom," in which Potter proposes his bioethical creed.

Despite the fact that Potter never epistemologically or methodologically defined what bioethics was or should be, it is possible to find in his work some interesting concepts that were important for the subsequent development of the discipline: (1) The concept of danger attached to the development of science (or knowledge); (2) progress and survival; (3) a moral obligation toward the future; (4) the control of technology; and (5) the need for an interdisciplinary effort to address new moral controversies arisen in medical, biomedical and scientific settings.

In this way, for Potter, bioethics assumes a global dimension that goes beyond the introspective gaze of science and, specifically, of traditional biology, whose reductionist knowledge comes fundamentally from the laboratory. Bioethics, then, should examine the nature of human knowledge in order to achieve a realistic understanding of our limitations to foresee and assume moral responsibility for the eventual consequences of our actions. On this specific point, Potter agrees with Jahr in that bioethics should detach itself from a purely immediatist, anthropocentric and reductionist intellection, by pointing out grounding paths to generate a true public policy to govern biotechnological research.

However, and beyond its original global and biocentric conception, over the years, bioethics, especially that of the United States, would take other directions, shedding its claims of universality and focusing its interest on clinical and biomedical issues, although both in Europe and in Latin America, scholars and practitioners would insist on extending its scope to other disciplinary areas related with it, both methodologically and epistemologically.

1.2 From biomedical ethics to European biolaw

As it has been stated before (Valdés, 2021), the birth of biolaw responds to a multidimensional history. While its first relevant epistemology was developed in Europe (Rendtorff & Kemp, 2000), the conceptual roots of what we could call "European biolaw," even having antecedents in Europe, originally grew up in the United States. Along with the historical circumstances that triggered the origin of this new field, its epistemological antecedent is certainly American bioethics, although as we already saw, its original expression was quite at variance with its current epistemological aspect. However, the first global dimension of bioethics could have inherited certain categories to biolaw. Therefore, its first echoes were a coefficient that turned out to be the factor of a true polynomial of historical and epistemological facts worth revisiting.

The Nuremberg Trials can be considered an epistemological antecedent of American bioethics, as well as of the extensive cast of instruments of UNESCO, the Council of Europe and the European Court of Human Rights, created to regulate biomedical practices, which originated the so-called international biolaw and European bioethics and biolaw (Rendtorff & Kemp, 2000). In fact, the Nuremberg Code of Medical Ethics was the first document that identified principles and procedures to rule experimentation with human beings, a controversial atmosphere that, upon later, the Belmont Report explored paradigmatically. Therefore, and as the epistemology of American bioethics deepened and extended the theoretical and methodological scope of the Nuremberg Code of Medical Ethics, by encouraging the emergence of essential categories for the conceptual configuration of international biolaw, we can affirm that the prehistory of biolaw begins in the 1930s. In fact, the original archetype of the Nuremberg Code emerged in German politics before World War II, specifically, between 1930 and 1940, a time when the German Medical Association was considered a democratic organization focused on public health. However, the final version of the Nuremberg Code, which established that explicit voluntary consent of patients is required for human experimentation, was drawn up on 9 August 1947, including principles such as informed consent, absence of coercion, proper formulation of scientific experimentation and beneficence, among others.

The Code is considered for many the most important document in the history of clinical research ethics, and it had a massive influence on global human rights. In fact, the Nuremberg Code and the Declaration of Helsinki represent the basis of the Code of Federal Regulations, issued by the United States Department of Health and Human Services for the ethical treatment of humans and biological material, and are currently used in the Institutional Review Boards. Furthermore, the idea of informed consent has been universally accepted and now constitutes Article 7 of the United Nations International Covenant on Civil and Political Rights. It also served as the basis for the drafting of the international ethical guidelines for biomedical research in humans, proposed by the World Health Organization.

However, the Nuremberg Code did not acquire conceptual density enough to give rise to bioethics or any other relevant epistemology. Something else had to happen for bioethics and biolaw to hatch in the international scenario.

In 1974, and already known the abuses that scientists inflicted on their eventual human subjects of experimentation both in Tuskegee and Willowbrook, the United States Congress ordered the creation of the National Commission for the Protection of Human Subjects of Biomedical and Behavioral Research, whose purposes were to discuss and reflect on the limits of biomedical research, as well as to evaluate the equation between risks and benefits of human experimentation. In addition, the National Commission was aimed at providing guidelines and criteria for fair and equitable selection of experimental subjects as well as reflecting on the nature, scope and meaning of informed consent when applied in biomedical settings.

After four years, the National Commission published the results of its work in a document that quickly became a key reference for the development of bioethics' epistemology, increased the precision of reasoning in decision-making processes and contributed to the optimization and creation of public policies to regulate experimentation with human subjects. The document, known worldwide as *The Belmont Report* (*The Belmont Report: Ethical Principles for Research with Human Subjects*), was intended to provide criteria to protect human beings faced with biomedical experimentation. The Report identified and defined a cluster of "basic ethical principles" whose value and epistemological and methodological scope became very useful quickly to analyze, understand and solve moral controversies arisen in biomedical and clinical environments.

As an important part of the conceptual grounds, principles, rules and procedures that the Report provides for bioscientific research were replicated, years later, by the Council of Europe and the European Court of Human Rights, originating international biolaw; it may be useful to expose the most relevant elements of the document synoptically.

The Belmont Report's main goals (National Commission for the Protection of Human Subjects of Biomedical and Behavioral Research, 2009) were to identify basic ethical principles to guide and rule biomedical research in human beings and develop procedural guidelines to ensure that any study is carried out in accordance with those principles. Its first goal was to abolish the excessive paternalism, both of scientific practice and medicine, which traditionally did not consider subjects and patients' self-determination as a criterion for carrying out research and conducting treatment. Therefore, the Report gives pre-eminence to individual autonomy, allowing human subjects to participate in deliberation and to make active decisions in biomedical and clinical settings.

Second, it was aimed at restoring respect for human dignity, by promoting the maximization of benefits in experimentation as well as demanding to reduce the potential risks and damages involved.

And third, the document stressed the importance of equitable treatment of subjects, granting them the same rights in several important research stages: (1) Fair methods and procedures to choose them; (2) equitable distribution of efforts to protect dignity, health and life of those involved; and (3) non-discrimination in research with human subjects, regardless origin, race and intellectual, social or economic status.

The Belmont Report can be considered as the first document in history to identify, articulate and define specific bioethical principles (Respect for Persons, Beneficence and Justice). Since then, those principles enjoyed a rapid and growing acceptance, not only in bioethical atmospheres but also in legal ones. Both the epistemological scope and the practical application of the principles by far surpassed the disciplinary context they were originally created for. In fact, the National Commission itself clarified that the principles were only general guidelines aimed at enhancing deliberation, reinforcing decision-making and moral reasoning, as well as providing criteria for choosing the right courses of action in each case. However, the principles turned into a theoretical framework strong enough to engender more specific rules that eventually would set up procedures to be applied very effectively at a practical level.

The Belmont Report still represents a guide to the protection of human research subjects. In the more than four decades that have passed since their publication in the United States Federal Archives on 18 April 1979, biomedical and socio-behavioral research companies have grown and experienced profound changes in knowledge, technologies, methodologies and capabilities. In the same way, the possible scope and consequences of the discoveries and advances in research contain a complexity that is often intolerable, not only for their correct social reception but also for their effective regulation.

These continuous changes in research surroundings, as well as the permanent and rapid enhancement of the biosciences, have raised questions about the proper application of the principles. The point is that not only bioethics is concerned with these issues. In fact, all epistemology and hermeneutics contained in the document have been extended, analogically, to the field of law, a phenomenon that supports its development under the hypothesis that all ethical dilemmas emerging in bioscientific contexts also imply legal quandaries.

For example, there is no legal agreement regarding the best way to balance or prioritize the principles in the context of clinical trials that compare the effectiveness of widely used therapies for certain disorders with others at an experimental stage, in order to decree if a methodology can reach better outcomes than one another. Questions about the application of these principles also arise in research involving human biospecimens (samples of biological material, such as urine, blood, tissue, cells and DNA) or unidentified genomic data. The same happens in community-based participatory research; human challenge trials conducted in emergency situations, such as the current COVID-19 pandemic; randomized study designs; and observational research involving big-scale databases, among others.

Additionally, while *The Belmont Report* did not explicitly point to a duty to participate in research, some people believe that as everyone is a potential beneficiary of biomedical and socio-behavioral research, everyone should feel responsible – when opportunities arise and risks are minimal or manageable – for taking part in the investigation. In this fashion, a large-scale voluntary collaboration would result in a greater understanding of human health, diseases and the effectiveness of proposed therapies in a broader and more indicative spectrum of society. This should lead, in the long run, to benefits for the entire population.

On the other hand, in the context of the principle of procreative beneficence (Savulescu, 2001), it has been profusely discussed if parents have or do not have the moral and legal obligation to choose or select the "best embryo possible" through preimplantation genetic diagnosis (PGD). Legal conflicts raised by the mandate contained in this principle are quite radical as PGD not only allows the selection of embryos with certain characteristics but also literally ensures that embryos with disabilities are produced when the parents so desire.

Thus, not just human research but all bioscientific inventions raise profound questions about our status as potential participants and beneficiaries of knowledge gained from biomedical and behavioral studies. In fact, the eventual application of principles that indicate fundamental values of a social state of law enjoying a constitutional status extends itself analogically to biomedical and bioscientific fields, demanding an intellection attuned with the legal nature of those new advancements.

On the other hand, the protection of human research subjects still represents an epistemological environment of profuse discussion. In clinical settings, for example, distinguishing between human subject research and activities designed to secure and enhance therapy can often be difficult to be carried out with certainty and accuracy. Furthermore, the feasibility of an optimal application of regulations – mainly developed in the context of biomedical research – to the entire spectrum of socio-behavioral research has been questioned for decades, both for the apparent conceptual utopia that this achievement encompasses and the lack of proper legal models that can make it possible. As a matter of fact, the Council of Europe, in the middle of the 1980s, began to reflect on this disturbing, and also imprecise, list of scenarios. In this way, it evaluated as very necessary to widely reconsider the legal and regulatory frameworks that governed, until then, research on human subjects.

Thus, what we could call European proto-biolaw, and known in its beginnings as life sciences law, (i) addressed contemporary challenges associated with human subjects' research, including emerging new possibilities opened by the biosciences; (ii) allowed the profusion, exchange and access to personal data within the European Community; and (iii) understood that risks to genetic privacy required creative, original and progressive legal, regulatory and institutional frameworks (Valdés, 2021). Certainly, this work was intended not only to improve the protection of human subjects (from a pre-embryonic state) in research but also, and very especially, to boost the investment in bioscience in order to obtain more and better knowledge to optimize individual and social well-being.

In this way, gradually the Council of Europe's jurisprudence, community law and European parliamentary law began, during the 1980s, to be grounded not only on *The Belmont Report*'s ideas but also on a constellation of new revolutionary concepts, contained in a seminal book called to become one of the most remarkable epistemologies of bioethics thus far.

Principles of Biomedical Ethics (Beauchamp & Childress, 2019), whose first edition appeared in 1979, is probably the most famous and influential bioethics book in the world. On it, the authors offer an epistemological and procedural framework for a deliberative model, made up of four principles with claims to universality, in tune with the specificity of biomedical ethics, which lacked such a reasoning platform at the beginning of the 1970s.

These four basic principles – Respect for Autonomy, Nonmaleficence, Beneficence and Justice – represent abstract mandates, namely, common morality norms, of general scope and rather vague normative content. These principles function as criteria to deliberate on complex moral conflicts arisen in biomedical surroundings. However, they are not categorical imperatives or absolute mandates. Its application admits exceptions, precisely because each of these moral referents represents a prima facie principle, that is, it has a specific normative weight that is theoretically equivalent to that of the other three. In addition, they are principles that indicate what we could call natural laws or universal precepts of reason. Indeed, it is highly unlikely that a human being, committed to morality and the laws, can reject in his mind the idea that a just society is better than an unjust one and that a free person is fuller and happier than an enslaved one. In this sense, the four principles, by representing those precepts shared by most of the individuals, encompass self-evident general mandates to human conscience and morality.

This model of the four principles, known worldwide as "principlism" – a term pejoratively given by two of its most notable critics (Clouser & Gert,

1990) – is based on the idea that it is practically impossible for humans to ignore these principles when executing any value judgment or when dealing with a moral dilemma. The idea of Beauchamp and Childress was, then, to provide a priority system of moral principles that would serve as deliberative guides in the solution of value conflicts. In this sense, the authors affirm that never an ethical theory or a deontological code has been able to design a system of principles emancipated from conflicts, exceptions or instances of judgment (Valdés, 2021).

However, the authors clarify that principlism does not represent all common morality but only a part of it. Talking about the universality of the principles is also a methodological resource to build an adequate deliberative framework for biomedical ethics. In this sense, the principlist theory does not seek to establish a list of basic principles of morality and law but rather defends the idea of a universal common morality that includes the four principles. In this regard, Beauchamp (2019) himself has emphasized that principlism does not reject the existence of particular morals, which is evident and profusely documented. However, it is clear that axiological diversity does not inhibit the fact that people coming from different traditions cannot agree on certain basic and fundamental moral standards, which are intercultural ones.

Therefore, common morality is not simply one more morality among many others. "Common" means that the principles are or can be shared by many or by all, without major reluctance or contemplation. In this sense, common morality mandates such as "Do not kill," "Do not cause unnecessary harm or suffering" or "Help those who are in danger" belong to what Beauchamp (2019) calls a "public system of norms" that transcends individual value barriers.

In this context of a universal common morality is where, according to Beauchamp and Childress (2019), the principles work much better. The content of each one of them not only gives light to deliberate on general or specific moral dilemmas but also provides a constellation of rules that contribute to the construction of principlist models of biolaw, such as the European one (Rendtorff & Kemp, 2000), for instance.

The influence of American bioethics in the emergence of European biolaw is then clear. However, saying that all bioethics constitutes the most notable influence for what was later called international biolaw is probably too much. As bioethics is an applied ethics that seeks to deal with very specific moral conflicts emerged in a very specific field such as that of biomedical sciences, this task is carried out by providing various deliberative models, among which principlism has been not only the most criticized but also, by far, the most successful and influential. Therefore, a large part of what can be called the influence of American bioethics on European biolaw or the transition from bioethics to biolaw is, in reality, the impact that principlism had on the development of most of the international instruments created to rule biomedicine and biotechnology's advances.

Another important impact of principlism on the emergence and development of European biolaw is that the founders of this field in Europe

(Rendtorff & Kemp, 2000), who have been severe critics of Beauchamp and Childress' principlist theory, shaped their proposal for European bioethics and biolaw, sustained in what they recognize as common morality principles, as American philosophers did in the late 1970s. Therefore, European biolaw is also grounded upon a principlist scheme, iterated from Georgetown bioethics, but with principles whose content is supposedly more in tune with European human rights culture and tradition.

Most biojurists in the world do not develop a comprehensive distinction between bioethics and biolaw and, rather, consider the former to be a presupposition for the latter, as biolaw should simply be a form of social regulation that seeks to establish a legal framework to determine a valid and pertinent law for the solution of conflicts caused by bioethical cases and problems.

The influence of American principlism in international biolaw has caused this new discipline to be mostly understood as a juridified bioethics, that is, as bioethics or bioethical categories applied to the biosciences' legal conflicts. This understanding of biolaw has also defined it as part of bioethics or as parasitical upon it (Singer, 2019, p. viii; Valdés, 2019, p. 43, 2021, pp. 31–58), that is, as an instrument of evolution of bioethics. Later on, we will address some epistemological and methodological problems that such conflictive intellection implies.

By now, we can emphasize that by assuming that law represents a constellation of institutionalized judgments prescribing specific standards to engender some expected social behaviors, the European philosophical-legal world understood biolaw as a bridge between ethics and law, fields that traditionally, and by influence of legal positivism, had been apprehended as separate from each other. Indeed, European jurists assessed that persisting in affirming the historical split between ethics and law was no longer procedurally successful in addressing the original and unprecedented problems raised by emerging and growing genetic technologies. In addition, as American bioethics had already created an effective deliberative model to reason on such issues, no one questioned the idea that biolaw should be based on bioethical epistemology (Valdés, 2021, pp. 85–123). As Kemp (2019) stated, "biolaw, then, became a bioethical demand."

That was a milestone for biolaw to become a disciplinary field that gradually gained epistemological status to cover all legal judgments and approaches linked to bioethical matters, regardless of the legal system where those decisions should be made. Thus, the jurisdiction of European biolaw was part of ethics and bioethics committees, international instruments created to rule new bioscientific practices, administrative ordinances concerning bioethics (commissions, colleges and councils, among others) and jurisprudence about bioethical conflicts and controversies.

Therefore, the institutionalization of biolaw in Europe implied that it was understood as a philosophy of law focused on legal issues within bioethics, to obtain more certainty on the relationship between ethics and law as well as on their ability to produce a model to help human beings adapt themselves to new demands imposed by new technologies. This institutional dimension of biolaw fractured its conceptual dimension, by obscuring any possibility to distinguish it from bioethics. As bioethical issues became disturbing and complex, society began to be aware of genetic and bioscientific practices that could affect the most delicate spheres of persons. In other words, the jurisdiction of biolaw turned into a bioethical one (Valdés, 2021, pp. 125–142).

Human rights in biomedical settings became a relevant issue in the European legal systems. This implied the creation of a life sciences law, which pointed to a legal framework of norms in matter of life sciences, grounded upon American bioethics' epistemology. In this way, an important convergence was also found between the fundamental principles recognized by the Council of Europe, especially in the Oviedo Convention, and those highlighted by the European Union based, on the one hand, on the European Group on Ethics in Science and New Technologies' recommendations and legal directives and, on the other, on the Charter of Fundamental Rights of the European Union, which emphasized the application of human rights doctrine to new technologies and life sciences.

Also, a new legal framework emerged, founded on key axiological concepts, such as respect for human dignity, respect for autonomy, nondiscrimination, right on the own body, protection of the vulnerable and respect for privacy, among others. This juridical evolution led to the legal recognition of ethics committees' role in creating regulatory standards for biosciences.

European law also fostered the use and consideration of certain fundamental principles, such as respect for privacy and equality. This allowed the emergence of new principles that, due to their epistemological construction, did not have normative content but rather encompassed ontological conditions – dignity, for example – as a result of reducing other principles' scope (especially in economic matters), by emphasizing the use of some norms linked to different relationships between the human being and biomedicine as well as recategorizing the legal status of the human body. In this way, fundamental rights started to be related to individuals not only as economic or social agents but also, and very especially, as embodied entities. Moreover, fundamental rights' application was not limited to the field of community law, so those rights gained the status of founding rules for European law, turning into key guidelines for the new political construction of Europe and the creation of a European citizenship.

The Oviedo Convention and the European Group on Ethics in Science and New Technologies helped seek a foundation for this new European law. The Council of Europe's specific task was to produce concrete answers to govern different genetic and biomedical techniques as they appeared and developed. Thus, the Council of Europe standardized, for instance, the legal status of blood products and eased the circulation of organs and tissues over Europe for transplantation and grafting purposes.

Nevertheless, lacking a general legal framework to permit progress in European regulation made very difficult to build transversal policies for synchronizing rights with biomedical practices' new challenges. This was aggravated by the lack of moral, political and ideological agreements on complex issues of not only legal implications but also social and anthropological ones. In this context, the European Community started to work on identifying, elaborating and defining principles to found a new law, understood as a symbolic normative atmosphere to govern new sciences and technologies and, at the same time, to help redefine human identity in new bioscientific settings.

Thus, the European Commission financed the *Basic Ethical Principles in European Bioethics and Biolaw* research project, which was conducted between 1995 and 1998. Such endeavor counted on the cooperative work of 22 members from different European Union's countries. It was intended to define and provide content to ethical principles related to autonomy, dignity, integrity and vulnerability, understood as four important grounds for European bioethics and biolaw. The research concluded that basic ethical principles could not be understood as universal ideas or eternal truths, but rather, they had the status of "deliberative guidelines" and fundamental values of European culture (Valdés, 2021, p. 28).

That work ended with the publication of *Basic Ethical Principles in European Bioethics and Biolaw* (Rendtorff & Kemp, 2000), which inaugurated biolaw as a new field in the world. With this milestone, the historical transit from American bioethics to European biolaw reached its pinnacle. However, the existence of diverse conceptions of biolaw was a problem for the correct intellection of the new field. We address this matter in the next chapter.

2 Biolaw in different parts of the world

2.1 Different epistemologies of biolaw

Biolaw has historically had an eclectic epistemology. Since its first relevant conceptual configuration (Rendtorff & Kemp, 2000), several conceptions have emerged and been legitimized in the international academic context. These theories (Valdés, 2019, 2021) differ very significantly from one another and define the meaning and nature of biolaw from divergent arguments, criteria and ideologies.

In this chapter, we analyze different biolaw epistemologies that have been developed so far. Those theories are deepened, by seeking to prove why none of them was able, over 20 years, to understand biolaw as a legally binding branch of law. Such conceptions have conceived biolaw from bioethics, by fostering different kinds of wrong relationships that have been called juridification, complementation, subjection, overlap, substitution, colonization and intersection (Valdés, 2021). As the theoretical evolution of those conceptions has been very limited, all of them have adopted classical bioethical categories, which makes them anachronistic regarding biomedical sciences' empowerment. In fact, except the European conception, different biolaw schools display an exclusively clinical vision of bioethics. Therefore, all conceptions explain biolaw from bioethics, in ways that can be different to one another but, at the same time, share two elements: (i) The ambiguous relationship between bioethics and biolaw and (ii) the idea that biolaw must be the work on bioethical (instead of biomedical) issues of legal scope.

2.2 European biolaw

This epistemology (Rendtorff & Kemp, 2000), characterized by the concepts of juridification and complementation, understands biolaw as a juridified bioethics. In other words, European biolaw is made of a set of common morality norms originally systematized by American bioethics (Beauchamp & Childress, 2019) and considered as ethical-juridical standards to rule bioscientific and biomedical practices entailing significant risks for human beings. The idea of biolaw developed by Rendtorff and Kemp was accepted,

DOI: 10.4324/9781003147848-2

deepened and disseminated in most of the countries of central and northern Europe, including England. For this reason, it has been called European conception (Valdés, 2021).

Rendtorff and Kemp (2000, pp. 25–56) identify the principles of European biolaw as autonomy, dignity, integrity and vulnerability, the "principles of European bioethics and biolaw." These general norms are considered as an expression of the European humanist tradition, which emphasizes the ontological value of the human being as well as its self-realization and development in society. In this sense, these principles would be binding guidelines to deliberate and rule legal and ethical controversies that emerged from biomedical settings.

The four "basic ethical" principles of European bioethics and biolaw (Rendtorff & Kemp, 2000, pp. 19–21) are intended to protect the human being when exposed to biomedical and biotechnological interventions. In this sense, the principles contribute to the development and consolidation of a "European Ethical and Legal Culture" by recognizing the human person as an end in itself from a human rights platform. Thus, "the ethical principles" serve as criteria not only for the protection of rights linked to self-determination but also for those rights implying life and privacy.

This conception of biolaw disregards some of the American bioethical principles to build its own principlist proposal. Indeed, dignity, integrity and vulnerability are considered as a counterweight for autonomy, mainly because they represent powerful decisional criteria to reason on the conflict presented between life and quality of life, when this dichotomy emerges in clinical or biomedical environments. For the same reason, Rendtorff and Kemp (2000, p. 19) state that their principles should be understood as expressions of "the concrete phenomenological reality of the human life-world."

As the principles of European biolaw work within the framework of the European humanist tradition, they are also eloquent of the importance to respect people as concrete human individuals, beyond their racial, religious or philosophical differences. Therefore, the basic ethical principles extend the protection of human rights toward biomedical fields, where controversial interventions are carried out on the bodily integrity of people.

The juridification of these European ethical principles is also based on the close connection that European biolaw admits between ethics and law, which is the main reason to think that common morality standards can be applied, indistinctly, as moral and legal norms. Nevertheless, none of the principles is ontologically preeminent regarding the others. In fact, Rendtorff and Kemp criticize the alleged authority that American principle of Respect for Autonomy seems to have over Nonmaleficence, Beneficence and Justice, by affirming that such superiority comes from its epistemological configuration rather than American society's cultural patterns.

Exposed in a very synoptic way, the principles of European bioethics and biolaw are as follows (Valdés, 2021, pp. 34–35).

Autonomy, which implies self-determination and self-legislation capacities by pointing the rights to (1) choose one's own way of living; (2) maintain individual life in privacy; (3) make rational decisions about one's body; (4) decide and act without coercion or external pressure; (5) consent or reject any medical treatment, therapy or experimentation; and (6) participate in the public space.

Dignity, which points out the substantial and intrinsic condition of each person's humanity. Every human being is an end in itself and is worthy of being respected as such and not be exclusively treated as a means to ends.

Integrity, which implies the right of every human being to remain unalterable in its genetic constitution and protect it from any damage and alteration. It is fundamentally based upon the right that every subject of experimentation has to protect its integrity and the consequent obligation to respect such integrity.

Vulnerability, which demands the respect and protection of the human being's intrinsically fragile condition. As the human being, conceived as a biological and psychological individual, is vulnerable, they are always exposed to damage. The procedural extension of this principle is greater than others because it is clear that in any legal and moral order, autonomy, dignity and integrity are subordinated to human beings' finite and mortal nature.

European biolaw shows why the relationship between principles and cases must be understood as a dynamic hermeneutical circle, where norms and rights are able to create ethical frameworks for biomedicine. While discerning between general and particular cases encompasses a tension between specific principles and situations, in the case of European biolaw, this tension does not imply an epistemological or methodological opposition between casuistry and principlism, as biojuridical principles are applied on cases and, on the other, particular cases give some content to the principles.

Understood as a legal principle, autonomy means the individual right to self-legislation and self-determination. This principle should be understood closely related to beneficence, which is very relevant in clinical environments. This means that patients' decisions should be respected even if physicians consider them bizarre or extravagant, as in clinical settings, autonomy means the right to pursue a good life according to self-determined wishes and beliefs.

At this point, it could be argued that this kind of theoretical interval for individual autonomy is rather a lax environment for individual rights, implying the risk of falling into a tautological dynamic of respecting individual decisions only because they are allegedly autonomous. However, this concept of an open space for law implies that there are no general legal solutions for specific problems. Legal controversies emerging by virtue of bioscientific advances entail such singularity that, thus far, an efficient legal framework to rule them has not been created. European biolaw enables individual decision-making regarding personal issues. This implies two premises: (1) Citizens are morally free and legally responsible for their decisions regarding their body and private sphere, and (2) it is not possible to apply general legal norms to unusual cases. Hence, the principle of autonomy emphasizes self-determination as a binding value and conditions its application to pressing conditions that every particular case may impose on a legal system.

The principle of dignity has a more naturalistic content. Persons' moral dignity is also legal dignity. This entails the categorical obligation to treat people as ends in themselves and not only as means for ends. In this sense, dignity implies to respect the intrinsic value of every human being and implies a legal indication arising from the ontological status of humanity, shared by all of us. Respecting the human body and its genetic identity implies recognizing ourselves as persons made of something more than a body. Dignity, therefore, is a fundamental legal principle for European biolaw, by ordering human beings' protection from possible harms that technological progress can provoke.

On the other hand, the principle of integrity plays an important role in the medical declarations and codes on the protection of patients and research human subjects. The legal definition of integrity limits biomedical interventions on the human body. The protection of physical and psychological integrity is important to formulate legal norms to govern genetic manipulation. The right to inherit an unaltered genetic structure is also a key component for any regulation based on the principle of integrity. Thus, the principle of integrity protects human beings' personal identity from genetic manipulation. This protection does not only concern people who actually exist but future generations too, because any germline genome manipulation can be passed on to the offspring. Therefore, any manipulation of human biology that entails a substantial change of genetic identity can be prohibited by following the legal normative content of the principle of integrity.

According to European biolaw, the principle of vulnerability is the foundation of any legal system as it is the ontological substance able to articulate individual life and rule social institutions. The whole juridical and political organization as well as legal principles and rules of any system should be intended to protect vulnerability of life, which is always exposed to risk and destruction. All legal systems should protect the weakest, the poorest and the most vulnerable against the ravaging consequences of discrimination, marginalization and other forms of abuse. Thus, a democratic and pluralistic society has punishment structures for those who, using their eventual position, power or abilities, harm others' life arbitrarily. Thus, the principle of vulnerability gives dignity more concrete content, by determining social institutions' regulation and becoming the main ontological basis of any legal order.

In short, the basic ethical principle of European bioethics and biolaw's goal is to build a normative framework for the protection of persons from biomedical and biotechnological applications. However, it has not achieved the status of a legally binding model. This epistemology aims to defeat normative antinomies between bioethics and biolaw, by considering biolaw principles as bioethical ones, so that they work as common morality norms and legal standards indistinctly. European biolaw, therefore, does not understand bioethics as a common law model or as a catalog of recommendations to regulate bioscientific practices. Rather, it defends that biolaw should be understood as a field that encompasses all legal judgments concerning bioethical issues and, therefore, should always be involved in counseling jurisdictional authorities, bioethics committees and courts about conflicts and controversies of bioethical scope (Kemp, 2000, p. 69).

Moreover, European biolaw has some naturalistic elements. As a matter of fact, Beyleveld and Brownsword (2000a, pp. 179–218, 2000b, pp. 15–44) criticize the traditional ontological and epistemological status of dignity, but at the same time, they consider dignity to be a possible criterion of argumentation in biolaw, from a human rights perspective. On the other hand, in their latest works, Kemp and Rendtorff (Kemp, 2019, pp. 19–32; Rendtorff & Kemp, 2019, pp. 33–40) argue that autonomy, dignity, integrity and vulnerability are ethical principles belonging to law. Thus, he emphasizes that the basic ethical principles of European biolaw should be supported by the idea of justice, which, at the same time, should be grounded upon the four ethical principles. Therefore, the principles should not be understood as ontological conditions but as reflexive guidelines for bioethics and biolaw, in the context of a plurality of discourses displayed in many different points of view (Rendtorff & Kemp, 2019, p. 39).

Rendtorff and Kemp's proposal is clearly the first substantive epistemological configuration of biolaw. Earlier on, biolaw was only a neologism pointing to a new sort of unspecified and unclassified law. They do not define biolaw as a specific branch of law; instead, they do identify it as a new hermeneutical model to rule biomedical practices that entail important risks to life as a whole.

European biolaw is also exhaustive in describing the contextual universe in which the new field should be applied. In this sense, there are different contexts of application for the principles, as well as these encompass general normative dimensions within European culture and tradition. Ethical and legal conflicts arising from bioscientific research must be approached from two points of view: Principles and rules. Principles work in general and theoretical environments. Rules are a kind of principles' particular and practical dimensions. This means that principles imply foundations and definitions and determine deliberation's epistemological scope. Rules, on the other hand, point to a procedural level where principles are specified. Therefore, these two deliberative levels (principles and rules) are complementary in European biolaw, and they need each other.

Also, this conception of biolaw is not an encapsulated and traditional intellection of legal problems. In fact, it works in a context of a globalized and technologized world where biotechnological practices demand more consideration and point to more complex ethical and legal quandaries.

On the other hand, as European biolaw's principles are traditional common morality norms culturally accepted by Western tradition, they are part of a cultural identity and work as guidelines for social cohesion and consensus in the civil space. Thus, their scope can be extended to create regulation to protect animals and nature from new biotechnologies' impacts and applications. In fact, whereas European biolaw does not develop substantial arguments about animals' and nature's legal status, it is promising in understanding biolaw free from being encapsulated within an anthropocentric legal model. This, now more than ever, when doctrine and international jurisprudence go forward in that direction, represents an important insight especially not only to reflect on the importance of morally and legally respecting animals and stop causing them unnecessary suffering but also, and especially, to modify our feed customs and, thus, stop approving, supporting and institutionalizing the absurd slaughter and unjustifiable suffering of animals in the world, which, as we will show further, impact negatively the possibility of a sustainable world.

Finally, although European biolaw does not configure a completely dense epistemology for the principles' normative content, it does improve the possibilities to achieve more effectiveness, not only in deliberation and decision-making but also in engendering new regulatory models to be applied in clinical and biomedical environments.

2.3 Mediterranean biolaw

This epistemology takes various theoretical and ideological bases from human rights, by considering the human being to be the first and only target of any regulation. Most of Spanish, French and Italian jurists have developed this idea of biolaw, which is why, despite being, strictly speaking, a theory born in Europe, it has been called the Mediterranean conception, as it is necessary to specify it and distinguish it, methodologically and epistemologically, from European biolaw (Valdés, 2021, p. 131).

Romeo Casabona and Romeo Malanda (2019, pp. 59–76) recognize biolaw as an autonomous field and define it as a legal discipline. They argue that there is an interdependence, both epistemological and methodological, between bioethics and biolaw. In this way, as bioethics has inspired law, this has also influenced bioethics (Romeo Casabona and Romeo Malanda, 2019, p. 68). That is a good reason to consider this conception characterized by the concepts of subjection and overlap between both fields.

These authors use different but complementary perspectives to explore some aspects of bioethics' methodology, such as its interdisciplinary discourse and its approach to conflicts provoked by bioscientific practices. However, while they affirm biolaw's disciplinary liberation from bioethics, they do not distinguish the epistemological and normative gaps between both fields. In fact, Romeo Casabona and Romeo Malanda (2019, p. 67) affirm that by virtue of bioethics' empirical scopes, law and biolaw should be integrated into it.

In addition, these authors propose a dichotomous definition of biolaw, which obscures its epistemological configuration. They claim that biolaw must be understood and defined by virtue of its purpose. If its goal is to regulate genetic practices that affect only the human being, biolaw should be taken as a biomedical law. In this way, law, by virtue of the human being's legal transcendence, should master biosciences' legal repercussions for persons, by integrating biology's contributions into biomedical and clinical settings (Romeo Casabona & Romeo Malanda 2019, p. 65).

As biolaw is intended to rule biosciences, which is able to impact not only human beings but also nonhuman entities, it would become a law of *bios*, by addressing new technologies' ethical implications for all living beings (Romeo Casabona & Romeo Malanda 2019, p. 61). The idea that biolaw should be understood from its relations of subjection and overlap to bioethics, becoming a subdiscipline aimed at studying, clarifying and eventually resolving ethical quandaries that biotechnological applications entail for life as a whole, clearly underlies Romeo Casabona and Romeo Malanda's conception of biolaw (Valdés, 2021, p. 40). Therefore, from this Mediterranean intellection, biolaw becomes an instrument of bioethics or, at best, part of it.

On the other hand, French biojurists consider biolaw to be a cast of bioethical laws (Lenoir, 2000, p. 221) or bionorms (Fagot-Largeault, 2000, p. 27), giving content to bioethics in order for it to identify what the best regulation for biomedical practices should be. Those bionorms should consider three elements: Facts, values and choices. From this tridimensional hermeneutical approach, defining specific laws or norms for biomedical sciences would be possible. Thus, facts need to be evaluated and judged. Only after that, a regulatory model could be chosen to address cases or practices.

French authors affirm a consubstantial relationship between bioethical laws and fundamental values of European society (Lenoir, 2000, pp. 222–223). In this way, the legally binding status of any bioethical law needs to be in tune with and be based on prima facie, nonbinding moral norms. This intersects Mediterranean biolaw with the human rights' doctrine, by making evident some characteristics this epistemology shares with the European and international conceptions of biolaw. These connections are (i) dignity as an overarching principle for governing biomedicine. According to Lenoir (2000, pp. 224–225), dignity has two distinctive features regarding other principles: (1) It overcomes the distinction between the I and the Other, because dignity implies to understand any person as oneself, and (2) it is a categorical principle, because its observance does not admit exceptions. (ii) Mediterranean biolaw encompasses a consubstantial relationship between bioethics and human rights, because it works with universal moral principles that allow the recognition of new fundamental rights such as to dispose of one's body and the right to a bodily integrity (Lenoir, 2000, p. 224).

Also, Mediterranean biolaw understands dignity as a restriction to individual autonomy, which must display itself in harmony with such ontological condition of the human being. In this way, dignity is a paramount value to guide biomedical settings' regulation. This intellection, as implies a coincidence between bioethics and human rights, reveals an instrumental status of biolaw, dependent on the optimization and evolution of bioethics.

Finally, Lenoir (2000, p. 267) affirms that biolaw has an important role to play, especially in balancing interests, protecting the vulnerable and empowering individuals when facing the new inventions of biomedicine. Therefore, not all biomedical practices or bioethical conflicts require a "new biolaw." Lenoir (2000, p. 267) states that biolaw can be especially effective in establishing a framework for bioethical principles as well as identifying a plausible range of practice to be complemented by regulations able to encompass specific casuistic applications and interpretations.

In Italy, Carlo Casonato (2019, pp. 77–91) considers biolaw to be an open, updated and attentive law. It is open because it is building laws for decision-making at the intersection of science and ethics. In other words, biolaw would also be an instrument of bioethics.

Casonato argues that international biolaw's instruments are grounded upon scientific aspects of philosophical and social scope. Thus, biolaw would be an open law to the scientific and ethical dimension of biosciences. Also, the evolution of international instruments (parliamentary law, jurisprudence) implies that European law has been molded by bioethical epistemology, which finally points out the instrumentalization of the so-called life sciences law as a key means for the bioethical colonization of European law.

On the other hand, biolaw is an updated law as biosciences changes its ethical and social understanding, which must be regulated by a new law. Two sorts of temporary laws can be identified in the field of life sciences: (i) A flexible nature of regulation's content is closely linked to changing scientific paradigms; hence, traditional law does not make sense because its object simply does not exist anymore, having been replaced by another, more accurate and evolved; and (ii) a second type of temporary legislation, which is not related to expected scientific changes, but to a supposed modification of ethical and social paradigms (Casonato, 2019, p. 85).

In addition, biolaw is an attentive biolaw, not only to bioscientific changes but also to individual needs. Thus, biolaw entails a legal flexibility in order to balance interests, which would be much more compatible with constitutional principles. Therefore, biolaw does not work far from constitutional law, being attentive to the changing complexities of biomedical science, whose legal approach should necessarily consider an initial bioethical debate.

As a conclusion, we can say that Mediterranean biolaw understands itself as a field tributary upon bioethics, as its theoretical and practical justification, as well as its legitimization to address juridical quandaries arisen from biomedical practices, strongly depend on bioethical evolution.

2.4 American biolaw

American conception encompasses a consubstantial relationship between bioethics and biolaw. We will see that this relation is determined by a bioethical colonization of American courts as well as a complementation between bioethics and traditional law. In fact, American biolaw would be a law supported by bioethics' epistemology, aimed at addressing legal issues emerged from new genetic techniques. In other words, American biolaw would simply be the law applied to new problems of bioethical interest.

Mekinoff (2001, pp. 1–3) argues that the American legal system has played a very important role in how public opinion understands the field of bioethics. However, it is not only the public mass that recognizes the intrinsic connection between law and bioethical issues but also the leading scholars in the field, paradigmatic books and bioethical organizations in general. All of them agree on the relevance that law has had in achieving a deeper and more mature understanding of bioethics.

In this way, the expression "law and bioethics" refers to a new field of traditional law evolving into certain not strictly legal areas. In this way, for American conception, "law and bioethics" (namely, "biolaw") implies a juxtaposition of legal doctrines, not related to each other but only sharing interests of bioethical nature (Tribe, 2000).

Johnson, Iltis, and Hinze (2008, p. 1) assert that biolaw implies legal perspectives in bioethics. Thus, although controversial, the intervention and intrusion of law, lawyers and courts in bioethics and their issues are, according to the authors, an indisputable fact. Besides being a traditional law, adapted to bioethical contingencies of the current legal conflicts provoked by biomedical practices, American biolaw converges with bioethics (Johnson et al., 2008, p. 1), pointing out a mutual influence between both disciplines. This relationship is analogous to the connection between law and ethics.

Johnson et al. (2008, p. 2) think that an obvious point of convergence between biolaw and bioethics would be the methodology used in both fields. They emphasize that common law system rests on a methodology that has been preponderant in the bioethical discourse. Indeed, as the essential method of common law model is law evolving from court's rulings, facts and circumstances examined case by case create priors for subsequent judicial decisions. In this way, common law principles emerge from the analysis of convergences and divergences of different concrete situations. This casuistry would also be remarkable in the evolution of biomedical law or biolaw.

Another linking between bioethics and biolaw emerges when the legal framework to address bioethical issues adopts moral norms and ethical models of reasoning. This often happens in the United States, where faced with decisions related to the end of life, most of the courts have explicitly implemented a principlist model, using the four principles approach to decide about biojuridical conflicts.

Therefore, for American biolaw, law is an institution limited not only by the legal standards themselves but also by the variability of the context and the lack of consensus on ethical standards. In fact, law establishes standards to determine a minimal ethical behavior and not an ideal ethical conduct.

Dolgin and Shepherd (2005, p. 7) ask themselves how much biolaw exists in the United States and how much of it will exist and should exist in the future (Valdés, 2021, p. 47). When they point to the new field, they use quotation marks as they understand biolaw as a law focused on bioethical issues, which has gradually increased the legal attention on medicine and bioethical conflicts in general. According to them, the approximation of biolaw to bioethical issues has been "piecemeal, uncoordinated and somewhat haphazard" (Valdés, 2021, p. 47). This is quite clear in federal and state courts applying common and constitutional law, as well as when state legislatures and regulatory bodies create statutory schemes and regulatory models. Thus, American biolaw is traditional law evolving in courts, case by case and jurisdiction by jurisdiction.

Therefore, biolaw can differ depending on the state, regarding its hermeneutical and conceptual approach to specific cases.

For this epistemology then, biolaw informs bioethics like law does it with medicine. This influence is rather procedural and comes into play when law is used to solve dilemmas related to clinical and biomedical fields. However, the epistemological distance between bioethics and biolaw is, in this conception, rather diffuse.

Dolgin and Shepherd (2005, p. 8) also affirm that, in health care's settings, American society has often used the right to ask and answer questions related to what is ethically correct to do among those who provide health care services and those who use or receive them. Thus, American biolaw is a reaction to the perception that something is going wrong in the health care field. As a matter of fact, over the past 30 years, federal laws have illustrated how American society has reacted, questioning law and requesting the creation of laws to end unethical behaviors and abuses in health care. In this way, "the legal resolution becomes a societal consensus statement on ethics" (Dolgin & Shepherd, 2005, p. 8), until the laws change themselves or modify the status quo.

By concluding, we can affirm that American biolaw's advance depends on jurisprudence's evolution, which implies unsystematic development and epistemological fragility in its configuration. Moreover, American biolaw is reactive and, therefore, is unable to create normative spaces with conceptual and hermeneutical density. Finally, American biolaw's evolution is not profound, and its theoretical inaction is easily perceivable. While new technologies' applications are profuse in North America, American biolaw seems not to have a promising future in reaching its epistemological consolidation.

2.5 International biolaw

This conception understands biolaw as a collection of international instruments mostly created by UNESCO and the EU, containing an extensive cast of nonlegally binding provisions and recommendations to be adopted in the European regulation of biomedicine. The whole catalog of recommendations, namely, all nonbinding provisions, come from the intersection between American bioethics and human rights. In this sense, all the provisions are an expression of prima facie moral principles lacking relevant epistemological density. Some instruments of international biolaw are Universal Declaration on the Human Genome and Human Rights, UNESCO, 1997; Declaration on the Responsibilities of the Present Generations Towards Future Generations, UNESCO, 1997; and Convention for the Protection of Human Rights and Dignity of the Human Being with Regard to the Application of Biology and Medicine, EUROPEAN UNION (Oviedo Convention), 1997, among many others.

All instruments share three elements: (i) The principles that tacitly or explicitly underlie the recommendations, (ii) principles' meaning and content and (iii) dignity as the overriding principle of each instrument (Valdés, 2021,

p. 49). In this order of ideas, Andorno (2013, p. 15) identifies three fundamental features: (i) The recognition of human dignity as the paramount and overarching principle, understood as a principle inherent to human beings' condition and, therefore, that radiates to any other principle; (ii) the use of the human rights framework, because this doctrine represents an exhaustive collection of universal moral principles, also based on the founding principle of dignity; therefore, those principles have the same epistemological composition as American bioethics' principles, being common morality norms, and thin-content standards of general and vague scope; and (iii) the widespread adoption of general principles, understood as optimization mandates, which must be applied to different degrees, depending on the circumstances.

Thus, international biolaw is an extension of international human rights and American bioethics to biomedical settings. This analogy is justified from an imprecise epistemological intersection of principles between both disciplinary fields. Therefore, this is a rather tautological conception of biolaw. Indeed, being a constellation of instruments and principles working as nonbinding provisions of international biolaw, those standards are replicated in most conventions and declarations. This means that the normative configuration of the principles is also similar and, in many cases, identical in most instruments.

Also, international biolaw is unable to materialize a conceptual and institutional dimension to reach a denser disciplinary status. Accepting that international biolaw is a constellation of international documents on biomedicine, based on bioethical categories, leads to conclude that this conception considers biolaw as a simple compilation of nonbinding provisions on biomedical practices.

Therefore, international biolaw does not create new legal knowledge. This means that it does not advance in understanding traditional principles of law that, in the light of the new bioscience's advancements, seem to demand and deserve a new interpretation. In this way, international biolaw is only a compendium of nonbinding recommendations, which become a soft law without a binding regulatory dimension.

It seems to be then that principles of international biolaw's ultimate grounds are, rather, metaphysical and, therefore, are often based on dogmatism and ideology. This means the arguments that provide normative content to the principles and provisions are not strictly conceptual (Valdés, 2021, p. 56).

2.6 Cosmopolitan biolaw

By cosmopolitan biolaw we mean a biolaw able to achieve an interjurisdictional regulatory scope so that the new field can become the basis for international governance and sustainability in a post-COVID-19 world. Indeed, as we have already stated in the Introduction, the virus has demonstrated the need for such a biolaw to deal with global governance and create good transition toward more sustainable international legal and economic structure. In this context, cosmopolitan biolaw turns into a relevant tool for the realization of the United

Nation's Sustainable Development Goals. In this way, biolaw is an instrument for creating a better relation between protection of the environment and the social and cultural development of society toward sustainability.

As cosmopolitan biolaw distances from other traditional conceptions as well as from bioethics, it is important to discuss its epistemological and regulatory features. In this sense, cosmopolitan biolaw constitutes a new epistemology for global governance and sustainability; a new deliberative and argumentative device to understand ethical and legal implications of global problems arisen by virtue of pandemics and new technologies; a new hermeneutical approach to read the real scopes of risky scenarios posed and raised by a pandemic world; and a new branch of law, able to discover, identify and define new categories to oversight and rule very conflictive scenarios' tributary upon global and existential risks emerging in our contemporary times.

Cosmopolitan biolaw is a new epistemology for global governance because it clearly has recognizable conceptual and institutional dimensions to be applied in global scenarios of risk. It is evident, as we have shown earlier on, that biolaw has a systematized disciplinary dimension, which has decanted in different conceptualizations with their respective institutional referents. These conceptions of biolaw, beyond their coincidences, have different theoretical density, categories, purposes, regulatory scopes, foundations and hermeneutics, by constituting eclectic conceptual approaches to the same event, which can be very workable at the time of analyzing and finding solutions for conflictive scenarios provoked by global threats that can fracture sustainability.

Moreover, cosmopolitan biolaw is competent enough to engender specific deliberative and argumentative frameworks to address disturbing legal controversies arisen by virtue of the proliferation of new biotechnological inventions and existential risks, as we will see at the end of this book. Therefore, a universal biolaw characterizes a new deliberative model within law, as it is able to develop articulations within the vast nature of global risks, as well as of governance and sustainability's issues, by inaugurating new juridical meanings attuned to the legal scopes of these new global challenges. Being a new deliberative model, cosmopolitan biolaw provides various criteria to understand and intervene massive problematic scenarios, which seems to be impossible for classical law and bioethics. Therefore, cosmopolitan biolaw, by consolidating itself as a new model of legal deliberation and argumentation, can identify and define criteria, guidelines, regulations and policies for a technological world as a whole. In addition, biolaw is able to recategorize other models already defined by law and coordinate and articulate them inter-institutionally and interjurisdictionally. In this way, cosmopolitan biolaw also turns into an instrument for the evolution of law and its institutions, by intervening and optimizing them.

Cosmopolitan biolaw is also a new hermeneutical approach within law. It identifies new criteria of interpretation to deliver legal certainty to global governance and sustainability's juridical implications. Moreover, it is able to identify new possibilities of damage available in the present world, by generating new institutional categories to predict and rule eventual harmful aftermaths. In the same way, cosmopolitan biolaw recognizes and defines new individual subjective rights related to those harms as well as new legal interests to be specified and considered in a world where international governance and planetary sustainability are at stake.

Moreover, cosmopolitan biolaw is a new branch of law that distinguishes itself from other traditional branches, at least in three elements: (i) Its juridical target: It is specific, precise and unique; namely, no other branch of law has as its main purpose to study, understand and rule latest bioscience's practices of global scope and impact; (ii) its regulatory scope: Unlike traditional branches of law, which seek to engender national regulation, cosmopolitan biolaw is able to build interjurisdictional and international regulation workable in different legal systems in the world, which is urgent in a globe where sustainability seems to depend on a cosmopolitan governance too; and (iii) its epistemological range: A universal biolaw has the ability to extend its categorical scope to other branches of law, irradiating and optimizing them. In this fashion, cosmopolitan biolaw can perfect civil law, criminal law, public law, constitutional law and public and private international law, by identifying and defining new regimes of protection for humans, new legal interests to be protected, new scopes for state responsibility when failing in the application of genetic practices, new subjective rights (biorights) and new forms of ensuring interjurisdictional governance and global sustainability in a post-pandemic world, respectively.

Therefore, from a general perspective, cosmopolitan biolaw is a new branch of law, applied to global scenarios, able, among others, to open new normative universes, by identifying new categories of unlawful damages, recognizing new individual subjective rights with constitutional value (biorights) and enabling greater legal certainty to rule biomedicine and global problems. Likewise, and specifically, cosmopolitan biolaw is not only a set of principles and norms to be coercively applied within local legal systems. Thus, a universal biolaw represents a legally binding model and approach, applied interjurisdictionally, as a basis for oversighting and ruling international governance and global sustainability's atmospheres.

Hence, cosmopolitan biolaw is not parasitical upon bioethics, as it is aimed at creating legally binding normative frameworks. Also, it has its own scope, different from bioethics, which is applied to moral controversies whose resolution does not necessarily generate legal-normative consequences. In this way, cosmopolitan biolaw has epistemological and methodological independence from bioethics, by inaugurating new normative universes, through the optimization and redefinition of traditional law's legal categories. At the same time, a universal biolaw identifies new categories of damages that traditional law never recognized before, which come from a contemporary world molded by global risks for governance and sustainability.

All global controversies coming from the advances of biomedicine, new technologies and the expansions of planetary risks have a biojuridical scope. In addition, the social relevance of global risks' legal implications is indisputable, as it is rooted in complex multifactorial relationships involving not only science and bioethics but also law and culture in general. Therefore, there is a need to identify and define new binding legal frameworks in order to understand new governance and sustainability challenges. This urgency becomes even more evident if we consider some objective facts evidencing traditional law's incompetence to address certain unprecedented legal problems that emerged from risk environments (Valdés, 2021, p. 136):

i. There are competing international legal positions regarding global governance, preventing juridical dialog from moving forward to consensus. This has paralyzed legislative work in several countries.
ii. Current legal hermeneutics is unable to address complex massive cases, as facts' interpretation is subjective (contingent on particular inclinations, beliefs, values and preferences), and authorities and legislators often declare ignorance about these matters.
iii. There are gaps and legal loopholes, as biojuridical international legislation and regulation are incomplete or inefficient to address global governance conflicts.
iv. Current international legal systems are incomplete in terms of biomedical regulation and, therefore, have problems to resolve biojuridical conflicts related to governance and sustainability.
v. There is lack of international policy on global governance, also due to the absence of legislation.

These facts point to an important inability of international legal systems to govern crucial aspects of governance and sustainability in a world strongly marked by global and existential risks. We argue that cosmopolitan biolaw can mean a milestone regarding that task.

Indeed, one of the most important contributions of universal biolaw to juridical science is to identify and define new rights in legal systems, which can work interjurisdictionally. Thus, cosmopolitan biolaw can create new normative universes whose legitimation in legal systems can be justified as follows (Valdés, 2021, p. 137): (i) These new biorights cannot be ignored in legal systems as that would imply a contradiction with constitutions and international conventions, and (ii) latest-generation technologies' scope and consequences cannot be accurately anticipated. This implies an interjurisdictional responsibility: Creating sufficient and necessary legal grounds to identify new kinds of rights that traditional law never recognized before.

Among these new biorights (Valdés, 2021, p. 137), we can identify, at least, *Right to genetic integrity*, which must be considered in relation to cultural and social identity, as it expresses the narrative coherence of any civilization. Damages and risks to relational aspects of individuals are then evident in the light of this new biojuridical category, which comprises the obligation to respect the right to preserve people's genetic integrity. Next is *Right to genetic self-determination*, which encompasses to reject predeterminism underlying nontherapeutic genetic techniques that can alter, diminish and even annul a life project, namely, persons' abilities to live their lives according to non-predetermined paradigms. In addition, using and trading with human genome and genetic information, without consent, also confront this right. Following is *Right to genetic privacy*, because using genetic information without consent hurts privacy, as it implies serious alterations and disturbances to individual life project's deployment; hence, the right to keep genetic constitution free from public scrutiny should be considered as a fundamental right of constitutional range. Then comes *Right to genetic diversity*, as nontherapeutic enhancement entails new forms of discrimination and social segregation, even worse than the current ones: Selective eugenics; universalization of esthetic and epistemological stereotypes; racial homogenization; and loss or, at best, erosion of genetic diversity, among others. This sort of genetic tyranny would determine the exclusion of minorities from public space, namely, the exclusion of the weak, the sick, the physically impaired, the esthetically unfortunate and the less intellectually gifted. This genetic diversity is a right to be respected as it can prevent society from moving toward new forms of marginalization determined by a social structure split into humans and transhumans.

All these rights have an interjurisdictional scope and can be integrated into international law and local constitutions indistinctly. Therefore, new biorights enable to identify new categories of global damages, which can have profound legal, political and social consequences.

Biorights can also impact other rights related to health, as well as they make visible the need to include new categories of damages when determining and calculating compensations. As one of the fundamental purposes of reparation is to observe principles of integral reparation and equality, neglecting new biorights would imply contradicting constitutional principles that all democratic nations agreed with. Learning from the European experience is important to foster the integration of biorights into legal systems, granting them constitutional status as fundamental rights. In this way, the constitutionality block can be workable for such integration. In fact, improving the constitutional protection of fundamental rights requires a constitutional reception of international legal criteria on individual subjective rights.

Thus, incorporating international jurisprudential rules and practices into local formal constitutions implies to configure the material constitution in relation to those rights. This does not mean an exaggerated categorical dispersion of constitutional norms but rather the extension of fundamental rights in harmony with the new possibilities of damage that biomedical techniques encompass. This extension should also imply the subjection or, at least, the adaptation of lower hierarchy local norms to interjurisdictional international norms.

We call biorights to not only subjective rights emerging from dogmatic evolution of international biolaw in the Council of Europe. Their basis is related to general fundamental rights specified into biorights especially when facing biojuridical quandaries. Therefore, biorights demand to reconfigure traditional legal categories of national systems, to improve juridical protection of human beings in global risky scenarios.

Biorights are also individual subjective rights related to the capacity to self-determine and self-preserve genetic identity. As we will demonstrate in the last chapter of this part, new juridical universes opened by biomedicine's empowerment are not duly regulated, and controversies arising as a result of the expansion of genetic techniques are legislated without epistemological conviction. Furthermore, the relation between biorights and fundamental rights points to their own content insofar as diverse legal systems recognize the protection of human autonomy and integrity as an essential dimension of constitutional democracies.

Moreover, human beings' protection is a juridical commitment of different states in the framework of international conventions. In this way, evaluating the specific conditions under those agreements on fundamental rights are inserted into national regulations as relevant. As biorights encompass human conditions and attributes threatened by new technologies, their protection and observance cannot be neglected. Their constitutionalization is based on how their effective protection must be conducted. Thus, how the states will allocate their resources to integrate these new biorights into juridical systems becomes a matter of public policy.

Biorights point to a new way of understanding the juridical institution of subject of rights. Rights of first (civil and political), second (economic, social and cultural) and third generation (rights of peoples, right to peace, right to a healthy environment, etc.) have been unable to extend their scope to face new controversies emerging from biomedical development and global governance issues. Instead, biorights represent new juridical categories that allow a more efficient protection of persons when loomed by genetics and global risks. Nowadays, subjects of rights are exposed to undeniable possibilities of harm in aspects that previously seemed to be improbable; for instance, their genetic makeup. All these harms can imply aftermaths for future generations. Therefore, biorights (a new generation of rights) improve human beings' juridical protection (Valdés, 2021, p. 139).

On the other hand, cosmopolitan biolaw is able to create new normative universes, identify new categories of unlawful damages, define new individual subjective rights (biorights), recognize new legal interests to be protected and provide greater legal certainty to rule biomedicine. Cosmopolitan biolaw imply a very important political task: It can merge competing positions regarding juridical implications of biomedical issues, which is key to move forward to agreements and propel legislative work. In this way, cosmopolitan biolaw is a more ductile and objective interpretative model, which circumvents excessive casuistry in order to perfect decision-making processes. As international legal systems regulation is overall not profuse, a universal biolaw promotes the proliferation of specific international juridical standards for biomedical and genetic developments by avoiding legal loopholes.

Therefore, cosmopolitan biolaw can determine (i) if existing international legal frameworks are workable to rule biomedical technologies and (ii) how biomedical and biotechnological empowerment impacts the prescriptive corpus of society. In this way, cosmopolitan biolaw can give biomedical practices more legal certainty and security (Valdés, 2021, p. 140).

Regarding cosmopolitan biolaw's methodological scope, most of the questions raised in biojuridical atmospheres are questions *inside-of* biolaw (Valdés, 2021, p. 140). On the other hand, asking what are the contributions of biolaw to international legal systems is a question *outside-about* biolaw. Thus, while cosmopolitan biolaw displays a double dimension able to address the legal-normative status of biomedical practices and how to rule them (*inside-of*), it is also able to inquire for its own nature and consequent relations to other jurisdictions (*outside-about*) (Valdés, 2021, p. 141).

The *inside-of* dimension implies the endogenous nature of biolaw, namely, *what* biolaw *is*, including its methodological and epistemological possibilities, and referring to what biolaw is regarding itself, without extending its scope to other disciplinary environments. The *outside-about* dimension implies the exogenous condition of biolaw, that is, its extension to other jurisdictions, which points to *what* biolaw is *for*, namely, what are the contributions of biolaw to other branches of law and epistemological fields. This double conceptualization is consubstantial as the exogenous dimension of biolaw cannot be vindicated without understanding its endogenous one (Valdés, 2021, p. 141).

Moreover, cosmopolitan biolaw represents an efficient legal device to protect new fundamental rights arisen from biotechnological settings. It also reinforces the state's obligation to protect those rights, by tending to their realization instead of their impairment. Thus, our proposal gets over, epistemologically and methodologically, the European soft-law-constitutional jurisprudence and also improves and optimizes the understanding of fundamental rights in contemporary juridical contexts. In this sense, cosmopolitan biolaw can endow constitutional legal systems with a new and more complete conception of fundamental rights, which allows the states to fulfill their international obligations by making such rights more efficient in domestic jurisdictional frameworks.

Therefore, the importance of cosmopolitan biolaw is not only based upon its procedural or doctrinal contribution to law and other branches of law but it also implies two significant consequences: (i) It speeds up judicial decisions on biomedical matters as it provides more legal certainty to reason on biojuridical conflicts at a legislative level, and (ii) it can guarantee the international constitutionalization of new individual subjective rights to make international jurisdictions more efficient and just.

In this fashion, cosmopolitan biolaw's power compared with traditional law is displayed in its capacity for providing more legal certainty to biomedicine, global governance and sustainability's scenarios, as well as to foster other branches of law's categorical expansion. This authority of cosmopolitan biolaw can be expressed through the following assertions (Valdés, 2021, pp. 132–133).

As traditional law is *literal*, namely, it recites phenomena of juridical scope by understanding their meaning, cosmopolitan biolaw is *hermeneutical*, that is, it interprets juridical phenomena by creating new meanings.

Traditional law is *reactive* as it rules after juridical incidents occur. Instead, cosmopolitan biolaw is *proactive*, as it is intended to rule before events happen.

Traditional law is *intradisciplinary* as it generally works fragmented and encapsulated in independent branches. However, cosmopolitan biolaw is *interdisciplinary*, as it displays itself attuned with other jurisdictional and epistemological fields and branches of traditional law.

Traditional law is *univocal* as it generally seeks and admits one answer possible to juridical and policy conflicts. On the contrary, cosmopolitan biolaw is *open* as it seeks and admits a plausible range of possible responses equally relevant to solve juridical and international policy quandaries.

Traditional law is *paradigmatic* as it based upon epistemological archetypes. Instead, cosmopolitan biolaw is *revolutionary*, as it is not necessarily grounded on epistemological prototypes.

Traditional law is *conservative* as it works with and from traditional categories of law. Cosmopolitan biolaw is *innovative* as it works with biojuridical concepts created from a categorial expansion of traditional law.

As traditional law is *reductionist*, meaning it does not identify new juridical categories, cosmopolitan biolaw is *holistic* as it irradiates, expands and perfects other branches of law.

Traditional law is *explicative* as it is not completely aimed at creating new knowledge. However, cosmopolitan biolaw is *extensive* as it creates new epistemologies.

While traditional law is *centripetal*, as its branches do not engender feedback with each other, cosmopolitan biolaw is *centrifugal* as it epistemologically irradiates other branches of law.

While traditional law is *anthropocentric* as it understands and thinks life as human life, cosmopolitan biolaw is *biocentric* as it thinks life as a whole by considering nature and animals as entities worthy of moral and juridical protection.

Finally, as traditional law is *national* because it rules inside legal orders, cosmopolitan biolaw is *international* as it engenders interjurisdictional regulations.

Therefore, cosmopolitan biolaw is very relevant, as it generates debate and discussion about the statute, not only legal but also ontological, of many concepts of traditional law, which can lead to an optimization of biomedical matters' regulation and legislation, as well as to understand global issues of governance and sustainability related not only to humans but also to animals and environment's rights.

3 Biolaw and society

3.1 Jurisdictional scope of biolaw

A compelling determination of biolaw's jurisdictional scope demands to clearly distinguish it from bioethics. Even though while analyzing different conceptions of biolaw, we have already explained some differences between both fields, it is significant at this point to provide more robust arguments to clarify this important matter, especially to prevent biolaw from being understood only from bioethics.

First, biolaw works in its own normative environment, which is different from that of bioethics. As bioethics points to deliberative settings, by designing models of reasoning for ethical quandaries that emerged from clinical and biomedical surroundings, biolaw engenders legally binding norms to rule biosciences and new technologies' practices.

Second, biolaw is not part of bioethics. It is not a bioethics' sub-branch that addresses legal scopes of bioethical problems. Biolaw does not study bioethics and its legal quandaries but juridical crossroads emerging from biomedical and bioscientific fields. Affirming that the new field is parasitical upon bioethics implies a dangerous overlap of distinctive normative dimensions.

Third, when biolaw assumes a principlist model (Beauchamp & Childress, 2019; Rendtorff & Kemp, 2000), it cannot be grounded upon common morality principles. This would entail to accept that there are no differences between bioethics and biolaw. Moreover, accepting that deliberation in biolaw must be based on general ethical principles points to a methodological and epistemological imprecision. It is a methodological mistake as it encloses the procedural scope of biolaw within the field of ethics, preventing it from being extended to the jurisdictional context of law. Biolaw is able to build juridical frameworks for biomedical practices' regulation. Traditional conceptions of biolaw do not consider such relevant imperfection, as all of them fail in giving biolaw a legally binding vocation. In this way, biolaw has its own epistemological status that is not similar to that of bioethics (Valdés, 2021, p. 126). In fact, biolaw configures an interdisciplinarity different from bioethics, with a wider scope to define and apply legal standards in biomedical surroundings. At the same time, biolaw can recategorize classic legal categories and foster new hermeneutics for legal argumentation.

DOI: 10.4324/9781003147848-3

As biolaw overcomes the limitations of traditional legal dogma, it can identify new individual subjective rights (biorights), to be integrated into constitutions and light legal systems interjurisdictionally.

Fourth, the normative content of biolaw is different from that of bioethics. Biolaw is not an instrument of evolution for biomedical ethics. It is true that both fields have colonized each other, which has eroded biolaw's legal status. However, such colonization has been mainly discursive, as it can be seen in the European Court of Human Rights' jurisprudence and in American courts' rulings. In any case, this demonstrates that there is a necessary relationship between the two fields. Therefore, biolaw can be perfectly justified or understood without bioethics.

Fifth, bioethics offers space enough to engender emotional models of reasoning, enabling the participation and consideration of very subjective aspects of deliberation. These include axiological considerations of values and preferences, as well as the acceptance of professional duties and third parties' expectations' clashes. While biolaw does not engender emotional normative models, it does seek social consensus, which is expected to be based on explicit social and public agreements, in order to avoid arbitrariness and partiality.

Sixth, bioethics belongs to a more eclectic normative universe than that of biolaw. Deliberation in bioethics can be conducted in any of its normative levels, such as ethical theories, prima facie principles, professional rules and procedures (Valdés, 2021, p. 127). This eclecticism leads to misperception when principlism is applied on conflictive scenarios. In fact, people do not know what to do with principles as those four prescriptive dimensions are not always consubstantial and often collide with one another. In its place, biolaw represents an integral and nonfragmented approach to legal conflicts arisen in bioscientific contexts. It does not impose deliberative phases disconnected from each other. As biolaw does not address juridical problems from fossilized legal theories or already existing norms of traditional law, it does create new prescriptive atmospheres, in tune with specific legal problems raised by new technologies' advances and bioscientific practices.

Therefore, the prescriptive dimensions of bioethics are encapsulated or intrinsic, as the normative scope of its normative stages is determined by theories, principles, norms or procedures. On the other hand, biolaw has an extrinsic normative scope, as it impacts other branches of law, by recategorizing institutions of traditional law, regardless of pre-established norms.

Having said that, we now have to determine where the authority of biolaw is coming from. Abbot (1988) used the term "jurisdiction" to conceptualize the relation professionals establish between themselves and different tasks they carry out. This connection is also made by the public sphere and people in general, by legitimizing a professional field in culture, social environments and academic atmospheres. Evans (2012) refers to a professional crisis in bioethics, especially concerning its jurisdiction, that is, the cast of competing ethical claims about medical and scientific practices (Valdés, 2021, p. 128).

Discussion on how biomedical practices should be governed boosted in the public sphere, implying that several social actors have gotten involved in different discussions to articulate professional approaches to the problem. However, opinions are not always coming from professional environments. Common people also impact debates, as it is understood that they have some authority to share expertise, knowledge or even common sense to complement public deliberation on new technologies. People and the public space, in general, recognize bioethics as the most authoritative field to get accuracy in analyzing and governing bioscientific developments and applications. As bioethics is an institutionalized epistemology, it has become legitimized as a professional field.

Nevertheless, we can affirm that bioethics lacks legitimacy to claim total authority over bioscientific matters, especially because of its epistemological diversity pointing to a multiplicity of professions coexisting within it. In this way, determining bioethics' efficiency to govern new technologies entails doubtful initiative. While bioethics is not legally binding, it reveals some inability to rule those practices beyond deliberative frameworks able to perfect reasoning on those matters. However, how can regulation be improved?

Responding to such question implies to understand biolaw as a transdisciplinary field instead of a multidiscipline. While biolaw converges with biosciences, ethics, philosophy, medicine and law, as bioethics does, it is thought that determining who is entitled to claim its jurisdiction is improbable. In this sense, various professions compete for biolaw's jurisdiction. This apparently multifactorial biolaw's status contributes to create confusion as well as to diminish biolaw's legitimacy in the public space. As different professions deploy different approaches to biojuridical conflicts arisen in bioscientific contexts, scholars have become skeptical regarding biolaw's efficiency to rule biomedical practices in comparison to bioethics' and traditional law's abilities (Valdés, 2021, p. 128).

However, it has been already demonstrated that biolaw is not a multidiscipline (Valdés, 2021), although it encompasses a multidimensional epistemology. In fact, biolaw is focused on juridical conflicts that emerged from biomedical settings in order to rule them, by being related to other conceptual disciplinary fields, such as ethics and science, but also, and especially, optimizing and refreshing other branches of law. This interaction and influence of biolaw over other legal contexts make it, in fact, a transdiscipline, meaning an epistemology that irradiates itself to other branches of law. Thus, biolaw's transdisciplinary scope does not mean eclecticism but rather ductility. In other words, biolaw has the ability to claim legitimacy to even influence, inspire and stimulate important jurisdictions other than law related to juridical implications of bioscientific practices, such as health care and organizational ethics, international governance and public policy (Valdés, 2021, p. 129).

On the other hand, biomedical sciences' practices need not only ethical but also legal regulation. While the legally binding regulation of biosciences is increasingly profuse in Europe and North and South America, it is, however, inaccurate, incomplete and, often, ineffective. This weakness is not due to an apparent biolaw's disciplinary eclecticism but to a prevalent ignorance about its nature and epistemological meaning, which has systematically prevented it from being institutionalized, in spite of its conceptual development that distinguishes it from both bioethics and other branches of traditional law.

Most of international regulation on biomedicine has been unsystematic lacking robust conceptual content. Therefore, the regulatory systematization of biolaw has been displayed within international biolaw's scope. However, we have already shown that international biolaw is rather a constellation of instruments and recommendations without legally binding force. In this way, regulation and jurisprudence appear as a result of social pressure for legislative or executive commissions to work on the matter. Nevertheless, there is some reluctance to request advice from people who have relevantly deepened into the intellection and understanding of bioscientific practices' legal implications. This creates some mistrust in biolaw, essentially due to four reasons: (i) The public space as well as many legislators and legal operators wrongly believe that these issues concern bioethics instead of biolaw; (ii) legal controversies generated by the inefficient international regulation of biomedical practices are ultimately an interpellation to biolaw; (iii) historical approaches to biolaw have been carried out from a promiscuous relation to bioethics; this sort of obsession in understanding biolaw from bioethics has also prevented this new field from being institutionalized and legitimized as an independent juridical space; and (iv) the evident naturalistic intellection underlying the different epistemologies of biolaw has built a barrier for it to become an autonomous branch of law. For these reasons, most of those involved in biolaw's atmospheres only achieve an oblique understanding of it, lacking the skills and knowledge to reason and, eventually, rule latest-generation bioscientific practices (Valdés, 2021, p. 131).

This misunderstanding of biolaw entails an important barrier for its social, cultural and academic recognition. Therefore, traditional authors, as many other social and academic actors, do not have the jurisdiction of biolaw as they have spread out a wrong intellection of it by pointing to a juridified bioethics, a branch of bioethics, a biomedical law or a mere collection of soft law's recommendations and nonbinding dispositions.

Biolaw guarantees an efficient legal device to protect new fundamental rights that emerged from biotechnological settings. It also reinforces states' obligation to protect those rights. In this fashion, our proposal gets over, epistemologically and methodologically, the European soft-law-constitutional jurisprudence and also improves and optimizes the understanding of fundamental rights in contemporary juridical contexts. In addition, biolaw can endow constitutional legal systems with a new and more complete conception of fundamental rights, which allows the states to fulfill their international obligations by making such rights more efficient in local jurisdictional orders.

Therefore, a cosmopolitan biolaw is very applicable in the light of constitutional texts. However, this points to a relevant condition of possibility: Understanding constitutions as normative texts rather than simply programmatic ones (Valdés, 2021, pp. 139–141). It is important, however, to recognize biorights as a key juridical platform that places fundamental rights in their deserved valuation range and works as an indicator for the state to protect those rights.

3.2 Societal challenges of biolaw

According to the World Health Organization (WHO) data, on 8 December 2019, the first case of coronavirus was reported in Wuhan, China. Since then, and with terrifying speed, the virus has spread to practically the entire world, causing a pandemic of catastrophic dimensions, whose definitive scope and final consequences are still unknown.

The latent danger of the virus forced states to take extraordinary measures not only to protect population's health and prevent an unmanageable number of deaths but also to ensure that health systems were able to tolerate the agonizing demand for beds and ventilators.

The world suddenly changed its way of living as well as of understanding concepts such as closeness and remoteness. Apocalyptic stories colonized the media. Metaphysical solutions were suggested. Praying and waiting could also be an option. However, beyond the ontological and onto-theological issues that COVID-19 has generated, a constellation of practical problems has been violently gestated that governments, health care centers, physicians, health care staff and ordinary people must deal with every day. Which distributive criteria should be used to allocate financial and clinical resources? Are human challenge trials ethically and legally acceptable? Should the citizens accept all the restrictions on self-determination imposed by the states?

However, as the pandemic advances, a whole constellation of practical questions related to biotechnological matters has also emerged. Should we intensify experimentation with human embryos and advance gene editing to avoid the occurrence of such catastrophic diseases in the future? Is there a bioterrorist conspiracy theory behind these contemporary dystopias? Clearly, pandemic challenges are not the only societal tests that biolaw has to deal with. Current biotechnological empowerment also raises important conflictive scenarios to be elucidated from a social perspective. In this context, we will synoptically analyze three societal challenges of biolaw: Genome editing, biosecurity and human challenge trials, which also raise global risks for contemporary times.

3.2.1 Genome editing

CRISPR/Cas9 technology is a molecular tool used to edit or correct the genome of any cell, including human cells. This mechanism works like a sort of molecular scissors to cut any DNA molecule in an extremely precise and fully controlled manner. That ability to cut DNA is what finally allows scientists to modify a sequence, by eliminating or inserting new DNA.

The acronym CRISPR/Cas9 was created by the Spanish molecular biologist Francisco Martinez Mojica, who discovered that functional sequence in bacteria's DNA, and it means *Clustered Regularly Interspaced Short Palindromic Repeats*. The second part of the acronym indicates the name of a series of proteins, mainly nucleases, that point to CRISPR associated system. This technique is based on a property that some bacteria (*Streptococcus pyogenes*) have to defend organisms against viral infections. These bacteria have enzymes that are able to distinguish between the genetic material of the bacteria and that of the virus. Once the bacterium discriminates the genetic material, it proceeds to destroy the virus.

The grounds of this mechanism were better known when the genomes of some bacteria and other microorganisms were mapped. It was found that a certain area of the genome of many microorganisms, especially archaea, was full of palindromic repetitions with no apparent function. These repetitions were separated from one another, by specific sequences called "spacers" that resembled others of viruses and plasmids. Right in front of those repetitions and spacers, there is a sequence called "leader." These sequences are known as CRISPR. Also, in relation to this grouping, some genes encoded a type of nuclease: the *Cas* genes.

When a virus colonizes the bacteria, it controls the cellular configuration and interacts with different cellular components. But the bacteria that have this defense system have a complex formed by an RNA-bound Cas protein produced from the CRISPR sequences. Then, the virus's genetic material can interact with this complex. If so, the viral genetic material is inactivated and degraded. But the system goes further. Cas proteins can take a small part of the viral DNA, modify it and integrate it into the set of CRISPR sequences. Thus, if that bacterium (or its offspring) meets that same virus, it will inactivate viral genetic material much more efficiently. It is, therefore, a factual immune system of bacteria.

In 2012 a team of researchers, led by Jennifer Doudna and Emmanuelle Charpentier (2012, pp. 816–821), published an article in *Science*, which demonstrated how to turn that natural machinery into a "programmable" editing tool, which served to cut any in vitro DNA chain. That is, they managed to program the system to go to a specific position of any DNA (not just viral) and cut it. The impact of this development was so intense that only eight years later, that is, in 2020, the Nobel Prize in Chemistry was awarded to Doudna and Charpentier.

The system designs an RNA molecule (CRISPR or guide RNA) that is then inserted into a cell. Once inside, it recognizes the precise spot of the genome where the Cas9 enzyme should cut. The process of editing a genome with CRISPR/Cas9 implies two stages. In the first stage, the guide RNA is associated with the Cas9 enzyme. This guide RNA is specific to a concrete DNA sequence so that by the rules of nucleotide complementarity, it will hybridize in that sequence (the one the scientist is interested in editing or correcting). Then, Cas9 acts, which is an endonuclease enzyme (i.e. a protein that is capable of breaking a link in the nucleic acid chain), by cutting the DNA.

In the second stage, two natural mechanisms to repair the cut DNA are activated. The first one called *indel* (insertion-deletion) means that, after the cut-off site (the specific sequence of DNA where the guide RNA was attached), a hole appears in the chain, or a small piece of chain is inserted. This implies the loss of the original function of the cut DNA segment. A second mechanism allows the incorporation of a specific sequence exactly in the original cutting site. For this, logically, the cell must be given the sequence that the scientist needs to be unified with the DNA.

Genetic editing is used to regulate gene expression, label specific genome sites in living cells, identify and modify gene functions and correct defective genes. It is also already being used to create animal models to study complex diseases including schizophrenia, for which there were no animal models earlier. Currently, scientists are also investigating to reprogram human cells to cut the HIV genome. In fact, in 2018, He Jiankui's human gene–editing clinical experiment caused profuse public discussion in the scientific and social community. The Chinese scientist recruited couples who wanted to have children. In order to participate, the man had to be HIV positive and the woman, uninfected. He Jiankui took sperm and eggs from the couples, performed in vitro fertilization with them and then edited the embryos' genomes using CRISPR/Cas9. In one case, twin girls were born healthy by mid-October 2018. However, it was unclear if there might be long-term effects from the gene editing.

Important interest has emerged regarding the possible applications of genetic editing, both for research and for therapy. The latest possibilities range from restoring normal functions in diseased organs or organisms, editing somatic cells, to preventing genetic diseases in future children and their descendants, by means of germline cells editing. The fact that these new genetic editing technologies can be used to make very precise changes in the genome, with high frequency and considerable precision, has driven a very intense attention on research that seeks to develop effective and safe therapies that use these new approaches offering new options beyond simply replacing a gene completely. Indeed, nowadays it is possible to insert or delete nucleoids, interrupt a gene or a genetic element, make small cuts and breaks in the DNA, modify a nucleoid and also attempt epigenetic changes to intervene genetic expression.

Genome editing can be used for (i) basic research, (ii) somatic interventions and (iii) germline interventions. Basic research can focus on cellular, molecular, biochemical, genetic or immunological mechanisms, including those that affect the reproduction, development and progress of a disease, as well as possible responses to a treatment. That research may involve working with human cells or tissues, unless such practice may have incidental effects in revealing information about identifiable elements of a living human being.

Most basic research in human cells is conducted on somatic cells, namely, nonreproductive ones; for example, skin, liver, lungs and heart cells. However, there is basic research that uses germline cells, including early cells of the embryo, ovules, sperm and cells that allow the growth and development of the testicles and sperm. These cases require very important ethical and legal considerations, mainly related to how these cells should be collected and what would be the purposes of their use, even if the research does not imply pregnancy and transmission of changes to the offspring.

Moreover, biomedical research points to interventions in human subjects. In the United States and in most countries with dense regulatory systems, it has been proposed that biomedical research should be supervised at a previous research stage in order for its clinical availability to be approved. The clinical applications of genetic editing that involve the use of somatic cells affect only the patient. For this reason, efforts to apply gene therapy for the treatment and prevention of diseases have been profuse, whereas germinal interventions can be used to alter the genome, by provoking a modification in the offspring's genome.

Many questions, of ethical, legal and social scope of gene therapy and reproductive medicine, can be raised. However, practices such as CRISPR/Cas9, which has turned genome editing into an efficient and precise practice, open up a huge constellation of possible applications that make it practically magic. Germline editing to prevent hereditary genetic diseases is part of its hopeful catalog. Other applications are related to enhancement editing, namely, alterations that go beyond mere restoration and protection of health.

Feedback and public space opinion are very important to approve the application of many bioscientific advances. Approving the introduction of new technologies into society, it is not possible to simply apply the figure of a social pact, as the possibilities of these new practices are so vast and crucial that they require an explicit agreement that must be reached through transparent and public instances able to create or optimize policy to engender regulation on these techniques. In this way, within the concept of "social collective," nonhuman entities must be included. In other words, nonhuman animals and nature are factors that should be included in any equation seeking to rule and supervise scientific practices, especially those related to genome editing.

Bioscience mobilizes the public debate beyond ethics and law, as it significantly concerns the whole social structure, mainly with regard to the true scope of this powerful and revolutionary invention. One of the controversies is that in the long run, this technique will prevent the birth of disabled children, which has generated an avid social discussion about the value and role that in a future society would correspond to disabled or functionally impaired people.

According to the National Academy of Science (2017), some criteria that can be used to build regulatory frameworks for this practice are the following (Valdés, 2021, p. 177):

- There is no reasonable and superior alternative to the practice.
- The practice is focused on disease prevention.
- The gene editing that can cause or have the disposition to provoke pathologies and disabilities is restricted.
- The genetic alteration is limited to improve human health.
- There is evidence that the practice will not cause mosaicism.

- There exists availability of clinical and preclinical data and information on the risks and potential health benefits of the editing.
- During the editing development, there is a rigorous supervision on its effects.
- The participants or patients' health is guaranteed.
- Long-term multigenerational plans are developed to respect autonomy and self-determination.
- There is maximum transparency and consistency with patient privacy.

Cosmopolitan biolaw proposes a model of argumentative and discursive consensus, where all those who may be affected by these new inventions (including nonhuman animals and nature) are represented in a deliberative process that concludes in explicit and reasoned decisions about the eventual proliferation and regulation of this practice, especially when it acquires a nontherapeutic dimension.

An efficient regulation of genome editing should consider that a correct understanding of it seems to demand a binding legal framework, especially for those applications that introduce deteriorations or disabilities resulting in objective harms for the future person, manipulated in his or her embryonic past. Therefore, legal systems must be updated, expanded and deepened through the legal recategorization of nontherapeutic genetic manipulation and the concept of legal existence of the person. Through this recategorization it is possible to recognize new harms, new individual subjective rights or biorights, new subjects of rights and new legal interests other than the genotype. This is necessary because any genetic alteration can be carried out in two ways: (i) The introduction of genes into somatic cells, which provokes a modification in the individual genetic structure, and (ii) the incorporation of genes into germline cells, by passing the alteration to the offspring.

Some principles that can serve as a basis for articulating a public policy and regulatory framework to carry out these practices with more legal certainty may be beneficence, transparency, precaution, responsibility, autonomy, equality, distributive justice and transnational cooperation (Valdés, 2021, p. 179).

Also, the following steps can be important articulating elements for international regulatory models (Valdés, 2021, p. 180): (i) Implement procedures and applications of genetic editing that promote the health and well-being of the individuals involved; (ii) guide practices to the treatment and prevention of diseases; (iii) minimize risks with a high degree of scientific certainty; (iv) ensure a reasonable balance of risks and benefits for any application or version of genome editing; (v) deliver and disclose sensitive information in the most comprehensive and timely manner possible; (vi) assume public input or feedback as a very important element of judgment in the processes of construction of public policies related to genetic editing, as well as with other new and disturbing technologies; (vii) proceed cautiously, under appropriate supervision, in a way that allows frequent and systematic supervision of these practices, in the light of future scientific advances and their scope, and considering the cultural and social opinions related to them; (viii) ensure a high-quality experimental design and analysis, systematically and permanently reviewing and evaluating scientific protocols; (ix) grant equal value to all individuals involved in research; (x) respect and promote autonomous individual decisions; (xi) prevent different abusive forms of research from occurring; (xii) do not stigmatize disability; (xiii) distribute impartially benefits and burdens in research; (xiv) ensure broad and equitable access to clinical applications resulting from genetic editing research; (xv) respect different national public policies that articulate regulatory models for this practice; (xvi) coordinate standards and regulatory procedures between different countries whenever possible; and (xvii) ensure transnational collaboration in the articulation of intercultural regulatory policies on genome editing.

3.2.2 Biosecurity

Biosecurity implies to implement measures and policies to stop introducing and spreading harmful organisms to humans, animals and plants into the environment (Ryan & Glarum, 2008). Biosecurity is intended to protect human health as well as increase and optimize the protection of agricultural products through prevention, control, oversight and management of biological risk factors. It also seeks to protect human beings, animals and natural life from acts of bioterrorism by preventing its adverse effects, as well as to offer advice on political and social changes that must be adopted by government regulatory agencies.

On the other hand, a bioterrorism attack involves the intentional release of viruses, bacteria, toxins or other harmful agents used to cause disease or death in people, animals or plants (Ryan & Glarum, 2008). These agents are normally found in nature, but they may be mutated or altered to increase their capacity to cause disease, as well as to be resistant to current medications, or to increase their power to spread in the environment. Biological agents can proliferate through air, water or food. Thus, bioterrorists tend to use biological agents because they are extremely difficult to detect and do not cause diseases until within several hours and even several days.

Bioterrorism is a disturbing weapon nowadays, especially because biological agents are relatively easy and inexpensive to obtain, can be easily spread out and can cause fear and panic beyond real physical damage. Nevertheless, it has some important limitations, as it is difficult to use a biological weapon to affect only the enemy rather than allied or local forces. Therefore, a biological weapon is useful for terrorists, primarily as a method of creating mass panic and disrupting the normal course of life in a state or country. However, it is worth thinking about the potential power that genetic inventions could imply for the development of bioterrorism.

Moreover, the use of agents that do not cause harm to humans, but that are capable of affecting the economy, has captured the attention of governments and international security agencies. A harmful pathogen in this context is the foot-and-mouth disease, a virus able to provoke vast damaging effects to the economy and, at the same time, to engender great public alarm, as, for example, occurred in 2001 and 2007 with the fever outbreaks in the United Kingdom, even it did not have the ability to infect humans.

Biological weapons take some time in infecting populations, but they have the ability to spread and impact large areas and a large number of people. In this way, biological risk assessments are carried out to identify acceptable and unacceptable odds of threats. Methods adopted to manage their control are an important field of research, and their eventual reduction implies the exchange of knowledge and advice in relation to policy and training needed for pathogens to be handled and controlled safely. In this regard, there are some nonbinding norms and recommendations to rule particular biological activities. Organizations, scientists and researchers can voluntarily agree to meet them. In this order of ideas, an important variety of risks that threaten health and biosafety have already been typified by most jurisdictions in Europe and Latin America. The Cartagena Protocol on Biosafety (1975) is a paradigmatic document for such effect, by advising to eliminate and prevent any (i) biological, chemical or physical agents, present in food, able to cause an adverse effect on health; (ii) biological agent that can be transmitted, naturally, between humans and wild or domestic animals; (iii) pathogen that can cause adverse effects on animal importation; (iv) species, breed, plant, animal biotype or pathogen, harmful to plant products; (v) pest that has a significant potential risk to the economy and that does not yet exist or, if it exists, is not yet widespread and is under official oversight; (vi) living modified organism that possesses a combination of unknown genetic material, obtained through the use of biotechnology, causing adverse effects for the conservation and sustainable use of animal biological diversity, as well as implying risks to human health; (vii) recombinant DNA organism acting directly or remaining in food, provoking adverse effects on human health; and (viii) animal species outside its natural past or present, whose introduction severely threatens biodiversity.

In conclusion, the design, development and implementation of effective measures to protect and guarantee population's health from a wide range of natural threats or bioterrorist attacks, through the use of biological agents, as well as the construction of protocols for protecting people working in laboratories and research centers (biosecurity and biosafety, respectively), are a new focus of interest for law, which requires a specific approach, determined by the specificity of the legal aspects that biosecurity encompasses. In this way, the biolegal scopes of biosecurity, in all its forms and meanings, need biojuridical approaches for its understanding, oversight and regulation.

3.2.3 Human challenge trials

In most regulatory regimes, vaccines take several years to develop, and their development typically proceeds through three phases of clinical trials. In Phase 1, small groups of people receive the trial vaccine. During Phase 2, the clinical study is expanded, and the vaccine is given to people who have characteristics similar to those for whom the new vaccine is intended. In Phase 3, the vaccine is given to several thousand people and tested for efficacy and safety. During this phase, participants either receive the vaccine or a placebo. The efficacy of the vaccine is determined by comparing the prevalence of infection in the group that was administered the vaccine with the one that received a placebo. If everything goes well, the hypothesis that those in the vaccine group will be infected significantly less is thus tested.

Under human challenge trials, participants of both the vaccine group and placebo group are deliberately exposed to the infection upon consent – thus, they are "challenged" by the disease organism. This is where the expression "human challenge trials" comes from. Proponents of the method believed that such trials could save valuable time in developing a COVID-19 vaccine, as researchers would not have to wait for participants to contract the infection under real-world conditions.

Human challenge trials have always been controversial. In fact, somehow the birth of bioethics, which represents a milestone in recent academic history, was because of these kinds of studies. In 1970, something disturbing was unveiled. Mentally retarded children housed at the Willowbrook State School in Staten Island, New York, were intentionally infected with hepatitis in an attempt to track the development of the viral infection. The study began in 1956 and lasted for 14 years. Researchers also wanted to determine the effectiveness of gamma globulin injections as protection against hepatitis. They justified their deliberate infections and exposures by claiming that given that there was a high rate of infection in the institution, it was practically inevitable that the children would become infected.

Despite human challenge trials in the context of the current pandemic are not alike the Willowbrook case, at the end of the day, they are human challenge trials. So, critics have questioned undertaking such trials for Covid-19, which is a potentially deadly disease for even those who are less at risk. It's known that an ethical concern of human challenge studies is the selection of human subjects and possible unduly incentives to get volunteers; for example, offering housing, food and the like to vulnerable people to get their agreement to participate, which is very common in some trials. It's clear that this can lead us to juridical dangerous slopes, as the unduly incentive context is able to create imprecise atmospheres to research and can also engender counterintuitive scenarios of diffuse certainty. The only way to accept this is under an oblique understanding of autonomy. It's clear that dignity is a value that is disrespected here. But the first principle to be violated is autonomy. The incentive in this scenario turns into a coactive element that virtually obliges the subject to accept participating in the study. Extreme need is not a good advisor to make self-determined decisions, and taking advantage of that perhaps is not ethical at all.

No doubt, this is a topic to be addressed more exhaustively, and as it's not the goal of this work, we will focus on the risks versus benefits equation. In this fashion, some critiques and concerns on human challenge trials are related to the following:

Broad consultation with the community: Probably, it is not fair to introduce practices, techniques, and clinical essays by assuming a tacit public agreement. In this fashion, the British figure of social pact is not the best one. Because of the important impacts, effects and consequences that human challenge trials can provoke on people, a deliberative or public engagement model seems to be better.

Risks to participants: Participants in coronavirus human challenge studies might face risks associated with the challenge infection and, in some cases, the experimental vaccine. Such risks should be minimized, for instance, via the restriction of participation in initial studies to healthy young adults and the provision of high-quality medical care, including intensive care, if required (Jamrozik & Selgelid, 2020, p. 201).

Background risk faced by potential participants: Individuals who are highly likely to be naturally infected with a pathogen during an epidemic (for instance, health care staff) might face a smaller increase in risk related to participation in human challenge trials than the general population (Jamrozik & Selgelid, 2020, p. 201).

Uncertainty for participants: Infection with unknown diseases might be associated with uncertainty (Jamrozik & Selgelid, 2020, p. 201). Unexpected aftermaths might occur and participants should be warned about it.

Risks to third parties: The potential for third-party risks must be considered in any human challenge trials' calculation.

Facing these ethical concerns, in a 2016 document titled "Human Challenge Trials for Vaccine Development: Regulatory Considerations," the WHO stated that human challenge studies have been conducted over hundreds of years and have contributed vital scientific knowledge that has led to advances in the development of drugs and vaccines. Nevertheless, such research can appear to be in conflict with the guiding principle in medicine to do no harm, namely, nonmaleficence according to principlism (Beauchamp & Childress, 2019).

The relationship between harms and benefits happens to be the most important calculation element to determine the utility of human challenge trials, so we have to say something about nonmaleficence to epistemologically justify our position. The principle of nonmaleficence reveals an implicit presence of utility as a criterion of moral correctness in bioethics. Despite establishing obligations of a categorical and unconditional nature, the principle of nonmaleficence is applied in deliberation following consequentialist balancing criteria. Utility is not explicit here, but it appears tacitly. Nonmaleficence's obligations differ from beneficence's ones. Whereas beneficence's obligations are laxer and more ductile, nonmaleficence's duties are much more binding because they ought to be followed impartially, and even, they provide reasons for punitive punishment when people do not respect them.

However, the greater binding weight of nonmaleficence does not imply, procedurally speaking, that it is applied categorically in deliberation. Reasoning and any decision-making process in the context of coronavirus should be utilitarian, as obtaining favorable consequences at the lowest cost possible seems to be a strong criterion to evaluate human challenge trials. Doing it differently can have pernicious effects, as it encapsulates deliberation in dogmatism and even ideological fundamentalism. It's true that a researcher should always have in view the obligation to do no harm and consider and understand it as a categorical and unconditional duty. But the procedural scope of nonmaleficence is, in fact, related to consequentialist criteria, because in the edges of life and death is where the true deliberative value of this principle comes into play. If we understand nonmaleficence as the highest standard, the paramount principle to decide, that might derive a dogmatic closure of the possibility of accepting residual risks and damages in order to obtain greater subsequent benefits.

Obviously, we refer to a rational and reasonable utilitarian application of nonmaleficence. As the main criterion is a consequentialist one and avoiding damage is always up to variable coefficients, and it depends on a multifactorial constellation of even random conditions that occur in every case, it is clear that utility in nonmaleficence admits exceptions and also rejects extravagant proposals. Thus, under the same criterion, beneficence may eventually take preeminence over nonmaleficence; for example, if a physician wants to kill a prisoner sentenced to death to remove his or her organs and, that way, save the lives of five innocent people. That seems to be unacceptable. This means that the principle of utility rejects perennial moral axioms, and the priority of one principle over another is always under review, and its axiological weight will depend on and will vary according to the circumstances. In these circumstances of pandemic and death, we think that nonmaleficence should be applied from its utilitarian understanding.

By concluding, we can affirm that any ethical and legally binding juridical framework to justify the utility of human challenge trials should consider, at least, the following criteria:

Speed or accelerated development: Replacing the Phase 3 can considerably reduce the licensure process time, making efficacious vaccines available more quickly. We think the risks this involves are completely justified by virtue of the benefits that we can obtain from accelerating the process.

Less number of subjects: Human challenge trials need a considerable smaller number of subject to succeed. This reduces not only the number of people at risk but also the potential number of infected subjects in the trial. The cost-benefit relationship is then critically optimized.

Maximization-minimization equation: Human challenge trials enhance this coefficient, both qualitatively and quantitatively. In fact, these trials maximize the benefits (speed, accelerated development) by reducing the harms (less deaths, smaller number of subjects to experiment). At the same time, human challenge trials can improve the amount of cured people versus the victims both of trials and the virus.

Residuality: Residual or marginal risks versus the potential and predicted benefits justify, rationally and reasonably, human challenge trials in pandemic times.

Tacit social pact: This agreement figure is plausible, acceptable and juridically defensible here. It's true that this model seems to be quite unsuitable to introduce new technologies into the world. In this fashion, an argumentative model, at Frankfurt School style, seems to be more reasonable. Just assuming that all people agree with the surreptitious induction of new devices or techniques and taking that for granted is not enough; for example, the recently created algorithm to read your mind in order to allow people with cerebral palsy to express their will as their thoughts are translated, in real time, into words on a computer screen, but at the same time, that algorithm can be used to literally read your shopping tendencies, preferences and, even, wishes. It's possible we need much more than a tacit agreement for that. But, in the case of the pandemic where rapid and tragic decisions need to be made, a tacit social pact seems to be a good epistemological platform for decision-making processes.

In sum, it's true that human challenge trials involve risks, but rejecting them obeys an oblique hermeneutic. Therefore, as WHO has stated, if human challenge studies are undertaken with prudence, caution and oversight, the information obtained clearly justifies the risks human subjects have to face, insofar the risks and harms are residual in comparison to the expected benefits to be gained.

Part II

The philosophy of biolaw

4 Philosophical foundations of ethics of biolaw

4.1 Bioethics and democratic politics

The legal policy and public debate of bioethics and biolaw are characterized by the fact that ethics is an integral part of democratic debate in the late modern risk society. This is based on an effort to protect the democratic society against biopower and totalitarianism, where the state increasingly rules over the body of the citizens. The background to the controversial status of bioethics in the public debate is an increasing legalization of many aspects of society that have not previously been regulated by law to the same extent. At the same time, the rapid development of medical technology has led to a permanent bioethical crisis of legislation, where judicial protection of the human body and the rest of the living world hardly fits into ordinary law. Welfare state politics is not solely a matter of social technology. In the legal policy debate, cultural and historical attitudes, substantial perceptions of values and society's view of human beings are crucial to the legitimacy of biolaw. This is a conflict between different perceptions of the good life in a pluralistic society. The public debate on governance of biomedical issues, including general health priorities, organ transplantation, genetic engineering, reproductive technology and so forth, is about fundamental values and not just about economic priorities.

Therefore, most governments and parliaments around the world believe that the political legitimacy of bioethics and biolaw must be based on a societal consensus and not just on narrow majority decisions. At the same time, judicial regulation of bioethical issues is an expression of political democratization, in which more people are involved in the decision-making process. These include patient and medical organizations, churches and other religious groups, industrial groups and so forth. We can speak of an increased proceduralization of ethics, where the individual countries, depending on their special legal cultures, set up different parliamentary commissions, ethical councils, advisory committees on bioethics or other bodies of governance.

The bioethical legislative process in a democratic society can be defined as a discursive and deliberative policy (Habermas, 1992, p. 349). The judicial process takes place in a tension between conflict and consensus. Deliberative politics means that a public democratic discussion, with the inclusion of

DOI: 10.4324/9781003147848-4

arguments and views from different groups in society, is the basis for judicial policy decisions. Such a democratic judicial policy, in which one listens to the arguments of the other, often risks being replaced by purely strategic action. Here it is important to point out the importance of the public. A political public is central to maintaining a common framework for discussion and negotiation for resolving political conflicts in a pluralistic democracy.

Therefore, no final governance decision or final justification can be given for the principles of bioethics and biolaw. The democratic politics in which biolaw is created arises in the daily political life of society. Deliberative politics in a pluralistic society means that a peaceful negotiation about the common good, based on conflict and different perceptions of morality (Engelhardt, 1986, p. 44), reaches a temporary consensus that is constantly open to revision. As part of society's social law, biolaw is created through a permanent negotiation on the formulation of legal principles, between different and free people, who in plurality must agree on a common perception of the good life in relation to each of the basic biomedical issues. The legal policy discourse on biomedical issues must necessarily be grounded in various ideological, philosophical, cultural, historical and pragmatic considerations, and a concept of the good and justice within the framework of a democratic state governed by the rule of law becomes the real basis for the legal policy rationality that must be made applicable in the bioethical debates.

The fundamental legal and philosophical significance of jurisprudence lies in ensuring that judicial management and governance of the human body take place with caution and not without careful consideration, as society here intervenes in the private sphere of human beings. In a democratic society, this is considered problematic, that is, as an intervention in privacy and in the freedom of a human being to rule over his or her body, which is a fundamental right (Lenoir, 2000). A society can become totalitarian if it develops incorrect moral norms for the individual's dealings with his or her body, for example, by interfering with the citizen's sexual behavior and religion. There is a risk that society manipulates the individual's body and makes it the object of common benefit.

In continuation of a legal policy reluctance toward progress, it can rightly be argued that judicial regulation of bioethical issues in this way can also help to aim at technological development in a democratic direction and thus strengthen democracy. The extension of the policy area to the health sector, research and experiments in the risk society, where the citizen is directly affected by technological development (Beck, 1986), can help to safeguard the foundations of democracy and the body of the individual. The human vision of the body that characterizes legislation and case law on biomedical issues can help protect the dignity and integrity of the individual in biotechnological development.

4.2 The threat of biopower

The negative premise of legislation and case law on bioethical issues in democratic societies can be termed as biopower (Foucault, 1973, p. 31). In modern society, different power strategies for dominance of the human body arise. Biopower consists in a dialectical logic between the same and the other, an identity movement that sets differences and strategically oppresses a human being by dominating over his or her body. The body is in fact directly placed in a political field that makes it a medical and technological object as part of society's political economy (Foucault, 1972, p. 31). Health science, in fact, involves a totalitarian intervention in the human body. It, like psychiatry, aims to expel madness and insanity from the productive order to ensure that citizens function and are disciplined in society's everyday life. Criminals are brought physically under control in prisons, where corporal punishment earlier in modernity functioned as a technology of power to discipline the soul of the prisoner (Foucault, 1972, p. 28).

There is a close connection among the discovery of the "functional utility" of the body (the human machine), the development of the "human" sciences, industrial commodity production and political power. Among these, the clinic and the medical gaze help to objectify the body and define norms of normality that, together with other techniques of power, can be placed in the social order and in industrial production (Foucault, 1964). The medical objectification of the body in this way leads to an increased control of the individual, which apparently is based on natural concepts of normality but, in reality, includes society's power strategies, which also apply to the state's general population policy management of fertility, ability to work, mortality and so forth, and this power is politically sovereign but anonymous and immanent, at once intentional and without a conscious subject, but at the same time completely determining the power of society over the experienced body.

Biopower unfolds in these contexts among science, mastery of the body and political sovereignty. It arises in the complex conditions that lead to state domination over the life and death of the citizen, as described by Hobbes in the theory of governance of society. In his critique of the Enlightenment's democratic rule of law project, Michel Foucault argues that modernity, instead of leading to greater freedom, has led to an intensification of biopower through the linking of business policy and mastery of the citizen's body through population policy mechanisms. This "bio-policy" becomes more pronounced as an "anatomy policy" with the demands of the economy for increased growth and the increasingly nuanced mapping of the body as a biological machine in medicine. The technological development of biomedicine has thus today given the state greater opportunities than ever to discipline and control the bodies of citizens at its own discretion. This connection among state, biopower and existence simultaneously leads to unification, a normalizing movement using various micro/macro power techniques that make the human body and its biological life part of a conformist social corpus.

The problem is whether biopower really works that way and whether it has made modern health science oppressive of human beings. One wonders whether it can be feared that technological rationality can also produce pure barbarism in today's democratic society or, in that case, contribute to an increased normalization and discipline of society's citizens. In such a case, it is a development in which modernity's project on healthy citizens can risk leading to health tyranny and becoming irrational. Here it is relevant to refer to Hannah Arendt's concept of "the banality of evil." In connection with legislation and case law on biomedical issues, we must be aware of instrumental rationality structures and developmental logics in the health sciences that, by virtue of the system's internal self-understanding, can lead to a moral blindness to the perceived human body. The rationality that manifested itself in the Holocaust of Nazism was possible only by virtue of the instrumental reason of modernity. The question is whether such moral blindness even today tends to characterize the development within gene and reproduction technology as well as euthanasia (Bauman, 1989).

The task of biolaw is to avoid moral blindness in the technological rationality in connection with the development of biomedicine. One must realize that technical-administrative procedures and a given health science practice can in fact be an expression of an "unreflected evil" (Arendt, 1964; Rendtorff, 2020g), which becomes part of the background mentality in the hospital sector, where doctors and health professionals, thoughtlessly and blindly captured by traditional practices without being fully aware of it and perhaps even believing that they are serving humanity, in effect exercise a human barbarism against other people. The danger is that moral blindness becomes an integral part of the background mentality of today's biomedical practices in hospitals or nursing homes and people are treated unworthily as machines or animals. The protection of the human body in technological development should serve as a safeguard against rationalized evil, and it is an essential task to counteract the threat of biopower in a democratic state governed by the rule of law.

4.3 Legal status of the body

This requires formulating the legal status of the body in connection with the development of biomedicine, but leading legal theories relate to the experienced body, the unborn life, the dead body or different body products and body parts in very different ways.

In modern natural law theory of, for example, Rousseau and Locke, the positive law is justified on the basis of the freedom and autonomy of the individuals, where they enter into a social contract with each other (Locke, 1993, p. 132). For Locke, the body is the property of the individual, over which it can freely decide from the outside, without anyone having the right to interfere. But precisely this norm of freedom is put to the test of the development of biomedicine, which can change the will, reason and freedom of the legal subject through genetic engineering and reproductive technology. And because it is based solely on human freedom, a contract theory has problems explaining why society should worry about future generations, fetuses, cells and so forth. These are not legal entities in the strict sense.

Although Jürgen Habermas does not relate directly to the body in his theory of the modern rule of law (Habermas, 1992, p. 109), he is aware that the protection of the person's life and integrity is central to the rule of law. It can be said that the body falls under the rule of law's protection of human subjective freedom and private autonomy. It is important to maintain the intimate connection between private and subjective rights and the protection of the human person (Ibid, p. 112). Personal rights and civil autonomy are two sides of the same coin. Private and public autonomy mutually presuppose each other. But this also means that manipulation of the human body touches on the preconditions of citizenship, that is, by the fundamental social and political rights when intervening in the personal integrity zone of a human being and his or her private sphere.

The so-called liberal and procedural legal models, which perceive a legal system as some procedural structures for securing basic duties and rights, but where the state must be neutral to the citizens' ethical beliefs, make the individual's right to decide over his or her body something fundamental. Here, the notion of the person's sovereign right of control over the body's private sphere is the central approach in understanding the problem of the body in bioethics and biolaw. In connection with euthanasia, organ donation, premature born babies and so forth, it turns out, however, that the self-determination of the individual alone cannot be the basis for formulating sustainable legal policy solutions.

These theories of the body as property, as a precondition for subjective rights and as a basis for self-determination can be supplemented with philosophical-anthropological justification of biorights. Here one can use the body's phenomenological conception of the person as a foundation for a judicial regulation of the human body. This approach is inspired by French personalism (Emmanuel Mounier) and the phenomenological movement in German and French philosophy (Bompiani, 1992, p. 171). It focuses on the human being as a psycho-physical entity, determined by the Husserlian dualism "Leib-Körper" and Merleau-Ponty's idea of "corps propre," where the body is constitutive of the person, and in this case, there is a close connection between the body as subject and object and person and thing. From a legal and philosophical perspective, this means that the basis of law is the bodily incarnated person who, as a legal entity, is granted basic rights. A body's phenomenological legal justification cannot be based on a metaphysical concept of person but is based on respect for the concretely experienced body as a basis for a democratic legal order. Human rights and biorights can then be claimed to be an expression of the legal primacy of the bodily incarnated person. A phenomenological theory of the human body can in this way form the basis for contractual theoretical and natural law justifications of the rule of law (Bompiani, 1993, p. 286). Here, the recognition of human self-determination is supplemented by respect for the individual's integrity, dignity and vulnerability.

This justification for protection of the human body implies a recognition of sources of law outside the law itself as a system of objectively given positive rules. Judicial regulation appeals to principles of respect for the life and dignity of the person, which also takes into account the place of human beings in the living world. An ethical appeal for justice that goes beyond the existing legal order also plays a crucial role in bio-judicial legislation and case law. The bodily phenomenological justification for this can be regarded as a third way, which, based on a human being as a bodily, historical-cultural being, is used to overcome the opposition between positivism and natural law.

4.4 The good life in ethics, law and politics

Biolaw must thus be based on a humanistic sensitivity to the fragility and vulnerability of the living. This involves a notion of the good life at the societal level. Thus, based on a theory of the bodily incarnated human person, and hermeneutics of the self, it can be justified that a notion of the good life must be the basis for a close connection between ethics and law. Both personal and societal commitment are based on a notion of "the good life for and with the other human being in just institutions" (Rendtorff, 2020f; Ricœur, 1990, p. 202), and one can add in cohesion with the living universe.

The ideal of ethics is, as Aristotle argued in the *Nicomachean Ethics*, the lifelong friendship with the other human being, based on the given and received between free people in diversity, generosity and reciprocity. The ideal friendship is based neither on interest nor on usefulness, but on the need, lack of and concern for the other understood as a happy, independent and responsible human being. Ethics is based on shared appreciation and reciprocity. This is in contrast to a focus on the demand of the other as an absolute imperative (Lévinas, 1961). The basis of ethics is not an unconditional duty but a mutual affection, where the appreciation of one's own perfection and the concern for the other's and the other's irreplaceability and fragility are the condition for personal and common happiness (Ricœur, 1990, p. 199).

This idea of ethics of friendship can be understood as the basis of the political community. The political community cannot be justified on the basis of technological rationality or strategic calculation alone. Justice must be based on the genuine desire of the people to live together in stable and just institutions. A fundamental precondition for political community and judicial organization must be sympathy and understanding between citizens, based on the realization of freedom in stable political institutions. The political community arises in an agreement to create a common world and civilizational progress by coordinating political opinion and practical action (Ricœur, 1990, p. 17).

At the same time, the political community is based on a preconception of the finitude and mortality of human existence. The task of politics is to ensure the survival of society by creating sustainable and stable institutions. This cannot be done without a fundamental awareness of the fragility and vulnerability of political society. No external standards can preserve the common exercise of power that can be dissolved in instrumental violence. In this perspective, the threat of biopower to the basis of the rule of law can be seen as an expression of such rationale of the political community.

The political practice that emerges in a public democratic space for deliberative politics seeks to counter the threat of biopower. The precondition for this is that law and justice are created as a result of society's basic narratives and notions of justice, that is, based on society's utopian and ideological self-understanding as a democratic society, a humanistic culture and so forth. In a humanistic vision of society and culture, therefore, based on the ideals of human freedom and diversity, respect for the sanctity of life and human bodily vulnerability are all very important in biolaw.

In a communitarian-Aristotelian perspective, one can, on this background, determine justice as a relationship among the individual case, the parties involved and the special nature of the situation as "the right middle" between extremes. This is a teleological conception of justice as an equal relationship in the distribution of goods in society to the individual citizen. This also applies within the sphere of justice in biomedicine.

The concept of goods includes not only secondary material goods but also primary existential goods in relation to the human person, namely life, bodily integrity and health. Aristotle's concept of "the mean in middle or center" aims at an overall equality while taking as its point of departure the special situation to ensure that the justice of distribution is not contrary to the nature of the relationship.

Michael Walzer's theory of spheres of justice (Walzer, 1984) builds on Aristotle's notion of justice as the right middle or center according to the nature of things. Justice is ultimately grounded in the shared values of society (Shared Values), which form the basis for a social distribution of goods and opportunities. This implies a complex equality, where justice cannot be thought of once and for all but must take into account the peculiarities of society's various spheres of justice. Complex equality means that the distribution must reflect the specifics of the different sectors of society, that is by the education system, the labor market and the health system.

On this basis, the biomedical field constitutes a sphere of justice in itself (Trappenburg, 1993, p. 269), which manifests itself in different ways within the individual biomedical areas. This is a concretization of Aristotle's notion of the right center according to a particular context. The notion of justice must be based here on people's common understanding of other people's vulnerability, and it is this care for the weakest that must motivate treatment and care in the health sector so that the bioethical notion of justice is not only dependent on the idea of equality but is also grounded in an idea of the inviolability of life and a notion of the good life.

Biolaw can be said to strive to realize the bioethical ideals of justice toward body and nature, which apply in the sphere of biomedical justice and which constitute the characteristic of the human view that is the basis of legal regulation.

4.5 The categorical imperative and the consideration of the weak and vulnerable

However, the right to live is not only dependent on common values and a vision of the good life. In order to be legitimate, the communitarian conception of law and justice must apply to all people. Jurisprudence must have a universal dimension. Therefore, a vision of the good life must be compatible with Kant's universalist justification for the rule of law. Kant's definition of justice is based on human autonomy, freedom and dignity. But in order for this not to end in empty formalism, it must be argued that a vision of "the good life for and with the other in just institutions" must be presupposed as the basis of Kant's moral philosophy (Ricœur, 1990, p. 237). At the same time, this means that practice in the area of justice of biolaws and biorights must not conflict with Kant's categorical imperative.

Consequently, a vision of the good life that must apply in the biosphere of justice (1) must be possible as a universal moral law that can apply to all people without contradiction. (2) In his or her body the human person must never be treated only as a means but also always as a purpose in itself. (3) The purpose of the moral law must be the people's own self-legislation in a realm of purposes, a society of free people.

The first formulation of the categorical imperative concerns the possibility of elevating the charge of individual actions to universal law. The individual human being cannot, without contradiction and contrary to the moral law, follow a notion of the good life that is contrary to other human beings' happiness. Within the realm of bio-judicial justice, one cannot, without destroying one's own dignity, perform acts whose aim cannot be abolished into universal law.

The second formulation of the categorical imperative, which perceives the other person as an end in itself, must likewise be interpreted in the perspective of the good life. The golden rule "treat others as you would like them to treat you" expresses that a notion of good implies a moral obligation. The statement "treat the other as yourself" contains a concern and respect for the other person's personal dignity. Within the health care system, it should be a basic principle that one must always respect the integrity and dignity of the individual.

The third formulation of the categorical imperative is the most important in a political perspective when it comes to institutionalizing a teleological notion of justice. Respect and concern for the other should lead to a common legal system in which individuals are ascribed universal social and political rights as citizens of a realm of purpose. This Republican ideal of popular sovereignty and universal justice in the institutions of society can not only be justified by the demand for individual freedom but must also be justified by the demand for common values that include vulnerable groups in society.

Respect for human autonomy and existence as a purpose in itself is at the societal level a fundamental aspect of the good life. Reference can be made here to Tristram Engelhardt's defense of human freedom and autonomy as a basis for good policy with a view to "res publica" (Engelhardt, 1986, p. 47). It must be made clear that society consists of individuals, each with their own perception of the meaning of their lives, and that in their diversity they must live together in a pluralistic society based on a common perception of the good life at the societal level. This respect for diversity in a secular pluralism in the health sector can lead to a tragic tension between the individual's self-determination and society's perception of the good when certain groups of citizens choose to reject a particular treatment. Respect for the individual's self-determination may conflict with the health care system's perception of what is good for the patient (Ibid, p. 79). At the same time, in Engelhardt's perspective, respect for personal autonomy becomes a central aspect of bioethics' (and biolaw's) vision of the good life in a pluralistic society with great scope for moral differences in private notions of the good life.

This theory of justice thus places great emphasis on respect for personal freedom and dignity as fundamental to society's notion of the good life. In jurisprudence, it can find support in John Rawls' contractualist argument for "Justice as Fairness" in *A Theory of Justice* (1971). Rawls imagines an original situation where a number of citizens behind the "veil of ignorance," that is, without knowledge of the place they will be given in a future state, must choose basic principles of justice for that state. Rawls argues that they must derive these on the basis of a "broad reflective equilibrium" among philosophical ideals, intuitions and concrete moral perceptions. This reflection behind the "veil of ignorance" can justify individual freedom and autonomy, and the task is to develop principles of justice that apply to all members of society. Both Rawls' first-level principles, "Justice as Fairness," that is, respect for citizenship and fundamental rights, and second-level distributive principles demonstrate a fundamental ethical concern for equality. Thus, the principle of equality before the law, the notion of proper distribution of goods, the principle that social inequality can only be justified if it benefits the weakest and the principle of mini-maximization, that is, that goods should be distributed with priority to those who need them most, are said to imply a vision of a common good that must be communicated in the public political discussion and the concrete judicial practice of society.

In this way, Rawls' theory of justice presupposes that society is a cooperative enterprise and that it must be built according to some basic principles of justice. But while a procedural and constructivist theory of justice is necessary to secure fundamental freedoms, the just cannot be separated from the good. Rawls' desire to avoid inequality that disadvantages the poor and the weak seems to build on this concern for the whole of society. Furthermore, to avoid empty formalism, one must interpret Rawls' principles of justice in relation to the particular historical situation, which he himself seems to be aware of in his later political writings, for example, *Political Liberalism* (1992) with the remark "Justice Draws the Limit, The Good Shows the Point" (Rawls, 1992) and with the idea of overlapping consensus as the rationality of society's reflections on the common good (Rawls, 1992, p. 133).

Rawls' critique of teleological theories of justice must be seen as directed at the inequality that purely utilitarian theories with the notion of "the greatest possible happiness for the greatest possible number" seem to imply. Social inequality, which only serves the most socially disadvantaged, cannot be justified because, according to the principle of difference, social inequality can only make sense if it serves to help the weakest. In this way, utilitarian values must also be subject to the principles of justice of society and respect the autonomy and freedom of the individual. While it is important to recognize that consequential ethical calculations must play a major role in judicial policy considerations in order to ensure the common good, one must at the same time be aware of the limitations of utilitarianism. Thus, utilitarianism must respect the basic principles of justice. This means that in order to ensure the protection of the individual, utilitarianism must be defined as a "negative utilitarianism," which aims to prioritize the most disadvantaged by minimizing misfortune and poverty among the fragile and vulnerable instead of seeking a general maximizing happiness in the many without thinking about the difference between weak and strong in society (Kaufmann, 1994, p. 161). Under no circumstances can biomedical conditions regulate the rights of the weakest, but it is a matter of respecting and supporting them in their fragility and vulnerability.

4.6 A new natural law?

As this notion of the good life is the theoretical basis of biolaw, can the classical natural law be resumed? Leo Strauss tries it in *Natural Right and History* (1953) and in *The City and Man* (1964). Here, modernity is understood as an expression of the crisis of natural law, where power and mastery of nature have triumphed over the human view of antiquity and the Middle Ages, which perceived humanity as part of a larger context, living nature and the universe. According to Strauss, the revitalization of the classical natural law of Plato and Aristotle is an alternative to modernity's focus on mastery of nature and society. Classical natural law is characterized by going to the case itself. The starting point is a reflection on the connection among human nature, the nature of things and the whole. Humanity interacts with the rest of nature and the cosmos, which are not primary in relation to human nature but must be included in the shaping of the good and just society. Society does not master nature but is embedded in a harmonious context with the universe and life in general.

Although, of course, we cannot reintroduce the classical natural law that was dependent on the cosmology and social conditions of the time, in the modern world, it is important to be open to finding the right connection among human, body, nature and the cosmos that breaks with the power of biopower. The right way must be based on a contract of nature, as claimed by Michel Serres in the book *Du Contrat Naturel* (1992). He talks about a nature contract between humans and the rest of living nature. The ecological challenge, the technical progress, the greenhouse effect and the pollution mean that nature, animals and plants can no longer be perceived as lawless. It is the task of society to recognize nature, animals and plants as legal entities instead of continuing the non-contractual state of war between human and nature that applies today. Humans' social pact must be expanded with a nature pact as a basis for a judicial organization, which means that nature is given legal status. It must be based on a symbiotic relationship between nature and human based on the human body and physical interaction with the natural world. It is important to emphasize here that the right of priority implies a new relationship with nature, which means that the living world becomes the subject of legal protection, so that limits can be set for society's ruthless exploitation of nature and of animals and plants.

In this context, jurisprudence must be based on human responsibility toward living nature. Hans Jonas argues in the *Prinzip der Verantwortung* (1979) that the domination and destruction of nature by industrial society have changed the ethical obligations of men. The situation requires that people become aware of their responsibility to protect the human and not wipe out all life on the earth. This implies that the right of supremacy must set limits to society's manipulation of the living and to its deterioration of the possibilities of life for future generations. The principle of responsibility is grounded in humanity's bodily cohesion with the living world, a re-experiencing of an organic anthropology that places human in the creative development of the universe and makes it a part of nature. As a biological being, human is a part of the living world, and by protecting this world, he or she helps to sustain his or her own life.

The obligation to protect the vulnerable and fragile life that characterizes the principle of responsibility in biolaw is an extension of the categorical imperative to also apply to future generations. A characteristic formulation of this imperative reads, "Act in such a way that real human life will continue to exist on earth in the future." This means that bio-judicial regulation has a forward-looking perspective that is about protecting the possibilities for real human life and real nature life in the society of the future. We are not going anywhere to want to change the people in order to adapt them to a future ideal state. The state of today is responsible for ensuring the protection of the biosphere of nature and the diversity of species in order to give people of the future and species of the future the best life opportunities.

At the political level, the principle of responsibility can be used as a basis for the formulation of the basic principles of jurisprudence, which precede realpolitik and pragmatic considerations. State responsibility implies an ethos of restraint, where society, based on the vision of respect for integrity, dignity and vulnerability, is aware of the consequences of its own actions and sets limits for a scientific and industrial development that threatens the community, nature and citizens' well-being.

However, the arguments for establishing a nature pact and making the principle of responsibility the basis of biolaw should not lead to the abolition of the difference between humanity and nature. Despite his or her bodily affiliation with nature, human, by virtue of his or her reason and freedom, is qualitatively different from nature. In *The New Ecological Order* (1994), Luc Ferry has rightly pointed out the difficulty of making animals, nature and plants legal entities on the same level as humans. The involvement of biolaw and biorights in nature, the body and future generations must not mean that animals, plants and the whole of nature are made the subject of judicial protection of exactly the same kind as humans themselves (Ferry, 1992, p. 35). It is absurd to claim that natural resources, animals and plants or the ecosphere as a whole have rights, self-determination and freedom on the same level as humans.

It must be emphasized that the incorporation of nature and the body as objects of legal protection by the biolaw is not independent of society's cultural construction of nature. Luc Ferry is therefore right that the ethical notions that underlie biolaw and biorights, such as concepts of fear of extinction, care for nature and respect for the sanctity of life, cannot be seen in isolation from society's democratic tradition and cultural self-understanding (Ibid, p. 127). The development of biolaw presupposes an advanced level of civilization, in which society, in a rational and self-critical perspective, treats animals and living nature as objects of judicial protection, without being legal subjects on an equal footing with humans.

This means that the foundation of biolaw can be neither deep-ecological nor anthropocentric but must instead be based on a democratic responsibility and a sensitivity that involves caring for and supporting the living world. François Ost is right that nature is given a new legal status that constitutes a third world between the subjective and the objective (Ost, 1995). The nature pact thus does not imply an absolute and undifferentiated respect for all life. Destructive life as an HIV virus must be fought in the light of society's notions of the common good. It can be said that the biosphere must be interpreted throughout the human society, that is, that the good life and the moral universality at the societal level cannot be isolated from the relationship with future generations, the animals and the rest of the living world, which, by virtue of the development of jurisprudence, become objects of legal protection.

4.7 The right to life and body

It is thus possible to mediate between deep ecology and anthropocentrism in biolaw by appealing to human responsibility and the spirit of democracy. The basis for such a democratic legal understanding of the human body is found in Ronald Dworkin's *Life's Dominion* (1994), where he argues that it is in fact cultural notions of the place of human in relation to the "domain of life" that are the background for legislation and case law on bioethics. Judicial policy discussions on bioethical issues such as abortion and euthanasia are based on a democratic balancing of the relationship among state responsibility, individual self-determination and respect for life's dignity, holiness and inviolability (Dworkin, 1994).

The right of priority is justified here in society's responsibility to safeguard the living, which is given a meaning in itself (intrinsic value) independent of society's utilitarian assessments of sustainability. This debate on respect for life, which must be said to be part of the deliberative policy of biolaw, is about the right way to protect the living in nature and society and is rooted in different moral feelings of life's holiness and inviolability among different social groups, for example, liberals, Catholics and feminists, who each have their own particular perception of the value of life. Dworkin argues that the obligation to respect life and the living should not be understood dogmatically but that it is a matter of balancing different considerations in relation to the specific case.

Thus, not all life is sacred, and one may be forced to intervene in the face of life that destroys other lives or refrain from technologically contributing to sustaining life that has become unworthy of living (Dworkin, 1994).

Dworkin's analyses of the American legal policy debate in biolaw on free abortion and euthanasia illustrate these points. In the United States, the fight for abortion has now been going on for 40 years since the famous Supreme Court ruling called Roe v. Wade. In 1973, Jane Roe accused the state of Texas of imposing an illegal ban on free abortion. The U.S. Supreme Court decided the case by 7 votes to 2. Any anti-abortion law in U.S. states that did not allow abortion until the third month of pregnancy was declared to be in violation of the Constitution's principle of personal liberty. The epoch-making thing about Roe v. Wade, however, was that while affirming the women's right to abortion, it set some limits to free abortion after the first three months of pregnancy. This establishes that it is the responsibility and interest of the state to protect the sanctity and inviolability of human life, even though the American legal tradition has never regarded the fetus as a person with rights and duties. Respect for the dignity of the fetus is justified on the basis of society's common values, and the background for abortion legislation is thus neither power-political nor rights-liberal but the state's ethical responsibility to protect life as an end in itself. Therefore, according to Dworkin, the decision by Roe v. Wade is not an expression of moral decay and American individualism but a balance of the constitutional principles on the question of respect for human life and society's common symbols and values (Dworkin, 1994).

Can one apply the same argumentation in decisions about end-of-life intervention? Does the state have the right not to allow the citizen to commit suicide or receive active euthanasia? And what about dying patients who are reduced to a biological and vegetative life or have lost all dignity in advanced dementia? Many people are horrified at the thought of having to end up as a biological vegetative life in a state where all personal self-determination has been lost. The U.S. Supreme Court has also dealt with euthanasia cases. In the case of Nancy Cruzan, the decision became a permission to turn off the ventilator. A young girl had fallen into a permanently irreversible coma after an accident. Her parents, who had filed a lawsuit against the hospital, believed that she had wanted to perceive it as beneath her dignity to live such a vegetative biological life.

The discussions on abortion and euthanasia are significant elements in the development of biolaw. Some may disagree with Dworkin's liberal position on these issues. However, it is not so much the actual outcome of the cases as the balancing process implied therein that is important for understanding the basis of biolaw. In connection with biomedical technologies, it is the state's responsibility to enforce society's respect for the living. But at the same time, it is the task of the state to respect the human life and the right to decide over oneself in connection with interventions in the body. Dworkin's point is to use "difficult" lawsuits on abortion and euthanasia to show how principles of respect for the sanctity of life, of the person's autonomy, of life's boundaries at birth and death play a crucial role in the judicial regulation of biomedical issues.

Against this background, biolaw can be justified on the basis of society's bioethical concern for the dignity of human life and for the placement of human freedom in its proper relation to the "domain of life." It is about balancing humanity's place in the world in the best way in relation to nature, the body and the cosmos. Biolaw is based on a balance between the state's responsibility to protect the sanctity of life and the individual's right over his or her own body. Consequently, the judicial system opens up to the body, the animals and the rest of the living world and makes them objects of judicial protection. The long-term purpose of judicial regulation can thus be said to be a protection of integrity, vulnerability and dignity, seen in the light of society's notions of the good life and the moral right in a universal perspective.

4.8 The creative function of judgment

Against this background, it is the task of judicial policy and legal judgment to create legal rules and court decisions for the protection of the human person in a tension between society's perception of the good life and respect for the individual's autonomy. This is the foundation for our approach to bioethics and biolaw (Jørgensen & Rendtorff, 2018; Jørgensen, Rendtorff, & Holen, 2018; Rendtorff, 1998, 2002a, 2003, 2008, 2014a, 2015c, 2016a; Rendtorff & Kemp, 2009). Judgment is thus crucial for the transition from bioethics to biolaw, when biolaw must aim to respect the good life and the moral norm in legislation and case law and institutionalize judgments and court decisions in the legal system.

The legally creative function of bioethical judgment as a society-integrating and conflict-mediating person can be understood here from Aristotle and Kant (Ricœur, 1995, p. 237). It consists of a tension between practical wisdom and practical reason that balances the relationship between general rules of law and the specific case in the individual situation. Practical wisdom is particularly relevant where it is difficult to apply specific legal rules. It is used, for example, in the various biolegal situations concerning organ transplantation, genetic engineering, euthanasia and so forth. Here one must weigh the relationship among common norms for the good life, respect for the morally valid in the universal sense and the concrete body of human. The bioethical workings of judgment can thus be defined as an interplay between general principles for the value of the body and the specific situations that require biolegal regulation.

One can refer to Hannah Arendt's interpretation of Kant's theory of judgment in *Kritik der Urteilskraft* (1790). Her analysis of judgment can be seen as an attempt to mediate between a formalist conception of practical reason and the situation in the political community (Arendt, 1982). Judgment can be perceived in both a political and a judicial perspective. Kant distinguishes between the determinant judgment that applies already given general rules in specific situations and the reflective judgment that finds new, not predetermined, general rules for new situations. The reflective judgment manifests itself in creative thinking. Although the reflective judgment in *Kritik der Urteilskraft* is about esthetics and natural teleology, it is of great importance for political rationality and jurisprudence. Judgment relates human as a being of freedom to the world of natural, self-organizing processes to which it belongs. Therefore, it is particularly important for the judicial processes of creating principles of biolaw in relation to the living world.

There is a logical and structural analogy among esthetic, political and legal judgment. Judgment can be characterized as a mediation between the particular and the general in a space of intersubjective considerations and discussions about concrete cases based on a common understanding of value and validity. The political judgment that forms the basis for the formulation of political opinions, legal texts and concrete case law can be described as an interaction among understanding, imagination, reason and common sense (sensus communis).

The exercise of judicial power can, with Ricœur, be defined as a peaceful path to the resolution of social conflicts (Rendtorff, 2020f; Ricœur, 1995). Here, general principles of justice are applied in specific situations. The judicial system, which is autonomous, different from and created in the public debate and during the legislative process, must be said to involve a rational discourse on justice. A certain respect and some basic rights even for those who are to be punished come here instead of the pure violence of the biopower.

Judicial regulation, therefore, has two overriding objectives: On the one hand, a short-term pragmatic resolution of conflicts and, on the other, a long-term shaping of a more just society. As a result of deliberative politics, the exercise of right through judgment has a teleological function, namely, as a solution to conflicts and to contribute to social peace in the light of the regulatory idea of progress in history and the perfection of mankind's "Ungeselige Geselligkeit." Given legal rules and legal principles cannot be applied directly in all situations but must be interpreted through reflective judgments in relation to new situations. The pluralistic features of social conflicts make the application of universal moral principles and of the hidden narratives of the court a question of dynamic interpretations, where new situations without precedent challenge legal standards and require imaginative and original solutions on the border of traditional solutions (Ibid, p. 185).

Biolegal and legal argumentation, in general, must be described as a communicative activity, which, on the basis of a common understanding, sees a notion of justice as a regulatory idea for legal practice (Ricœur, 1995, p. 163). Argumentation and decision-making must be described here as a movement between concrete situation and abstract justification, between common preconception and critical rationality. This balancing procedure aims to find fair laws and decisions. In the judicial system, this discussion of justice involves a relationship between arguments that are tested in relation to facts, rules and beliefs. Therefore, judicial decisions and rulings cannot be reduced to mere questions of judicial positivism. Instead, they are guided by a teleological vision of social peace and a notion of what is good for the individual and society. Ricœur describes this concept of judgment as a fair distance (Rendtorff, 2020f; Ricœur, 1990), the right place between the parts of the conflict, the right distance in relation to the actual situation made possible by the court's formalized rules of the game to assess the specific situation. The ultimate goal of judgment is a joint recognition of the judgment by the parties involved in the case, which in this way makes it possible to build an understanding of the case despite its painful and tragic preconditions.

One must emphasize the distributive nature of judgment as the distribution and protection of social goods in the broadest sense. In biolaw, it is especially about life and body. Judgment must ensure a fair distribution of goods between individuals as part of an exchange system. Thus, judgment helps to delimit the spheres of society in relation to one another and to determine the sphere of biomedical justice. As it creates social justice, judgment presupposes the idea of society as a cooperating entity. The communitarian idea of society as a fragile and vulnerable context lies behind its efforts to create social peace and justice. But the distribution of good in different spheres of justice may conflict with common beliefs. Here reference must be made to the universally morally valid and the respect for the autonomy of the individual. In some cases, the individual's disagreement with the prevailing view of the good can lead to civil disobedience in the name of an unwritten law, and the corresponding "difficult trials" that constitute an appeal to rights and principles must be seen as a new way to ensure legal peace and coherence in the judicial system.

Legislation and case law on biomedical issues thus illustrate the requirement for the secondary court to be able to solve new and unexpected problems. The possibilities for intervention in the human body and for manipulating fetuses and embryos require reflection on how the principles of dignity and respect for the body may apply to future generations and potential individuals. In the following, it is a question of how these questions should be seen in relation to the perception of the human legal subject as a bodily incarnated being between person and thing and how judgment should concretely shape society's legal responsibility for the body. Embryos and fetuses are human life and thus require some treatment as purpose in themselves, but on the other hand, they are not properly regarded as persons and can therefore not be attributed rights and duties on a par with adult persons. This is about balancing the principles of the sanctity of life, the autonomy of the individual and society's responsibility for the living in relation to one another. This takes place in a tension among a common preconception, universal principles, collective experiences and democratic traditions.

5 The legal history of biolaw

5.1 The body between person and thing

Based on the theoretical basis of jurisprudence, it is possible to account for the body's role in European legal development as a background for an analysis of legislation and case law within the areas of jurisprudence. The question is how to ethically and legally make the body a legal entity between person and thing as a basis for legislation and case law within the sub-areas of the different parts of law. European legal thinking has divided the world into persons, actions and things. Although today we take this division for granted, it is important to keep in mind that it is a matter of legal construction and systematization, which presupposes law as a process and legal judgment as staging of reality (Baud, 1993, p. 13). The distinction among persons, things and actions originates from Roman law (Cook, 1962; Villey, 1972) and is fundamental in the *Code Napoléon* (1804). The human person is understood here as the basis for the organization of the legal order. An old legal principle makes the body a part of the person's private sphere that must not be touched (noli me tangere). At the same time, Roman law refers to different types of things, such as res nullius and *res sancta* (i.e. sacred things and things that cannot be bought and sold). These provisions have had a great impact on the legal status of the human body, yet the relationship between person and body has been a pervasive legal theoretical problem. The question is what significance the body must have for the legal definition of human as a legal entity and whether the body can possibly be a legal entity independent of the person (Dijon, 1991, pp. 63, 167).

There are, thus, three possible definitions of the legal status of the body. (1) The body is part of the legal subject's intimate, immovable and private sphere. (2) The body is one thing among other things. It is the person's property. (3) The body is both a thing and not a thing. It belongs to the personal integrity of the legal entity but, at the same time, has the status of a special thing that must be treated with special care.

All three perceptions are central to the development of jurisprudence. It is important to understand when the body should be considered part of the person's being, when it can be exchanged in ordinary trade and conduct and when it becomes a special thing with its own rights. When the body is defined

DOI: 10.4324/9781003147848-5

as a legal entity or an object of special legal considerations, law can no longer be understood as a question of a legal relationship between persons and of the distribution of things between persons (Arnoux, 1994, p. 17). The legal question then concerns not only who has the right to dispose of the body in trade and conduct but also how to weigh the consideration of the body as such by virtue of the intrinsic value it possesses as part of the living.

A real case where the judiciary was given the task of defining the status of the body between person and thing can shed light on this legal balancing process among perceiving the body as part of the person, as a thing and as something living in itself that is entitled to judicial protection (Arnoux, 1994; Baud, 1993). It is about a famous lawsuit from California, the John Moore case (1986–90), or "the case of the man with the gold cells." John Moore had been in treatment for a leukemia disease for years but discovered by chance that his doctors had at the same time extracted a rare medicinal product from his cells; indeed, they had made millions of dollars from manufacturing and selling the product. Moore sued the doctors for intervening and using his body without his informed consent. He argued that the body had to be his personal property and that he, therefore, had share in the money that the doctors had earned from using his cells to extract the precious medicinal product.

In the first judgment, the Court of Appeals upheld Moore's appeal, referring to the person's ownership of his body. The court ruled that human himself has the right to decide over his or her body. This decision could have been inspired by John Locke's legal philosophy, where the citizen's right to his or her own body is a natural right that precedes the social pact. The doctors were not allowed to use his body to manufacture and sell medicinal products without Moore's consent, and they were sentenced to let Moore have a share in the profits from the sale.

However, the case was appealed to the California Supreme Court, which found it problematic that a substance from Moore's body had been used for product extraction and sale. The Supreme Court held, citing the body as part of the person, that Moore violated his integrity and dignity by selling drugs from his body as a simple commodity. However, the real background to the commercial success was not Moore's body parts per se but the doctors' work and creative research. And although the Supreme Court would not recognize Moore's ownership of his body, it was held that it was wrong that the doctors had not asked Moore if they could use his cells to manufacture the medicine. The person has the right to decide over the privacy of the body, even though the body cannot be perceived as a property. This issue, however, was not the subject of actual litigation but settled with a settlement between the parties, in which Moore received financial compensation for wrongful interference with bodily integrity.

The two sentences in the John Moore case illustrate the scope of the challenges to bioright when it comes to determining the body's status between person and thing. The judgments express the difficulties of balancing the various considerations in relation to one another: The person's integrity and dignity, the right to decide over their body and society's interest in materializing the body for consumption and respect for the body as a living organism with its own values and rights. Admittedly, one must respect the person's right to dispose of his or her body, but this must not conflict with the person's dignity. At the same time, the body is a useful thing that can be exploited for the good of man, but there are limits to the commercialization of the human body. It must not conflict with society's general notions of human dignity and respect for the living. However, it is just as difficult to see the body solely as an expression of the person, as excreted genetic material, organs, sperm and body tissues can no longer be said to be a direct part of the person. The body, therefore, acquires a kind of independent being that cannot be fully covered by the person as a legal entity. The legal judgment must, therefore, include the personal integrity, the individual's ownership of his or her body and the body's intrinsic value in the balancing process, and then the body appears as a third kind of "thing" between person and thing.

5.2 The body in phenomenological perspective

The ontological basis for the body's duality between person and thing emerges clearly in a phenomenological analysis of the body's various dimensions. The starting point is humanity's experience with the body as a center of perception and action. When, for example, in Edmund Husserl or in everyday speech, a distinction is made between "Leib" and "Körper," it is because the body is both "Leib," that is, basis for a subjective world experience, and "Körper," that is, an instrument or object among other instruments and objects in the world (Husserl, 1973). Phenomenologically, in a health science perspective, a distinction can be made among the experienced body, the body in the human subjective disease experience, the body as the subject of the doctor's treatment and the body as the health science object (Nerheim, 1995; Thombs, 1993; Zaner, 1988).

The French philosopher Merleau-Ponty has studied the perceived body of a human being as the fundamental basis of its existence. He believes that in order to understand man's bodily cohesion with the rest of the living world, we must overcome the sharp distinction between subject and object. As a lived body, a human being "is" his or her body, but he or she neither "owns" nor "has" his or her body. The experienced body expresses the peculiarities that are characteristic of the individual person's bodily incarnation (embodiment) and determines a person's sensory experience (Zaner, 1965) in a bodily behavior and attitude that suits it. The experienced body appears as a field of meaning in a unit of bodily intentionality, original meaning and the organization of the body's symbolism, as well as different body meanings and Gestalt forms. Merleau-Ponty speaks of a "belief of the senses" based on the sensing body, "a core of meaning" (Merleau-Ponty, 1945, p. 158), which summarizes the subject's experiences in time and space; its experiences in past, present and future; its physical and social environment; and its moral and ideological situation.

The human body experience, despite this sensory unity, is characterized by some profound tensions, which Jean-Paul Sartre in particular has portrayed in

L'Etre et Le Néant (1943). He distinguishes between three dimensions of human existence of great importance to the body experience: For-oneself-being, in-oneself-being and being-for-the-other. Being-for-oneself refers to the consciousness's pre-reflexive and reflexive experience of itself and the world as a free, experienced self-relationship. Human is committed to existence and organizes the world as the world through his or her projects. This free consciousness, however, is embedded in an existential facticity, a bodily condition determined as in-being. The body is experienced especially as a thing in the encounter with the other human being, in the human being-for-the-other, where the body seen from the outside with the other person's gaze becomes an object among other objects in the world.

Health and illness, well-being and pain are not just some physiological processes in the human organism but also subjective experiences and experiences of the body (Thombs, 1993, pp. 27, 33) that must be understood in the light of a human being as a lived body. One can here distinguish between subjectively experienced disease and disease objectively considered as defects in the physiological functioning of the organism. The body is quite different in the patient who suffers and the health care professionals who have to deal with the ailments at a distance. From experiencing the body unreflected, the patient becomes aware of his or her body and experiences this change in the body experience. When health science treats the body as an anatomical object, the patient simultaneously becomes aware of the body as a neurophysiological organism. One must thus distinguish between (1) a pre-reflective experience of the body, (2) a subjectively conscious experience and (3) the body from the outside considered as a functional instrument or a thing among other things in the world (Ibid, p. 51).

Merleau-Ponty expresses the duality of *Phénoménologie de la perception* (1945) in the relationship between the experienced body and the body as object by talking about the ambiguity of the body (ambiguité) (Merleau-Ponty, 1945). As a material object, from the other person's perspective, our body is a neurobiological organism, a biological substance that is different from myself, but at the same time, we are generally not involved in the objectifying scientific processes that observe and treat our body as a neuro-physiological organism. In the perceived body's sensing and action life, that is, as the subjective center of meaning, the objective body, such as tissues, organs, brain and skeleton, is invisible. Sartre says that when you write a letter, you experience that you write the letter but never really the act of writing as such. In order to be able to experience the body as an object, that is, as in-being-being or being-for-the-other, one must reflexively abstract from one's experienced body. It can happen in confrontation with the other person's gaze, where we become aware of our bodily facticity and in borderline situations such as illness, pain and sexuality, where the person can experience the body as "foreign" (Thombs, 1993, pp. 60–61; Zaner, 1981, pp. 48–55). If we have cramps, we can, for example, experience the body as a painful resistance and thus become aware of the "object-body's" hidden presence in our experienced body.

Consequently, illness can be understood as an interruption in the experienced body life (Thombs, 1993, p. 62). The disease interrupts the body's presupposed mode of being in the world by changing its senses, inhibiting its actions and transforming its experiences of space and time. When the disease intervenes in our body, for example, if we suddenly lose sight or hearing, we feel the importance of the body as an instrument. Illness limits the projects that the individual has set for himself in everyday life and weakens the body's life possibilities (Zaner, 1988, p. 53). The possibility of death becomes present in a constant fear of the future, and life develops into a struggle against the decomposition of the body. Disease brings chaos in the human experienced body. It creates disorder in the self's relationship to its body, and it is not only a threat to the body but also a threat to the balance of the person and the self as such (Thombs, 1993, p. 70). The borderline and limit situation of the disease experience thus leads to an alienating and involuntary objectification of the experienced body. It testifies quite clearly that the body's being as a well-functioning "object-body," instrument-machine and physiological organism is a prerequisite for the experienced body.

The point is to show that the body as a biological basis for human existence gets meaning from the experienced body, for which it itself is the prerequisite. The inhibited diseased body lets the physical body, which is constantly present in human existence, come to light. The paradox of the disease, that the human being becomes aware of his or her body, but cannot escape from the body, testifies to the duality of existence between self-being and in-being-being, between person and thing. Therefore, one must really talk about the "hiddenness of health" (Gadamer, 1995, p. 133), which is revealed by the disease when it degrades the experienced body and allows human fragility, finitude and vulnerability to appear.

5.3 The concept of disease and medical judgment

Against this background, it is possible to define the concept of disease in medical science in a tension between experienced and biological body. In the famous work *Le normal et le pathologique* (1943), the French theorist of science Georges Canguilhem deals with a positivist physiology that perceives disease as an objective physiological condition. According to Canguilhem, the concept of the normal is esthetic, moral and social and not just purely scientific (Canguilhem, 1943, p. 23). Disease can not only be understood from a physiological and biochemical description. There is nothing in the disease that is not first in the consciousness. This means that the concept of disease always has a subjective and individual dimension. Human is more involved in creating his or her own pains and ailments than in passively suffering under them, as something inflicted from the outside. Medicine and culture are closely linked, and disease is just not a "device failure" in the organism's causal processes but always takes on a broader meaning as being closely related to culture's normative concepts of good and evil.

Despite the fact that the concept of disease is a social construction, one cannot escape the fact that biological normality plays a major role in our understanding of pathology. Illness can be defined as a "non-value," which as a negation of man's desire to live is the prerequisite for all the negative in human life. Disease destroys the power of life, man's vital ability to live, to love, to work and to think. Instead, one wants to live with the organism by feeling the body as little as possible in a lasting joy over life (Canguilhem, p. 74). This means that the normal function of the organism as the subject of an objective physiological description is of great importance for the goals of medical science. According to Canguilhem, there is a built-in pulsating normative force in life that becomes a value concept for medical science. This means that biological anomaly, abnormality and deficiency are not in themselves the subject of a biological and pathological description, but that such deficiencies seen through the normative glasses of the experienced body and medicine will express suffering and powerlessness.

Therefore, health and wellness can be defined as normative concepts that refer to the normality of the organism. Being in good health expresses the organism's possible reaction against diseases (Canguilhem, 1943, p. 86). The disease is a condition that one fights against in order to continue living. There is a close interplay between the normal functioning of the organism and the experience of it through the experienced body. The normal human being thus lives on the basis of the organism's functional norm, whereby the biological norm coincides with the subjective experience of good health. The healthy person thus lives in accordance with the body's biochemical and physiological norms, which become co-determining for the body's experienced life (Canguilhem, 1943, p. 98). The characteristics of the human species manifest themselves in a normativity that is at once biological and social, where the biological structure of the organism is the basis of human life as an experienced body with an infinite desire for life.

The differences among the experienced body, the biological-physiological aspects of the body and the body as a useful instrument, as a social resource and as a scientific object have become greater as a result of the development of health science. In many cases, health sciences have reversed the picture. The dead body has become more and more a model for the understanding of the experienced body. To the same extent that the body is objectified, the subjective experience is also explained with objective concepts. The medical gaze disregards the experienced body and describes the body's organs, structures and functions as physiological processes and causal mechanisms. Medical science has recently gained knowledge of the body's function through dissection and anatomical examinations of dead bodies. The understanding of the dead body has been transferred to the living body (Baud, 1993; Foucault, 1962; Thombs, 1993; Zaner, 1988). This has made it easier to come to terms with the fact that the body is a thing and a useful social resource. Today, the medical gaze penetrates deep into the objective body in a massive utilization of all its functions for organ transplantation, genetics and reproductive technology and so forth.

In the meeting with the clinic, the experienced body is transformed into a scientific object. The human person dissolves into neutral objective data and diagnoses. This reification threatens to erase the perceived body and thus the integrity and dignity of man. Therefore, an understanding of the body's duality between person and thing is of great importance for the treatment philosophy. Richard Zaner argues in *Ethics and the Clinical Encounter* (1988) that health science is a social practice that seeks to restore the patient's bodily integrity and natural balance (Zaner, 1988, p. 224). The health sciences and the rules of medical ethics (which are reflected in the law of biolaw) must therefore take into account all the dimensions of the body, both the objective disease reality and the person's subjective world of life.

In this way, medical science is at once science and medical action (Honnefelder & Rager, 1994, p. 15). Research into the structure and function of the body for the purpose of medical treatment is the goal of the medical profession. Here, diagnosis, therapy and prognosis become the central elements of medical treatment. When a patient is ill, it is the doctor's task as an outsider to know the body's pathological processes to understand the disease, that is, make a diagnosis and then intervene in the disease with a specific therapy and prognosis of cure so that the disease is cured or so that the patient's disorder is alleviated (Ibid, p. 17). Not only scientific knowledge is expected here but also concrete action. Therefore, according to the physicians Ludger Honnefelder and Günther Rager in *Ärtzliches Urteilen und Handeln* (1994), action and judgment are central elements in the art of medicine. Based on diagnosis, therapy and prognosis, judgment, as a creative translation of rational and intellectual insights into concrete action, must ensure responsible intervention in particular situations vis-à-vis specific individuals (Rager, 1994).

When a physician makes a diagnosis and puts the patient's disorder in relation to an already known disease picture, he or she makes use of the determining judgment, which is the ability to subsume the individual case under a general law. If it is a disease that the doctor does not know about, its disease picture must first be developed, and the judgment becomes reflective when it has to search for what is considered as the general in the situation in the light of the pathological processes, that is, the purposefulness of the particular case of illness (Ibid, p. 23). The medical judgment, where the theoretical knowledge is applied in practice, cannot be learned but is practiced through the doctor's practical experience. In a body phenomenological perspective, judgment is based on a holistic understanding of the patient's self-understanding, life project and perception of the good life, which is then again grounded in an ethical view of man.

In the treatment of the human perceived body as an organic, functional system and a biological object, the physician cannot fail to orient himself toward the human person. Making a diagnosis, developing a concept of illness and performing a subsequent treatment based on a prognosis about the probable course of the disease become an ethical act, where the doctor's concept of illness must be put in relation to the person's experienced body and existential self-understanding. The doctor does not get around the body's duality between person and thing in the treatment process, where he or she, on the one hand, must ensure that it proceeds medically soundly and, at the same time, must comfort and support the patient. The doctor must find a balance between the correct medical treatment and consideration for the patient's understanding of life as well as experience of his or her illness. As a practical science of the human body, the art of medicine must at once rely on medical knowledge of the bodily functioning of the body, fit this knowledge into a holistic understanding of disease and health in the light of a human view and make sure to restore the body's balance or at least alleviate patient suffering.

5.4 The body in the perspective of cultural anthropology

It is necessary to look at the body in a broader cultural anthropological perspective to truly understand the tension between person and thing, not least because the development of Western civilization can be seen as a process that increasingly distances itself from the natural spontaneity of the body and emotions (Elias, 1968, p. LXII). The social organization simply consists of a number of norms and prohibitions of civilization coming to regulate the relation of human to his or her body; for example, the cannibalism ban, the incest ban and the homicide ban, which have general validity. Norbert Elias argues that civilization, in contrast to barbarism, is characterized by norms of operational control, self-control and courtesy and by rules that distinguish between cleanliness and uncleanness (Elias, 1968, p. 60).

The civilizational relationship with the body is, therefore, characterized by a tension between order and disorder, moral behavior toward a culturally and border-breaking operating life. To get below the surface, Georges Bataille distinguishes in this connection between the homogeneous and the heterogeneous. The homogeneous is the useful and rational that belongs to production, work and social life, while the heterogeneous does not fit into the ordinary categories and concepts of everyday life. It manifests itself, on the other hand, in frontier-breaking parties, religious excesses and the political revolt (Bataille, 1933–34 and 1943). The experienced body is in the tension between the heterogeneous and the homogeneous. By virtue of sexuality, violence and ecstasy, it transcends the sphere of homogeneity, and when it transcends boundaries, it can destroy civilization. Society, therefore, seeks to control the human body and establishes a body-suppressing monopoly of power as a basic principle in the civilizational process.

Society's relationship to the body between person and thing is consequently seen in the tension among the sacred, the profane and the grotesque (Baud, 1993, p. 90; Eliade, 1988) in Western culture's most peculiar relationship to the dead body (Baud, 1993, p. 30). But the everyday tendency to live the experienced body and forget the sick and dead body is a general anthropological problem. Sickness and death are heterogeneous elements that human beings tend to displace. It is obviously very difficult to relate to the body as mere material fact and to forget oneself as a lived body.

It is clear, on the other hand, that society's formulation of norms for dealing with the dead body testifies to its civilizational self-understanding. The relationship with the dead body is characterized by ambivalent emotions. On the one hand, it is a thing, and on the other hand, it arouses disgust and or awe as a remnant of a living and as a symbol of the divide between life and death, which in a religious context is turned into a divide between time and eternity, the earthly and the heavenly. The dead body acquires both grotesque and sacred features. Jean-Pierre Baud believes that this is because the dead body makes us particularly aware that not only the body expresses the living person but that the living person also presupposes the material factuality of the body. The feeling of grotesqueness toward a skeleton or a corpse makes me recognize my body's mortality and finitude that comes from the body's facticity as a physical/biological organism (Ibid, pp. 37, 90).

The "material reality" of the body in the dead body is the starting point for the distinctions and norms for dealing with the body as a thing that characterizes Western culture. The physical reality of the body means that its products can be divided into something sacred and life-giving, something trivial and something harmful. Blood, semen and organs have been considered sacred and life-giving in various periods of Western history, hair and nails as something trivial and excrement as something harmful. This division of the body's products into the sublime and healing, the banal and the dangerous, has been the starting point for the norms of dealing with the body and defined the pure and impure, the commanded and forbidden.

As a result of Christianity, Western culture has perceived the dead body as a sacred thing. In Catholicism, the believer in the sacrament can receive life and strength from Jesus' body and blood – likewise by touching on a saint's bodily remnants. The saint can symbolically transfer life to the one who lacks life, whether he is sick or dead. The Christian notion of the body as a sacred life-giving medicine is perhaps one of the reasons why Western culture, unlike the Japanese, for example, has found it so easy to treat organ transplantation as an acceptable medical practice that is not considered barbaric (Ibid, p. 35). Organ and blood donation show that body parts can be used for therapeutic purposes. This is a different ritual treatment of the body than in certain pagan cultures that advocate cannibalism. Cannibalism in our culture transcends the forbidden and does not respect the rules of the sanctity of the body that have developed in continuation of the Christian tradition.

Society's treatment of the human body, however, may risk exceeding reverence for the sacred and ending in the grotesque. Body and body products become ordinary things that are exchanged in trade and conduct. Exchanging the body's waste products such as nails or urine is not a problem. But when progressive physicians in the early nineteenth century wanted to make the body a recycled object, the moral boundaries of society were put to the test. The grotesque occurs when society transcends its civilizational boundaries and disregards the fact that body and body products are not just dead things but the remains of a living person. Depriving the dead body of its living past leads to a grotesque banalization. The Nazis' attempts at living people as if they were dead and the use of dead bodies for the production of soap products in the concentration camps express a ruthless lack of respect for the sanctity of the body, thereby transcending the civilizational boundaries of our culture. A radical secularization of culture's religious and moral notions of the sanctity of the body can also have socially dissolving consequences. Most cultures have, for good reasons, formulated strict moral laws for the treatment of the human body, and the laws have been sanctioned both by unwritten cultural norms and by explicitly formulated rules by elites in society such as jurists, doctors and priests (Ibid, p. 140).

Society's moral distinction between the homogeneous and the heterogeneous, the grotesque, the profane and the sacred depends on the legitimate management of the body's status between person and thing. On the one hand, a total banalization and reification of the body risk leading to a grotesque violation of the human personality as a perceived body. On the other hand, an excessive sanctification of the body as an expression of the person cannot fail to displace the permanent reality of death and the material character of the body. A societal concern not to exceed moral boundaries is necessary to maintain the divide between culture and barbarism, which is expressed both in society's ordinary everyday etiquette and in the basic civilizational prohibitions.

5.5 The body in European legal traditions

Legal regulation using formalized norms has also helped to determine society's civilizational boundaries in relation to the human body. European legal tradition thus contains important case law and legal reflection, which form the basis for understanding the problems of modern cinema law. The heterogeneous status of the body in the tension between the grotesque and the sacred has resulted in it being difficult to relate to the living body within a rational legal discourse. During the process of Western European civilization, the law has thus not been able to give the body an actual legal status but instead has defined it as a thing either completely outside the legal transactions or as part of the person as a legal entity (Arnoux, 1994, p. 35; Villey, 1972). A legal historical analysis shows that jurisprudence has been fundamentally ambivalent in relation to the body and despite the secularization process has had more and more difficulty in fitting it into the judicial system.

In archaic societies, the body was elementally present in the judicial system. The judicial order was sacred, and harsh corporal punishment was used for violating the law. The individual's attachment to the judicial community functioned as a concrete physical obligation based on the division, eye for eye, tooth for tooth (Baud, 1993, p. 94). Judicial transactions found expression in bodily symbolizations such as bloody sacrifices of humans and animals. Archaic law was grounded in a higher cosmic order of divine origin.

Admittedly, Roman law can be said to have helped to demystify and desacralize the body by distinguishing the experienced body from the dead body and determining the dead body as a sacred thing outside the legal realm, but this provision is, at the same time, paradoxical. Thereby, the experienced body disappeared in the long run in the secularized legal subject. By not allowing the body free independent status in law and rejecting its legal significance, European legal tradition created a vacuum in the law and made the body homeless. In its zeal for civilization and rationalization, jurisprudence, as part of the profane sphere of homogeneity, has also refused to know the heterogeneous, sacred and grotesque aspects of the body and consequently shut it out of the legal universe.

Jean-Pierre Baud regards the *Code Napoléon* of 1804 as a culmination of the body constriction of jurisprudence, which stands in strange contrast to the ubiquitous presence of the body outside the legal universe in the ordinary life of society. We mean, by the way, that Baud goes with these claims too far in his emphasis on the body constriction of law. After all, it is possible to demonstrate some aspects of the body's legal status in European legal tradition that can deepen and put into perspective the contemporary discussion of biolaw and biorights.

Although Roman law developed an abstract legal system, it continued to rest on a natural law foundation. This meant that the relationship among man, nature, the political community and the trial in the specific case played a major role in the judiciary. For example, it was forbidden to formulate rules of law and judgments that transgressed against human nature, just as it was forbidden to fabricate "hybrids" or "monsters" that perverted human nature. Adoption rules were also justified on the grounds of the order of nature.

Thus, it was not allowed to adopt a human being who was older than oneself. Nature served as the norm for the judiciary's formulation of adequate legal rules. This natural law justification for the law's regulations can put into perspective the situation in modern cinema, which ultimately may also have to be based on "human nature."

The rationalization of the judicial system also implies a more humane relationship with the human body. Abolition of corporal revenge or torture as a result of a humane judicial procedure is one of the most important features of judicial systems in civilized countries. Admittedly, like Foucault in *Surveiller et punir* (1973), one might think that the establishment of modern prisons by biopower leads to barbarism in the modern legal system that will purify the prisoner's soul through isolation and strict control. On the other hand, it is difficult to ignore the fact that a rationalization and differentiation of criminal law is a condition for a more humane model of conflict resolution in a modern society.

This can be seen by some aspects of the concept of person that are of great importance to modern cinema. European legal tradition thus contains, as we have seen before, a notion of the private sphere or the "non-patrimonial rights" of the legal entity (Arnoux, 1994, p. 149), which obliges the law to protect personal integrity without the person being able to said to own his or her body. From this develops the idea of personal dignity and inviolability and of the person's right to rule over his or her body.

The universal aspect of the concept of person that confers legal protection on human, not because of status or merit but solely because of his or her being a person, must also be emphasized. In particular, criminal law as part of personal law has historically protected bodily integrity. The concept of person and the legal subjectivity of Roman law and the *Code Napoléon* are the precondition for human rights' protection of the person's life and body, and the development of jurisprudence, which makes the body the subject of legal protection, can rightly be seen as an effort to complement the political and social human rights.

5.6 Theology and the art of medicine

Although Roman law contained these possibilities to make the body subject to judicial protection, its definition of body and body products as res nullius (nothing) and res sanctus (sacred thing) meant that the formulation of society's norms for dealing with the body was also taken care of by two other social groups, the Catholic Church and medical science. The norms of the church were to secure a pure soul for human by treating the body as a sacred thing and avoiding immoral life. It formulated laws and regulations for dealing with blood and semen, masturbation, incest and homosexuality. Suicide and gross neglect of the body were perceived as a mortal sin. Medical science initially perceived the body as a therapeutic object that needed hygiene and a healthy lifestyle but later also as an object of research, something that with the dead body as a model could be described with scientific methods (Baud, 1993, p. 166; Foucault, 1964). The church made the individual morally obligated in relation to his or her body, because the body was the abode of the soul and the expression of human as living. The purity of the soul depended on the purity of the body, and therefore, the church defined the body as a sacred thing with its own rights (Baud, 1993, p. 106).

This interest in the concrete body of human and the church's care for the body as a sacred thing manifested itself in the development of the poor and the establishment of hospitals, where the sick was taken care of. Unlike the established legal system, which did not introduce social rights, the church claimed that everyone had the right to food and shelter. It helped the poor and in extreme famine situations could even justify a crime such as theft (Ibid, p. 122). The canon law made the care and nurturing of the concrete body something fundamental to develop the religious and ethical strength of the individual. Sickness and poverty were fought as part of a moral project to drive out sin and give human a pure soul, ready for salvation after death. This mixture of a hygienic-sanitary and a moral religious project of improvement and care is clearly expressed in exorcism and sacramental actions (Ibid, p. 130).

In this way, the church's interest in the human body gained a great deal of importance for the process of Western civilization. The church established a close connection among body, ethics and law through the ideals of care and solidarity with the weak and the sick that we find in the modern welfare state and public health care. The religious notion of the church as the body of Christ, "corps mystique" can mentally historically be said to have been reformulated into the secularized idea of the state and the population as a collective body that has been behind much population policy and health science in the nineteenth and twentieth centuries (Ibid, p. 155).

However, the church lost its hold on the body of the individual as a result of the secularization processes of the seventeenth and eighteenth centuries. Instead, it gradually became medical science that came to act as the norm-setter for the proper handling of the body. In the beginning, the church's moral care project was continued, and clinics and hospitals were built to heal the sick and ensure the individual's natural and healthy relationship with his or her body. But eventually, medical science broke with the church's religiously justified care ideals and replaced them with biological health ideals as the basis for bodily care. In the industrial society, it is the hygienist's ideals of light, air and cleanliness that triumph (Ibid, p. 156). He perceives society as a collective biological organism that needs to be maintained and purified. This is done through various forms of hygiene policy, for example, by rules for sexual behavior and medical criteria for healthy and unhealthy (read "moral" and "immoral") body hygiene. The hygienist combines Social Darwinism with eugenics. He wants to create stronger, better and more beautiful people and to avoid the weak, the ugly and the stupid. The hygienist fights the decadence and pollution of the body in the name of science and health (Baud, 1993, p. 157).

At the same time, another type of doctor emerged, the scientific researcher. This physician is mainly interested in the body as a biological object that can be explored as a mechanical functional context. Unlike the ancient medical science that would help man to feel well in the body and restore the body's natural balance, the dead body here became a model for the understanding of the living. As a result, modern medical science as the norm for dealing with the body relates to the mechanical structure of the body and easily forgets the patient's perceived body and an understanding of the care-related and communicative aspects of the patient-physician relationship (Nerheim, 1995, pp. 21, 373; Thombs, 1993).

Both the hygienist and the doctor as a scientist are characterized by a moral blindness to the sacred and moral dimensions of the experienced body. Medical science no longer perceives the body in a sacred perspective but as a biological spare part that can be cut up, repaired or reused in other bodies. The experienced body is in this perspective only a biological machine, where the model for the understanding of the living is the dead body, the skeleton. This oblivion of the experienced body and the moral dimensions of medical art was evident in the reification of Nazism and experiments with people in the concentration camps. Dr. Mengele, who in Auschwitz with a mixture of moral blindness and diabolical evil cut the eyes out of gypsy twins to examine their interesting color, is a sinister sign of what a completely morally blind medical science can lead to (Müller Hill, 1984). The experienced body is here reduced to something trivial and banal in a complete displacement of its holiness and inviolability. The result is morbid and grotesque, but the morally blind medical researcher can or will no longer see it.

In the face of this tendency to extreme de-humanization of humanity, we must cling to a medical science that is fundamentally in the service of life and falls neither for the useful ideology of the hygienist nor for the grotesque moral blindness of Nazism. As a therapeutic art, health science should not fall victim to bureaucratic or technological rationalization either. It is important to maintain that health science is a normative and therapeutic art that seeks to restore and support the living spontaneous power of the body and organism. Health science is committed to restoring the individual's bodily balance and subjective sense of well-being and zest for life (Canguilhem, 1943). The inherent power of nature and the body's own purposefulness as a biological organic organism, uncovered by the biological and physiological sciences, have always been important landmarks.

But at the same time, it is the ethical responsibility of health sciences to be clear that criteria for the pathological and nonpathological are not objective in the scientific sense but are part of general social and moral notions of health, illness and good health. This is not least at a time when the foundation of health science in the body's inherent balance and physiological structure is being challenged like never before. With the development of new technology that enables genetic engineering of the human body, we may one day be able to develop a radically different health science that is no longer dependent on the biology and physiology of the organism as its normative foundation. And yet this is "science fiction" for ordinary disease treatment. Here, health science must still use the objective physiological description of the organism's behavior as basic technical knowledge, which, at the same time, as its therapeutic and curative endeavor takes subjective part of life's inherent normative power to restore the organism's balance and harmony as middle and anatomical harmony (Canguilhem, 1943, p. 128).

5.7 The transformation of law in the risk society

As the only norm-setter for the handling and use of the body, medical science no longer seems to respect the person's bodily integrity. At the same time, the intensified violence against the body in modern industrial society means that the lawyer and the legislature can no longer turn their backs on the human body but are constantly confronted with abuse and encroachment on the body. It has become necessary to take a stand in social conflicts that are about respect for the individual's body. The reality of modern human beings is largely bodily determined. The culture industry and the media constantly remind us of the finitude of the body. The utopia of "a healthy soul in a beautiful and harmonious body" belongs to the elementary ideal formations in today's risky society. At the same time, humanity is constantly confronted with things that destroy his or her body: Industrial accidents, traffic accidents, chemicals in food, pollution, medical experiments and medical malpractice in hospitals and so forth. This permanent physical pressure is the background to the current need for legal regulation of the human body in the risk society.

However, the risk society has also led to a change in the way the legal system works. Many more citizens are involved in the management of the body and the decisions are made by those in power (Beck, 1986). While the concept of liability was previously considered to be a well-defined legal concept that went on the question of whether a person could be considered to have been the one who had committed a particular act, its conscious agent or not, one must, as we have seen, in day with a philosopher like Hans Jonas counting humanity's responsibility for future generations and its duty to care for the weakest and most vulnerable as his responsibility (Ricœur, 1995, p. 41).

In other words, there has been an expansion of the content of the concept of responsibility, which means that today one can also be responsible based on legal and ethical norms, even if one has not made a mistake or a criminal act at all. In the case of the welfare state, the responsibility has come to include the duty to take care of all weak, hungry and sick people in society, no matter what emergency they may find themselves in. The extension of the concept of responsibility in our time implies that the welfare state in legislation and case law must take over the protection of and care for the individual's body, which neither the church nor medical science is any longer able to take care of.

The takeover of the church's care project in legislation and case law is evident not only in civil and criminal law but also in labor, social and health law issues. Labor law and social law have thus changed the basic divisions of civil law into actions, persons and things. These are no longer just contracts between legal entities, but through marriage cases, pornography cases and other cases on the border of the private sphere, civil law has taken over the church's ideal of protecting the rights of the body. Likewise, criminal law no longer speaks of revenge or retaliation as a basis for judicial policy decisions but rather understands the court's task as a preventive measure, which aims, on the one hand, to resocialize the criminal and, on the other hand, to provide the victim with therapeutic care.

In labor and social law, it has long been possible to follow this process. In his book *L'Etat Providence* (*On the Modern Welfare State*), the French philosopher François Ewald shows how the risk society compensates for accidents at work, illness and social distress by establishing insurance systems – for example, work and health insurance – as collective care schemes that oblige companies and society to provide compensation for social misfortune, even though neither society nor the individual firms are legally responsible for the random fate of the individual. In this way, a number of social insurances arise as a counterpart to society's attacks on the human body. The industrial environment attacks the civilian environment and, in a sense, responds to charges. Therefore, one can no longer ignore the importance of the body for legal development in the risk society. Legislation and legal expertise are forced to put their traditional body displacement and body censorship behind them and face the new challenges (Ewald, 1984).

5.8 The body in the modern legal system

Against this background, we would like to point out some features of modern legal development that set the framework for legislation on the body. Most constitutions in the European legal tradition have institutionalized a protection of bodily integrity as part of the fundamental rights of the legal entity. The welfare state has taken the church's care project further in the form of an expanded state responsibility based on comprehensive collective insurance schemes. Legal subjectivity also includes the weakest and most vulnerable. Finally, concrete legislation and case law on biomedical issues have meant that the body is increasingly present in the judicial system as the subject of judicial regulation.

In the European constitutions on the European continent, a development can be traced toward a more comprehensive protection of the fundamental rights of the legal entity. Here, the legal entity is no longer determined only as a participant in a contract but as the subject of the law's protective function, which has become central. The legal entity has become the one "worthy of respect and care." The law serves to protect the dignity, integrity and vulnerability of the individual. In particular, southern European countries, such as France and Italy, have incorporated such respect for human rights (by virtue of the 1789 tradition) into their constitutions. In 1994, France introduced a law on "respect for the human body" (Law n ° 94–653 1994), which gives the body as inviolable and an expression of human dignity a legal protection that extends beyond the traditional legal entity. But also, Central European countries such as Germany and the Netherlands have developed some new constitutional rights aimed at protecting the integrity of the body. The German constitution of 1949, which is inspired by the principles of natural law, thus states that "die Menschenwürde ist unantastbar." And the Dutch constitution connects self-determination and integrity by pointing out the individual's right over his or her own body (Leenen, 1994, p. 15). Although human rights do not play such a huge role in the Danish constitution, it can still be said that the notion of protecting bodily integrity is a basic legal notion in health policy issues (including the Medical Practitioners Act).

This development of the connection among fundamental rights, person and body must, as has been said, be seen as a consequence of the expansion of the welfare state and the risk society into a state of care and protection. This is the basis for current developments of bioethics and biolaw (Jørgensen & Rendtorff, 2018; Jørgensen, Rendtorff, & Holen, 2018; Rendtorff, 1998, 2002a, 2003, 2008, 2014a, 2015c, 2016a; Rendtorff & Kemp, 2009). The regulation of the members of society by law moves from being grounded in contractual relations between free and equal legal persons to be a collective responsibility that also includes the body between person and thing. Jurisprudence can be said to be based on a common solidarity between members of society (Delmas, 1992). It largely recognizes human self-determination but, at the same time, has a collective responsibility to set limits on the individual's disposition of his or her own body. The biolegal norms for the human body must therefore be seen in a broader ethical perspective. Where ecclesiastical law in its time justified its care for the human body on the basis of a higher divine order, the jurisprudence of the welfare state must be based on a reference to a human view that can legitimize the law violating the individual's sovereign right to his or her body. It must, so to speak, secularize the ecclesiastical law's understanding of the body as a sacred thing that has its own right. The concepts of dignity, integrity and vulnerability are modern expressions of the respect the body's being between person and thing is entitled to. The legislation's protection of the body and the specific biolegal issues must be seen in the light of this human rights–oriented duty of care that has developed in the welfare state.

Judicial policy debates on blood donation were the first modern expression of the body's presence in law. European laws on blood transfusions are good examples of a modern view of man that understands the body as a sacred thing with its own right between person and thing outside of ordinary legal transactions. Based on the idea of mutual solidarity, legislation on blood donors is based on the idea of a generous gift of an intimate bodily nature (Baud, 1993; Titmuss, 1970). The biological uniqueness of the blood as a life-giving medium between people has helped to break down a categorical distinction among people, actions and things. Society here has had to formulate rules for how to treat parts of the body as something living and exchange them between members of society. The legislation in many cases refuses to commercialize the blood and yet gives permission to let it enter into a societal exchange, and in this way, one tries to find a place for the body between person and thing. These discussions about the sanctity and dignity of the body in connection with the social exchange of body parts today necessarily also concern organs, sperm, fertilized eggs, genetic material and information and so forth.

The principled legal discussion about the biolaw and biorights of the welfare state is thus about defining the body's right place between person and thing based on the idea of society's care for the person's body and respect for the living (Dworkin, 1994). It can rightly be emphasized that we must not fall back into an invisibility and bodily repression, but neither must we end up in a barbaric and grotesque reification of the body. However, excessive sanctification of the body can also be an obstacle to giving it real legal protection. In connection with blood donation, it would be a dangerous exaggeration to claim that this is a patriotic sacrifice of the individual for the sake of society. Judicial policy must take care to reject any intervention in the human body and the exchange of body parts as an uncivilized barbarism and thus return to mythical body worship that taboos the body as immovable and sacred. This would make a sober discussion about the trivial and harmful dimensions of the body impossible. Instead, within each of the sub-areas of sub-law, one must carefully weigh the different dimensions of the body in the relationship between person and thing. It is about finding the right middle ground among respect for persons, the sanctity of life and the societal exchange of human body parts. On the one hand, the legal policy debate is about the extent to which it is possible to materialize the body without violating the sanctity of life; on the other hand, to avoid that the dignity of the body and the sanctity of life are absolute to such an extent that we displace that the body is also a thing.

The judiciary must therefore try to define the status of the body on this basis. Here the Italian legal theorist Stefano Rodotà speaks of "legalizing the body". A biolaw and theory of biorights that is based on the tension between responsibility and care must try to clarify these different dimensions in relation to the body within the individual sub-areas of the biorights. For the time being, the legal status of the body, which combines three dimensions in the human relationship with his or her body, can be determined on the basis of subjective rights, objective legal goods and protection rights (Arnoux, 1994, p. 295). Faced with the threat of biopower and the rapid technological development, legislation and case law on bioethical issues must take place on the basis of these rights in an interplay with a notion of human nature in relation to a historically and culturally mediated humanistic view of humanity.

6 Toward Homo sapiens 2.0: Bioethical challenges to biolaw in the twenty-first century

6.1 Purpose of biomedicine: Immortality?

In our time we are experiencing a radical change in our livelihoods through technological interventions in the relationship between the organic and the mechanical, which has led to the emergence of many different forms of "technological creatures," such as genetically engineered mice and rats for experiments, organ pigs for transplants or cloned sheep as breeding animals. Furthermore, humans have increasingly become artificial creatures, where we become one with technology as test tube children or as creatures that use machines to survive, for example, by transplanting artificial organs, having a "pacemaker" implanted or being totally dependent on computer technology. In the imagination, we are strongly influenced by these notions of creating new beings. The science fiction literature is full of examples of new forms of interaction between humans and machines and of the use of technology to develop new species that fuse the organic and the mechanical: We can mention the film about the "Terminator" warrior, where a machine has got the human body, or the classic *Body Snatchers*, in which aliens take over the human bodies. It is often about how "living machines" threaten human reality but also about how machines help humans survive (Rendtorff 2002d).

Central to technological development and our imagination about the future is that many different creatures will populate the future planet. This clearly challenges the ethical and moral reflection, and it becomes necessary to find new principles of bioethics and biolaw for the coexistence between the different life forms (Jørgensen & Rendtorff, 2018; Jørgensen, Rendtorff, & Holen, 2018; Rendtorff, 1998, 2002a, 2003, 2008, 2014a, 2015c, 2016a; Rendtorff & Kemp, 2009). At the same time, the possibility of improving the human being with genetics and robotics has raised the question of the meaning of the human condition in a different way. It can be argued that the ultimate consequence of development is that we ourselves will decide what kind of people we want to be and that in the long run, we will become fully and completely masters of our own destiny. The question, therefore, is quite simply whether there is anything about the human and the human species that we would like to preserve for posterity. Immediately, one would say that it

DOI: 10.4324/9781003147848-6

would not be so bad if we could live longer and become more beautiful, wiser, stronger and more intelligent and that technology will help us develop in this direction. On second thought, the answer is not so simple even. We will now show this by examining some of the basic dimensions of human being that are challenged by technological development.

One of the most characteristic features of the scientific advances in genetic engineering and biomedicine in cloning, gene therapy and active genetic engineering with the human genome is that they ask the question of human dreams of immortality in a new and different concrete way. What if science became able to give us bodily and earthly immortality? One would like to find the human age gene and manipulate it in a way that allowed us to live for 150 to 200 years. Or what if they manage to clone individuals in such a way that one can also restore their memory and individuality, just like in the movie *Alien 4*, where the main character is resurrected by cloning after being dead for a few hundred years. This would mean that it would be a matter for public debate and joint political decision-making, to what extent society might regard prioritizing earthly, bodily immortality as an important political task.

Addressing this problem, however, requires a discussion of the significance of death for the meaning of life, which is a central issue in modern philosophy. Martin Heidegger shows in his analysis of death in the main work *Sein und Zeit* from 1927 that it is death and finitude that characterize the human way of being. Our existence is determined by the fact that we are temporal and historical beings who will one day die. Human understanding of death determines all our actions and goals with life, even though they tend not to want to face this truth. Therefore, people pretend not to die and live with a trivial understanding of life, as if death did not come to them and life should last indefinitely. In reality, however, humans are aware that death is the ultimate horizon of life. When one thinks about life in a conscientious moment, one does not escape the fact that the real being of man is the determined, anxious "being to death" in self-choice and lonely freedom. Death is man's only sure possibility that determines all his actions and other possibilities in the world.

Contrary to this notion of death, the French philosopher Jean-Paul Sartre in *L'Être et le Néant* from 1943 dispels the idea that death can give meaning to life. For Sartre, death is not to be regarded as humanity's sure possibility but rather a borderline case in existence and "the absurd" per se excellence. Death is not an option but the destruction of all the possibilities of the individual. Sartre argues that man cannot find meaning in death because man with his freedom and his projects of acting in the world can be described as an infinite striving to live and seize the world. According to Sartre, humanity will always be characterized by a striving to overcome death. Humanity's living conditions are characterized by an infinite desire for omnipotence and omniscience, to gain dominion over the world and in the presence of life to become one with the world. Therefore, death is incomprehensible and meaningless. And that explains our fear and aversion to death. Death makes man's pursuit of omnipotence and presence absurd and tragic because it puts an end to all the individual's dreams and life projects.

The American bioethicist Leon R. Kass also relates to human death and its pursuit of immortality in his highly readable book *Toward a More Natural Science* (1988). As the title suggests, Kass will make our general conditions of existence the norm for biomedical development. For him, human consciousness by virtue of the body is embedded in a natural world. The body tells us about our vulnerability, our freedom and so forth. Today we move more and more away from this by virtue of all the new manipulations: Organ transplantation, plastic surgery, artificial insemination, gender reassignment surgery and the dream of being eternally young and beautiful in a body that does not age. We want to get rid of the body's natural compulsion by being able to control the body with will and consciousness.

Faced with this quest for the omnipotence of immortality, Kass defends human mortality as the meaning of life. Kass thus differs from both Heidegger and Sartre. He does not look at life as pessimistically as Heidegger, who emphasizes finitude. At the same time, Sartre's attempt to get beyond chance by seeking infinity is rejected. Kass argues instead that life and death are closely linked, so transience must in reality be seen as a gift of life to be respected, because human temporality is the precondition for it to be happy and for life to feel important and meaningful. Kass is well aware of the randomness of life. We are as perishable as the leaves that fall from the trees in winter, flying randomly here and there with the wind, until they fall to the ground and rot up. We are determined by the necessity of time. We must die because we are, as we are, part of the biological processes of life.

Thus, when we emphasize that human life is about giving meaning to the temporal randomness of life in the tension between the infinite and the finite, we can understand the meaning of technological development. The purpose of biomedical sciences, in contrast to short life and chance, can be seen as an attempt to control age and achieve a better life with better health, but this pursuit of a long life can be understood in different ways. Of course, as we already do today and in which there is nothing wrong, one can avoid diseases and accidents and have a higher standard of living. However, a different radical struggle against age could be that we stop the aging functions of the body and become eternally young. In addition, we could slow down the aging process by finding the age gene. At the individual level, it is difficult to prohibit the individual's right to do so if the technique is available. But a general extension of life expectancy of, for example, 50 years would have incalculable social consequences. What would it mean for the family's structure and leisure time, and what for working life if the 80–120-year-old now suddenly had to work?

The proponent of earthly immortality will say that life must always be good and death evil. Therefore, a long life in which the individual, his family and friends remain healthy and sound for as long as possible must be the right thing to do. Of course, there should not be an infinite extension of life, but a few decades longer life for all people must be welcomed. Not least because death for many people today can no longer justify life. In the secularized society, a human being will live indefinitely because he or she is sure that there is no heavenly kingdom and a life after this life. Our desperate desire for immortality is linked to the experience of the security of death as terrible and relentless. In this perspective, it is pathetic, life-denying and theorizing to claim that natural coercion and our biological limitations can be a moral good. "Better a slave on earth than a king in the realm of the dead, Hades," as the war hero Achilles told Odysseus when he was visited by him in the realm of the dead.

But what would really happen if our life expectancy were generally increased? Would the enjoyment of life be more intense if, like another Don Juan, one could make love with 1,000 instead of 500 women? Yes, what should you really take the time to go through when you have done the things we usually do over and over again?

Kass claims that it would be difficult to take life seriously if it were to last forever. And that would surely imply a strong persistent boredom. Most of our chores are determined by the fact that we do not have enough energy and not enough time. There is a close connection between finitude and the poetic sensuous beauty of life. It is our knowledge of fragility and finitude that motivates our urge to create the eternal. By virtue of its understanding of the perishability of the ugly and the disgusting, man is able to experience and pursue the beautiful.

In addition, it can be argued that the greatness and beauty of human nature, of the individual's personal integrity and identity, its ability to act morally, is determined by its mortality. This also applies to humanity's ability to be generous with his or her own life and to give and witness his life to another human being or to a life task. A commitment to a cause must also be seen in this perspective. Most moral virtues and abilities are related to our vulnerability and finitude. The existential pain and suffering, of engaging with one's friends and family and of choosing in life, is necessary because of the limitations of man.

A further weighty argument against proponents of earthly immortality is that they have not understood the true meaning of immortality for man. Our pursuit of immortality is not to be understood as a longing for more life in the "quantitative" sense. On the other hand, the longing for immortality must be seen in the light of the Greek philosopher Plato's descriptions of the tragic pursuit of love in the dialogue Symposium. Plato claims here that human nature is carried by an erotic force that strives to unite with the beautiful and the good in eternity. Love is an earthly reflection of this pursuit. When we long for love, it is because human desire expresses a lack of goodness and beauty, and we seek to reach eternity by becoming one with the other human being.

As an earthly desire for eternity, which by virtue of its perishability is the lack of the good and the beautiful, man seeks wholeness, goodness and wisdom to become harmonious through the eternal and immutable. But this means that death is not in itself the problem but just one among many expressions of life's shortcomings. One could, for example, well live for quantitatively longer time without life as such would get better. Giving man a longer earthly life would not necessarily fill his need and longing for infinity. Just "more of the same kind" would not be able to fill human needs. Even the Christian notion of the resurrection is not understood as such an idea of an infinite continuation of earthly life, where the bodily needs we have today, food, sex, diversion and so forth, simply persist for a few hundred more years.

The objections to bodily immortality are a desirable ideal challenge to technological advance. Immortality is useless if it is not seen in the context of human beings' other, social living conditions. And here the establishment of the right of current generations to a longer life inevitably poses some global resource and justice problems regarding the relationship between generations. If current generations were to have 50 to 100 years' longer life expectancy, would not that slow down the possibility of future generations and upset the balance between young and old in society?

Wanting to live indefinitely is very characteristic of an individualized culture, where the purpose of life has become the fulfillment of the individual's desires and where the individual people want to maintain themselves and their lives at all costs. The paradox is that even this endeavor gets its meaning from the human nature of being bound to a tragic condition of existence. The paradox of human life is that a human being lives as an ambiguous synthesis between the infinite striving for freedom and the temporality of the body, where it is the joy of temporal life that makes sense with the pursuit of the eternal.

6.2 The body and sex: Reproductive technology

Aldous Huxley's famous book *Brave New World* (1932) is also about understanding human life in the technocosmos. Huxley describes a fertility clinic in the future society. All reproduction takes place in special reproduction rooms, where eggs are mixed with semen from a large semen mass in test tubes and then incubated artificially in special incubators. Eggs are examined for suspected abnormality, and A-, B- and C-humans are created with different characteristics for the purpose of well-defined functions that they will later fulfill in society. In Huxley's future world, sex between many different partners has replaced romantic love, and the word "mother" is an unmentionable taboo. Huxley's book illustrates an old theme in philosophy that is already present in Plato in the State, where it is discussed whether to exclude Eros and eroticism, which are bound to the striving of the body, out of the ideal state. A close connection between reproduction and love is not very rational, because reproduction is about the survival of the state, while love and desire express the human longings of man.

The contemporary development of reproductive technology has made Huxley's utopia topical. Future reproductive technology involves mixing semen and eggs in test tubes, pre-implantation diagnostics, incubators, transplanting ovaries, using eggs from aborted female fetuses, artificial uterus with fertilization and pregnancy completely separately from the human body and so forth. One must also imagine that men can one day become pregnant with the help of an artificial uterus and that whoever wants it will be able to clone himself to have a child identical to himself. It will probably also be possible through active hereditary hygiene to improve the genes of future generations as well as to abolish the generational succession and the general family structure.

In the light of the philosophy of the existentialist feminist Simone de Beauvoir, it could be argued that boundless reproductive technology may not be so stupid even as it involves a complete liberation of the woman, a radical *Endlösung der Frauenfrage*, which means that the woman no longer has to be forced to give birth to children. The woman will be able to be completely freed from her "biological disability" and finally live on an equal footing with the man without the obstacles of pregnancy along the way. Changing the natural reproduction does not have to mean that society becomes asexual, but it does free the woman from a cursed and unpleasant pregnancy.

This confrontation with the compulsion of nature and society as central to the liberation of women is basal in Simone de Beauvoir's famous work *Le deuxième Sexe I-II* from 1949. She sees the relationship between the sexes in the light of Hegel's famous description of history as a struggle for recognition between masters and slaves, where the slaves – afraid of death – are forced by the masters to work for them. It is now Beauvoir's point that the woman has been isolated from this male struggle for recognition. She has historically been made into nature and irrational in relation to humanity's creativity and reason. The space of technology and politics is the world of man, of which woman has been shut out as "the other." For the man, she is only present as a mother or mistress but never meets him as an equal with respect and dignity.

Simone de Beauvoir claims that it is the biological, historical and economic conditions that have created the male and female roles. You are not born a woman; you become one. Because she was physically weaker and had to have children, the woman was banished to the home and displaced from the man's public world to a life not even worthy of a slave.

However, this bondage has also gone beyond the man who has not been able to get the woman's recognition when she was not considered a human being on an equal footing with him. It is, therefore, also in the man's interest that the woman becomes free. She must become a covetous subject who, in authentic love, is not just pure use or pleasure for the man but both subject and object. This authentic love is based on friendship between man and woman rather than on the erotic relationship. The woman must be free on the same terms as the man for the achievement of mutual recognition. But this leads to an objection that Simone de Beauvoir actually thinks of the man's premises when she claims that the woman must be recognized in the man's universe, and then her struggle to overcome the woman's natural compulsion may in fact contribute to the suppression of the particularly feminine.

Contrary to Beauvoir's homage to the possibilities of technology, the French postmodernist Jean Baudrillard claims in his book *La transparence du mal* from 1990 that we live in a society that is in the process of eliminating the gender difference. Our reality has become unisexual and asexual. Reproduction by cloning one's own cells as the "ultima ratio" of reproductive technology expresses the resolution of the gender difference in "the same" and the cessation of any sexual reproduction. Any alienation is destroyed by the identical reproduction of genes and cells, as you no longer need a sexual partner to have children, when everything happens in the genetic code, which can then be restored indefinitely in identical copies. The development of technology means that the individual is no longer in a relationship with something else. It has no parents. It is outside the generational order and therefore does not have an authentic relationship to death.

In the fantasy of the technological universe, genetic reproduction no longer takes place on a subjective human level, but an infallible genetic model for possible bodies can be compared to the identical images in the series or mass media production of computers. Baudrillard says that the subjective experience and gender difference of the unidirectional science are now nothing more than an irregular "metastasis" in the genetic model. Cloning is a genetic incest that is so radical that everything is identical and "the other" is no longer present at all, and where we only meet ourselves again and again. Such a society is reminiscent of death, the pure narcissistic repetition of the same without the possibility of meeting the other and the stranger through the creation of life.

These critical analyses challenge our separation of sexuality and reproduction. Instead of making everything identical and similar and thus erasing the gender difference, perhaps in order to counter Baudrillard's postmodernism with a contemporary French feminist Luce Irigaray, one could move beyond Simone de Beauvoir and formulate a feminism that transcends the man's premises and thinks of the female from the nature of the woman.

In his book *L'éthique de la différence sexuelle* from 1984, Irigaray develops an ethics of caress based on gender difference as fundamental to the human. Philosophy is criticized for not understanding the body, the caress and the significance of eroticism for the beautiful life. The technological culture that creates an increasingly artificially fabricated world is an expression of a masculine, intellectual dominance, alienation and forgetfulness of being, of which cloning and reproductive technology are merely eerie examples. Here the woman, like another prostitute, is used as an instrument of the man's technique.

Inspired by Emmanuel Lévinas, Irigaray and Beauvoir's philosophy of recognition radicalizes by consistently understanding the woman as the "other" without making her equal to the world of men. The caress is central because it points beyond itself toward the other's experienced body in the borderland between person and thing. It expresses the encounter with the stranger that creates a new reality between concrete "I" and "you" that are both identical and different. In its sensuous sexuality, the body is freely giving and receiving toward the other, and this almost prelinguistic openness is par excellence an expression of a nonviolent, searching and attentive relationship with the other human being who respects the other as another. A human being becomes him or herself in duality, in the intimate love life of the other. The preconditions of ethics do not arise in the anonymous public life of mass society but rather in the singular encounter between man and woman, and here it is the difference to the other and not the hell of self-identity that enables human happy existence.

Irigaray says that a feminine philosophy based on the ethics of caresses differs from the Western identity thinking, which is characterized by wanting to dominate nature, for example, by a calculated control of the reproduction.

Instead of fabricating the world from the technical transparency of identity, philosophy must be open to the mystery of the other, which is expressed in the body and femininity. This is evident in the metaphysical astonishment that "there is something rather than nothing" in the joy of the fertility of love and sexuality. Instead of forgetting and displacing the bodily nature of the woman as an irrational instinct, it is for Irigaray to spiritualize the desire, the body and the natural world by integrating them into the realization of the subjects in the ethics of the caress.

At the same time, it means that Irigaray will radically break with any attempt to subordinate sexuality and love under the state's "identity-logical reproductive rationality," as in *Brave New World*. Rather, it is about releasing the feminine in the culture as a personal understanding of the other person's freedom. The perspective is extended to the relationship with other generations, races and cultures, where it is about understanding the other as another. The ethics of caresses becomes a democratic philosophy of respect for difference and diversity.

Irigaray's pointing out the ethical significance of the gender difference problematizes our current culture of equality and identity, where everyone becomes equal. But at the same time, the anchoring of ethics in the given conditions of human nature becomes far stronger than in Simone de Beauvoir, who points out the transcendence of the given as necessary for ethics and who, therefore, perceives the separation of sexuality and reproduction as a liberation. Although we have some sympathy for Irigaray's phenomenological feminism, the question is therefore still to what extent we should allow ourselves to be determined by our compulsion of nature. One could argue that Irigaray in vain in the technocosmos searches for the lost immediacy by justifying the ethics of body and caresses and that it is more meaningful to do away with the arbitrary, natural conditions of man. It must then be possible to technicalize reproduction and society in general without leading to a single-sex culture. And yet Irigaray's vision of a caress ethic seems more human in a postmodern society that fantasizes about a total separation of sexuality and reproduction, with asexual cloning as its ultimate consequence.

Judith Butler's development of critical third wave feminism focusing on queer theory can be said to formulate the consequences of the postmodern critique of Beauvoir's first wave and Irigaray's second wave of feminism. Butler's theory originates in the discussions of Beauvoir's and Irigaray's philosophies but moves the discussion of feminism toward the broader concepts of queer and transgender and demonstrates the discursive and constructive dimensions of gender and sex (Butler, 2006). In terms of bioethics and biolaw, this represents a challenge to nature-based concepts of human bodily autonomy, dignity, integrity and vulnerability. A postmodern vision of phenomenological respect for the human person must include these dimensions of respect for queer and transgender identities when determining respect for ethics of reproductive technology. Indeed, respect for basic ethical principles in postmodernity must be open for the complexities of postmodern families, not only with traditional concept of male and female but also with new concepts of gay, queer, transgender and other possible family forms. Furthermore, the development of the different waves of feminism into concepts of a social critique focusing on intersectionality of forms of repression where people from a particular race, class and gender (e.g. immigrant women of color) are being submitted to oppression from the different sectors is important for respecting human autonomy, dignity, integrity and vulnerability. In the cosmopolitan perspective, it is important that bioethics and biolaw integrate the perspectives from intersectionality and the different waves of feminism.

All in all, the discussion among Beauvoir, Baudrillard, Irigaray and Butler shows that the new technology is challenging our human vision of the future of humanity. Furthermore, a rejection of *Brave New World* is based on a belief in the ethics of caresses, which compares sexuality and reproduction. But is that a sufficient justification for rejecting technology, and how do we avoid an unacceptable moralism where thinking falls short without absolute arguments? The only thing we can say is that the body-determined view of human beings emphasizes the importance of the sexual difference and the ethics of the caress for reproduction. We need to be aware of the different forms of oppression of the body in technological development. But here the limit of ethics goes, as a human view can only justify itself, and, therefore, is always open to criticism from other perceptions of the role of class, race and gender for human reproduction in the technocosmos.

6.3 The technological creatures: Goodbye to humanity?

The discussions of mortality, reproductive technology and genetic engineering contain a premise that should be investigated further. This is the notion of the human and ethics as a construction that, in the end, cannot be based on preconceived ideas about the natural essence of man. Constructivism argues that it is pointless to justify ethics on the basis of human mortal life, body and gender, because these concepts are not absolute but merely random historical constructions that will soon be gone as technology evolves. And one cannot help but ask whether we are not already in an age of total manipulation, where it is absurd to refer to the natural. This was true both in the notion of immortality and the beautiful new world, but it is also expressed in the discussions about the creation of a technocosmos. As mentioned, we are not far from living in a technocosmos with a diversity of human variations. Here you can refer to the many new creatures, where you have mixed the organic and the mechanical. Here it no longer makes sense to talk about the natural, but everything is constructed. It could be argued that the argument about protecting the human in a technological age in fact presupposes a harmonious nature. And one wonders what consequences this radical reality of constructivism has for biotechnological ethics. Does it even make sense to talk about ethics and humanity in a world where man has become a machine? And does it matter?

Baudrillard gives a characteristic of our time as a world after the orgy. In the explosive postmodernity, we have in many ways transcended traditional contradictions. In the postmodern age, it is no longer possible to distinguish between evil and good, the true and the false, beautiful and ugly. We live in an empty culture characterized by an infinite series of superficial references that do not refer to anything. According to Baudrillard, natural human beings no longer exist, but bodies mixed up with animal cells and organs, machines and prostheses that relate to each other in an infinite symbolic programming. The metaphors no longer refer to an underlying essence. All genres and categories have been dissolved. The sexual difference no longer applies. We live in a Xerox copy culture where originals no longer exist. Communication has become without reference, and we live in a reality of the transpolitical, the transsexual and the transesthetic.

Postmodernity is also characterized by a fictitious economy where everything has become virtual. It is information technology that has taken over our reality, and we live in a kind of virtual economy based on information rather than economic realities. It is Baudrillard's point of view that evil in such a reality must be understood as an inexplicable virus in an information system and that a series of "androgynous" forms emerge that no longer have a relation to a natural conception of the human. We can, therefore, not get around a semiotic reality in which the human body has become an information machine that no longer acts on the basis of a soul or a consciousness. The Italian porn star Cicciolina, or the pop stars Madonna and Michael Jackson or Lady Gaga, are prototypes of such a plastic, constructed human being who constantly reshapes himself as an inert computer program. Moreover, in the age of queer and transgender, a biological naturalist conception of the human body is increasingly challenged.

Baudrillard's diagnosis of the postmodern society of the time takes on a nightmarish character when he claims that in our culture, we are far beyond the traditional notion of radical evil as based on human subjective intentions. That we have transcended the opposition between good and evil means that we can no longer distinguish between them. We doubt the existence of the concentration camps, and in the persistent sum of the media we become indifferent – indifferent to the biggest bloodshed in other countries, for example, Rwanda, Kosovo, Iraq or Syria. The problem is that in a time when absolute truths no longer exist, and each one lives after dissolving the difference between the same and the other, good and evil, we still cannot hold down evil. The terrorist attack on the World Trade Center on 11 September 2001 is a good example of this irrationality of evil. It was impossible for the Western world to understand the motives and actions of the terrorists. Evil thus returns with renewed strength as inexplicable events, a kind of fate that unpredictably breaks the logic of society's systems. Breaks and terrorism occur in all types of information systems, and we become unable to control reality.

The Irish anthropologist, philosopher and so-called cyborg-feminist Donna Haraway has developed a radical constructivist conception of the human body, which can be said to be assertive in the development of biomedicine. Haraway sees bioethics as a kind of biopolitics that is about taking constructivism seriously. She, therefore, does not go directly against all the creations of biomedicine, as she rejects any idea of the original nature of humanity, but instead, through her biopolitics, she wants to influence the constructions created by technological development. Her starting point is that today we must all be considered as engineered organic hybrids, that is, we are all to be regarded as a kind of machine-humans, or as cyborgs. This should not be understood exclusively in a negative way, and despite her shrewd demonstration of the eerie in our "androgynous hybrid life," where we are, as mentioned, on the way to dissolving the gender difference, Haraway also wants to formulate a kind of cyborg utopia that, what we must boldly try to show, expresses a postmodernist search for ethics and humanity.

She says in her famous Cyborg Manifesto, *A Cyborg Manifesto: Science, Technology and Feminist Socialism in the 1980s* from 1989 that society is evolving toward the formation of the cyborg as the coming human being. A cyborg is a "cybernetic organism, a hybrid of machine and organism, a creation of social reality, as well as a fictional creation." At the same time, the cyborg is a "monster" that breaks down our traditional understandings of nature and humanity. Haraway describes the cyborg as an expression of the technological development and therefore a construction that we must relate to in order to survive in the technological society. According to Haraway, modern medicine is full of mixtures between organisms and machines, and the many cyborgs must be understood as some, self-creating and self-governing, information-coded systems that are characterized by sexuality, intimacy and open to a power never seen before in human history. The cyborg idea also helps to turn modern times into a mythical age, where we are all chimeras, planned and fabricated hybrids between machine and organism.

Haraway perceives modern technology as a result of the Western philosophical tradition, expressing an antifemale, racist and dominant capitalist technocracy that exploits nature as a resource. However, this tradition has looked down on the cyborg and tried to maintain the sharp boundary between man and woman, man and machine and man and animal. It is such "artificially created boundaries" that biomedicine challenges and that cyborg feminism wants to problematize. It, therefore, becomes the task of cyborg philosophy to be responsible and aware of our construction of boundaries. It thus becomes part of this theory to help devise a world without gender, nature or creation, because in reality we are all constructions. The cyborg thus lives outside our common perception of the development and history of mankind, and it cannot fit into the Western notion of apocalypse and salvation. The cyborg philosophy does away with the notion of an original unity and possible identification with a harmonious nature. According to Haraway, the human machine, the monster, the cyborg, is an illegitimate child of Western capitalism.

Haraway emphasizes that the cyborg as a figure helps to break down all the metaphysical and power-political structures that have hitherto been constructed by Western metaphysics. She says the cyborg is dissolving the traditional biopolitical boundaries. This applies to the distinctions between man and woman, between man and animal and between man and machine, as well as the distinctions between the physical and the nonphysical. This shows the modern machines that are no longer large heavy devices but as microchips or biotechnology are everywhere and merge with the environment. Machines are built around information or biotechnology, and they, therefore, challenge the male-oriented symbolic language of traditional technology about power and strength. Therefore, Haraway cannot help but see something positive in cyborg's cross-border possibilities, even though she is also aware that the cyborg characters can easily become a kind of monster that, like new ghost creatures, freely flutters through the old world's categorizations and, at the same time, becomes a picture of our shared reality.

Our cyborg existence must thus be understood as a general living condition in a postmodern age that has been created by the development of technology. This has led to fragmentary identities and fragmentation of the individual. But at the same time, it must be highlighted how certain individuals take on their negative identity and try to live out their cyborg identities. Haraway mentions the reaction against the oppression of male society in reducing all types of isms such as paternalism, colonialism and so forth. The proponents of cyborg identity are against all types of isms. They maintain their negative monster identity in the face of the idea that something natural or original should exist. The cyborg has understood that no essence is given, that we have lost the innocence of all of us. Therefore, cyborg reality also becomes a powerful instrument of struggle against those in power who oppress the others and the other.

When there is no essence of woman, man or machine, but where they all collapse into new and unexpected constructions, we are set free like never before, and we can, as never before, do away with gender, class and racial discrimination in capitalist techno-societies. Cyborg constructivism thus expresses a reflexive thinking that begins to break down social and cultural boundaries. Our traditional contradictions between consciousness and body, animal and human, organism and machine, public and private, nature and culture, men and women and primitive and civilized have all been challenged by the new technologies. Information and biotechnology do away with our distinction between instrument and concept, historical knowledge and actual possibilities, and it can be said that by virtue of the new technologies, we are re-creating a heterogeneous world without destructive boundaries.

Within modern technology, it is communication and information that, like new power structures, hold the world together. This can contribute to the creation of more biopower and the oppression of the human body, where the beautiful new world is totally dependent on electronic technology. Haraway says that modern states, multinational corporations, military powers, welfare states, labor control systems, medical constructions of our bodies, commercial pornography, division of labor and even the churches have all become addicted to computer technology, thus constituting a pervasive biopower, which softens the boundaries between all traditional categories. An example of this is the dissolution among home, market and work in the technological home-work economy that characterizes the computer industry. This is also evident in the technology's resolution of the difference among animals, humans and machines, in xenotransplants or in artificial insemination, where it is in particular the woman who is responsible for the treatment.

Haraway expresses the critique of civilization by claiming that we did not originally choose to be cyborgs and well cannot escape the fact that the power mechanisms of society will create even more of that kind, but that even though we are not to blame for our own creation in postmodern culture, we must be fully and completely responsible for our lives as cyborg machines. This can be illustrated with the character Rachel in Ridley Scott's cult film *Blade Runner*, which is designed as such a perfect replicator that she is at once identical to a machine and the ideal human being that the protagonist falls in love with despite being a machine. We cannot justify our actions on the basis of our original nature, but we must take our lives as cyborgs seriously. This means that the distinctions between nature-nature, body and soul and so forth no longer matters. The cyborg theory knows that the cyborg body is not innocent. It ironically does away with traditional dualisms. We must recognize that we cannot get around the machines, that they are a part of ourselves and our body. This implies an acceptance and constant challenge of traditional boundaries.

A bioethics and biolaw based on this thinking recognize postmodern reality by opposing the production of universalizing and totalizing metaphysics; one can say that it is based on concrete social relations and tries in an acceptance of the limitless possibilities of technology to reconstruct boundaries that are not based on unreflected power relations. A cyborg feminist conception combined with the perspectives of queerness and transgender attitudes to the world will thus at once build and destroy machines and other societal constructions. One could say that this expresses a morality for a technological age in which we must recognize that, despite our bodily mortality, we cannot escape the fact that we are mechanical constructions.

6.4 The dream of better people: Genetic manipulation

Despite the fact that we can thus well understand the liberating power of cyborg philosophy, the bioethical and biolegal defense of human bodily, mortal, temporal life means that we can maintain a certain critical skepticism about the dream of creating better people through the use of genetic manipulation. If Kass and Irigaray are right in their emphasis on the beauty of the human condition, it is not certain that the use of technology to construct new and better people is necessarily a success. In addition, we cannot overlook all the consequences of our actions, and there are chances that we will end up creating an eerie monster over which we no longer have power. This is the story of Frankenstein, in which an unhappy monster is created that was almost the total opposite of the perfect human being. There is a risk that the myth of creating the beautiful, wise and perfect people will turn into its opposite. One can imagine a Pandora's box, where numerous evils suddenly spring out of the box with the consequence that utopia turns into a nightmare.

It is true that genetic engineering and enhancement can be used to help the genetically ill and weak in society, but there is a risk that this will lead to a perverted ethics of pity. Going back to a more realistic discussion of genetic manipulations, we cannot escape the fact that society imposes narrow standards of quality of life and that certain lives with certain genetic defects are not considered worth living. Based on preconceived notions of a happy and normal human life, society claims to be entitled to manipulate or eliminate lives that do not live up to the norm. And the question is who is to decide which defects and diseases are to be treated by means of genetic manipulation. In our technological intervention, we cannot avoid creating more cyborgs and monsters that never reach our perfect notions of the human.

At the same time, it can be argued that it is not at all realistic ever to give humanity the earthly immortality by technological intervention, due to the enormous complexity of the genome as such and the hereditary system of the individual. Therefore, radical improvement of man with genetic engineering will also not be possible for the next many years. The complicated relationship between heritage and the environment may in fact mean that our genetic predispositions are not even that important. The possibilities of gene therapy can thus be naturally limited, and it will be impossible to calculate the risk and consequences of both germ cell and body cell interventions.

Even if we could now make better people with extensive genetic engineering, the problem is whether one can now also really know which genes need to be changed. Science has far too high expectations for the outcome of the analysis of the human genome. It tends to see a human being as a static function of his or her genes without taking into account the influences from the environment to which he or she is exposed or to the freedom with which he responds to his or her living conditions. It is far from a given that genes alone determine human development and existence. Many traits arise in a complex interplay between heritage and environment. We do not yet know much about which combinations of hereditary systems "determine" abstract thinking, creativity and our notions of good and evil. Many human traits cannot be genetically defined at all but are created in the human being's experienced interaction with the environment. Analogous to the universal grammar of the linguist Noam Chomsky, genetic structure can be perceived as a formal basis for the personality that acquires content and character in the experienced life. With an analogy to the philosophy of language, one can say that the gene structure is a framework that the personal identity or the individual life event fills.

This relationship between structure and life course means that a human being can never be identified with his or her genes. The experienced body cannot be reduced to a biological phenomenon. By virtue of our freedom and our consciousness, a human being is able to behave reflexively in relation to his or her genetic structure. Our personal identity is rooted in a context of meaning that is grounded in the social and cultural world of human life. Our consciousness and reflexive self-relationship are formed in our experience of the body's interaction with the outside world, which cannot be described with the language of genetics. There is a subjective dimension to our desires, love and life with other people that is the result of our motives and actions. An analysis of the human genome can only capture the objective presuppositions of human existence in the world, but it can never capture the existential dimensions associated with human actual life in the world.

However, the genetic description of the objective preconditions for human existence in the world is not without consequences for human identity and self-understanding. The knowledge about the hereditary systems that the analysis of the human genome can obtain when, for example, it identifies disease predispositions or genetic defects, it radically changes the human perception of life's possibilities. The description of the hereditary systems influences the notion of life as an open horizon. Knowledge of our genetics can influence our choices and life plans. Justice and respect for bodily integrity in genetic testing (by the individual human being or his family members) must therefore imply the individual's right to decide for himself over his genetic information. One must have the "right not to know." In other words, the individual must be guaranteed a right to refrain from receiving information about the genome if he wants its future to appear indefinite and open. The indeterminacy of fate is an important aspect of our defense of the temporal coincidence of life, because it emphasizes a respect for every human being's right to find his own way through life and be a surprise to himself.

This can be compared to earlier rejections of divinations or the oracle from Delphi, where man also did not want to know about his fate but even live his life as new and unpredictable. The right not to know is not just about not wanting information about one's genetic predispositions but about respecting the human right to be a product of life's creative randomness and arbitrariness. One could call it the right not to be pre-programmed but to understand life as a gift, that is, to be freely condemned to create his own identity. Respect for personal integrity thus implies the individual's right not to let the genes decide for themselves nor to let his or her personal identity change radically by manipulating the hereditary systems.

The question is whether the "right not to know" is so absolute that it also applies to the family members affected by the genetic analysis. By refusing to gain knowledge about a particular risk, the individual not only chooses for himself but he also takes a risk that has consequences for children and family. The genetic knowledge about future generations, children's health, disease dispositions in the family, choice of partner, choice of children at all, career opportunities and so forth can be argued to be so important that we can no longer naively believe in a "genetic innocence" where one can totally disregard the progress of science. And not everything is left to the doctor's paternalism if one refrains from letting the genetic information determine the health treatment. Perhaps in some cases, you have a "duty to know" and let your partner and family share the necessary information if it can form the basis for better health or if you can prevent having children with serious genetic defects. In these cases, it would be selfish to ignore genetic knowledge and the "right not to know" conflicts with the solidarity of the individual and the responsibility of his fellow human beings.

This "duty to know" can be related to the health system's and the state's right to knowledge about the individual's heredity through genetic testing and genetic screening, but here the "right not to know" is far more obvious from the point of view of the individual as an end in itself, even if that precedes the utilitarian interest of the state in genetic information. This is especially relevant in connection with screening of fetuses and newborns. Does society have the right to record genetic information about its citizens when it contains information about the basis of their development opportunities? Such information can be misused and can upset the balance of society, which is why the right of the individual citizen to decide over them should be affirmed as a fundamental democratic principle. It is a matter of avoiding and counteracting the development toward a surveillance and registry society, as portrayed by George Orwell in his dystopia book *1984*. The right to the protection of the genome is no less important in the development of gene therapy. The dream of earthly immortality is related to the Roman ideals of *mens sana in corpore sano*: "A healthy soul in a healthy body." It can be argued that it is in the interest of future generations to be genetically engineered if they can become healthier and more beautiful.

This would be a civilizational advance for humanity, which could now seriously become "homo faber" by constructing perfect individuals for the ideal state. The utilitarian will claim that we will be able to avoid unnecessary suffering by allowing genetic engineering. Gene therapy on body cells will be able to help the weakest in society by improving their genetic predisposition. However, it is difficult to distinguish between the diseases to be treated and the genetic defects that are not to be treated. An important argument for genetic engineering here is that it serves to protect the unborn life against genetic defects, which one can thus cure instead of abort. But why expand gene therapy when you already have prenatal diagnostics to cleanse genetically defective fetuses? Applying gene therapy to body cells may also imply a narrowed concept of normality. Perhaps the personality traits are perceived as genetically defective, which in the human life world and experienced body are included as components in excellent traits. The creativity of great artists such as Toulouse Lautrec, who was manic-depressive, and Beethoven, who became deaf, shows that the connection between genius and particular hereditary systems is not unambiguous.

Germ cell therapy must be considered even more problematic, as it applies not only to actual persons but also to future generations and has a direct impact on the coherence of their characteristics. The individual human life is no longer unpredictable but can to a much greater extent be programmed by society. At the same time, genetic engineering with future generations in mind will affect, standardize and shift the overall gene pool, without it being possible to foresee the consequences. Perhaps individual defective and disease-causing genes have an important significance for the organism that we are not aware of but may prove to be indispensable for future generations. A further argument is that genetic engineering breaks with evolution and the great connection of life, in which the defective genes are of great importance. Genetic variation and diversity are undoubtedly part of the richness and beauty of nature and the human species. Therefore, a few good arguments for not intervening in the gene structure are far more important than the arguments for genetic engineering, considering that the interventions can lead to irreversible defects in the organisms being manipulated. Furthermore, the interplay between different human genes is so complicated that it is illusory to believe that by manipulating individual genes, one can improve the entire genome and definitively get rid of genetic defects. The prevailing metaphor of heredity as a "genetic garden" where one can isolate and cultivate certain traits is naive and can therefore have catastrophic consequences for humanity. It testifies to a lack of understanding of the complex interplay between heredity and environment that forms the human personal identity in the experienced body.

One can compare genetic engineering with parents who put their children in a better school, to do what is best for them, but in such a way that it changes their very nature: Their eye color, physique, height and so forth. When we have free school choice, why not a genetic supermarket that some philosophers have argued for. He talks about a free, private eugenics, where the parents of the future must be able to choose properties for their children in the same way as they buy goods in the supermarket. The English philosopher Jonathan Glover argues in *What Kind of People Should There Be* (1984) for a liberal utopia, in which a pluralistic society that respects the individual's right to self-determination over his life and accepts a human "zoo" recognizes a wide variety of life forms and views of life. Although we have a lot of sympathy for such a utopia, it is a question of whether the parents' free right to manipulate their children's genes will really be in the children's interest. Another option could be a "mixed model" in which the state, based on ethically sound principles of justice, restricts citizens' right to manipulate children's genes.

It must be in the children's interest that human genetic inheritance can be protected as far as possible, but this must not preclude the repair of any serious genetic defects they may have. However, genetic engineering that goes beyond such repair in order to restore the body's "normal" balance would mean that the very interaction between children and parents would be different. Future generations will be "programmed" based on today's notions of valuable qualities, morals and esthetics. The problem is according to which ideals we must improve future generations. Ideals and notions of the good life are historically conditioned and provide no assurance of "better" people by utopian genetic engineering. All the less so that it cannot be ruled out that the ideals and norms held in our time in the future will be perceived as foolish and inappropriate. The principles of justice can shift, and future generations can, at worst, become slave people. When we are long dead and gone, our descendants will fight with themselves in their genetically engineered body and will not be able to hold the present accountable for its inventions.

It is thus a matter of ensuring justice for future generations. It is a responsibility between generations. Today's society is committed to justice for future people. Based on the notion of universal respect for man as an end in itself, future generations must have the opportunity for "the good life with and for the other in just institutions." This means that we must cherish the opportunities of future people to live a "real human life" and for their right to "be a surprise to themselves." Neither our individual lives nor our collective history can be isolated from our relationship to the future, and we have in no way the right to turn the people of the future into therapeutic objects. Civilizational development and shaping of society must be seen in the light of humanity's long generation chain: "The Great Generation Chain."

Consideration of a human being's freedom to shape his or her destiny and live his or her own life should be crucial. We must not by force adapt future individuals to a historically determined standard of normality but try to create social institutions that can form the basis of a more just and humane society in the civilizational process toward the kingdom of ends.

6.5 The ethics of vulnerability: The concern for humanity in the technocosmos

So, what ethics should apply in the future technological society? Is there an ethic that can take into account reproductive technology, genetic engineering and, what cyborg created, monstrous human beings who are increasingly becoming a machine? Are there common ethical principles in a multicultural society? Is there an ethical concept that can apply to all people despite completely different perceptions of religion and morality? These issues have been addressed in a European research project at the Center for Ethics and Law in Denmark from 1995 to 1998. Among other things, we investigated the concepts of self-determination, dignity and integrity. But it was almost impossible to reach agreement in the understanding of these classical ethical concepts. On the other hand, it is extremely interesting that most people, when talking about morality, immediately refer to the notion of vulnerability. Vulnerability expresses the fragility of human identity and sets limits to our dignity. We all take for granted that it must be the task of society to combat human suffering and vulnerability by helping and supporting sick and weak groups. The ethics of the welfare state is a continuation of the ideals of Christianity and the humanism of the Enlightenment. Vulnerability indicates the most universal thing about human living conditions: That we are all finite and mortal. At the same time, the recognition that something is vulnerable evokes a moral appeal to consideration and care.

However, the American bioethicist Daniel Callahan criticizes this struggle to overcome human vulnerability. He believes that modernity is marked by the "agenda of the struggle against vulnerability." We believe that, in principle, it is possible to overcome all forms of human vulnerability. It is a widespread dogma that civilization will be able to eliminate human suffering. The welfare state, therefore, optimistically fights biological, psychological and social threats to create a happy and perfect society. But the problem is that the fight against vulnerability is happening in a wrong way, where one does not have an eye for the paradoxical dimensions of human mortal life, desire and the pursuit of happiness. We are captured by the utopia of "a healthy soul in a healthy body" without being aware of the complex impact of suffering and pain on the happy life. It also means that medical science helps to create greater vulnerability, for example, when it uncovers genetic predispositions for future diseases. Then the healthy person no longer exists. Life becomes "a deadly sexually transmitted disease"; we are all potentially ill, and the medical opportunities to partially cure various diseases have, in effect, led to more people living longer lives with poorer health.

Yet, health science is intensifying the fight against vulnerability, for example, by genetic diagnostics or other interventions, but it then threatens to narrow the concept of normality, thereby making many groups in society more and more vulnerable. Illness is not an objective condition but depends on how man defines himself in relation to his surroundings. If normality is a social construction, the question is whether we can force the non-normal to live up to the norm. Disability organizations in the United States have paradoxically argued that the sharp distinction between the sick and the healthy means that "disabled lives" are perceived as less valuable than other lives. Some deaf parents, therefore, want their children to be deaf. They will not be discriminated against and believe that deafness as such has a value. They do not believe that they are sick but that their lives are quite "good lives," as long as they are not discriminated against by the other citizens of society. And yet the struggle against the vulnerability of disability to all of us is so obvious that the "healthy" can hardly see the objections of these people as anything other than group selfishness.

The paradoxes of our "natural" struggle to eliminate suffering and vulnerability are also evident in the use of antidepressant pills and drugs for mental illness. The so-called happiness pills are used to help people overcome grief and worry and avoid psychological vulnerability. The existential disorders and depressions are made here a disease. The expanded concept of illness creates even more vulnerability that should actually be combated when the healthy person actually appears as a sick human being who has not yet been properly examined. But when we are all thus potentially sick, the healthy human being no longer exists. The medicalization of the vulnerability is total.

The fight against vulnerability in the welfare state also contributes to the victimization of most people in society. The appointment of the vulnerable groups in an incapacitating care system – unemployed, single mothers; immigrants; the mentally ill; incest victims; alcoholics; and drug addicts – means that these groups contribute to their own victimization and claim that their actions are determined by their own vulnerability. We can claim that victimization has become so widespread that people use the role of victim as a survival strategy and as a basis for personal identity. Today, the majority of the world population has been made victims. It can be said that an unconscious fight against vulnerability contributes to the so-called empowerment strategies, where the individual identifies himself as a vulnerable victim who is exposed to the injustice of the state and then uses this situation to fight for survival. This becomes extra absurd when the internalization of the victim role becomes so perfect that sex offenders or perpetrators begin to justify their own actions on the grounds that they have fallen victim to the social system or that they have had a bad childhood.

The sacrifice applies in particular in the social field. When it constantly makes the individual a victim, the welfare state helps to create more vulnerability. This is happening by breaking the traditional bonds of society in an individualized culture of care, where we are all lonely and isolated victims who are becoming more and more neurotic. In this narcissistic reality, the individual is cultivated as an object of care, detached from personal responsibility and existential obligations. The fact that the treatment society explains away human motives in the light of its psychological, social circumstances merely underlines this sacrifice. The many ego-centered survival strategies in modern society help to create more social clients. This manifests itself in a health and body cult – a lifestyle culture that, in fact, expresses the extreme psychological vulnerability of individuals. The welfare state's victimization of the individual as an object of care has paradoxically contributed to greater vulnerability and marginalization of the citizen.

These paradoxes in the fight against vulnerability show that a more well-thought-out understanding of vulnerability as a basic ethical concept is necessary. The question is whether vulnerability can be meaningful without being defined as a disease. Is it possible to think of vulnerability without being captured by the victimization strategies of the welfare state? Are there vulnerabilities that are enriching for our lives and thus should neither be made sick nor eliminated but should instead be preserved and cared for? The problem is whether vulnerability has a value in itself despite technological advances. It is not certain that we should eliminate suffering and vulnerability from our lives at all costs. One can imagine that a society of people without fragility and vulnerability would be impossible to live in and how does ethics avoid becoming a new sacrifice of man that merely contributes to fixation on man as unable to take care of himself.

Here the French philosopher Emmanuel Lévinas argues in the masterpiece *Totalité et Infini* from 1961 that it is not a human being's active commitment to the world but rather his or her vulnerable reception of the world that is the basis of existence. For him, human humanity is characterized by being fragile and vulnerable. This means that my ability to act morally arises on the basis of the experience of my own vulnerability by virtue of my bodily being in the world in space and time. If the individual was not vulnerable, he or she would not be able to understand the other person's vulnerability as the basis of the ethical claim. Thus, it is the individual's experience of his or her own finitude and vulnerability that makes the commitment of the other human being the demand of ethics. It is an existential understanding of vulnerability that recognizes finitude and fragility as an important part of human life.

Some would argue that this philosophy expresses the ultimate victimization because vulnerability is no longer psychological and social but rather an existential basic condition. Yet, one cannot escape the fact that it is our openness to the vulnerable in ourselves that allows us to understand that we must protect the vulnerable in the social and cultural world. Although it may be typical of the time, it is a great step forward when the participants in the already mentioned European research project agreed on the following interesting definition of the principle of vulnerability. Vulnerability expresses two basic ideas: (a) It expresses finitude and fragility, and with them, a human being is incapable of being totally autonomous; this vulnerability justifies the possibility and necessity of morality; (b) Vulnerability is the subject of a moral principle that requires care for the vulnerable. The vulnerable are those whose autonomy, dignity or integrity are capable of that. All beings who have vulnerabilities are protected by this principle, but the principle requires not only noninterference with the autonomy, dignity and integrity of living beings but also that they be helped to realize their potential, that there are positive rights to integrity and autonomy that justify the ideas of solidarity, nondiscrimination and community.

Thus, ethics should not pervert the fight against vulnerability so that it ends up in autonomous survival strategies, nor should it help to create more technological solutions and machine-humans but instead be aware that respect for personal self-expression is based on an understanding of the importance of vulnerability to human living conditions.

Part III

Biolaw, organizational economics and health care

7 Corporate governance, social responsibility and stakeholder management

7.1 Sustainable development, CSR and corporate governance

The structure of our argument is a review of sustainability and corporate social responsibility as the basis for a stakeholder analysis in business and organizations as the basis for understanding the role of governance in health care organizations, businesses and hospitals. This analysis is based on the theory and practice of philosophy of management (Rendtorff, 2010a, 2013a, 2013b, 2013c, 2013d, 2014b, 2015a, 2017c, 2019d). Thus, in this chapter we develop the theoretical foundations in governance and management theory to be included as the foundation of hospital management and management of health care organizations. With this, we move beyond more traditional theories of hospital management like scientific management, systems theory, contingency theory and behavioral management theory. As the foundation of bioethics and biolaw, the chapter aims to develop the theoretical foundations for hospital heath care workers' and health care managers' work with policy decisions, governance, budgeting and accounting and organization of the work and functions of health care organizations and hospitals.

The aim of the chapter is to relate corporate social responsibility, business ethics and stakeholder management to hospital management and hospital organization. Thus, we begin by investigating the idea of sustainability and corporate social responsibility (CSR) in organization ethics. The idea is that the sustainability, CSR and corporate governance debate should be seen as a discussion of the possibility of defining corporate good citizenship in society (McIntosh, Leipziger, Jones, & Coleman, 1998, p. 193). The basis for this is a normative definition of the stakeholder model, where companies' social responsibility contributes to realizing the company's long-term survival and protection of the individual stakeholders (Bonnafous-Boucher & Rendtorff, 2016a, 2016b, 2016c, 2016d, 2016e, 2016f). The concepts of sustainability and justice are developed as the basis for good governance. This should be seen as an ethical framework for the company's strategic management, which is clarified through the managers' ability to "moral thinking" and reflective judgment.

DOI: 10.4324/9781003147848-7

The company's social responsibility can be seen in the light of sustainable development, which, as the purpose of ethical business operations and business, can be seen as the basis for the company's good citizenship (Crane & Matten, 2004, p. 21). The concept goes back to the Brundtland Commission, the World Commission on Environment and Development, which in 1987 launched sustainability as a common political goal for the international community (World Commission on the Environment and Development, 1987) and which has been later developed by the Sustainable Development Goals (SDGs) from 2015. Sustainable development was defined as the core concept of environmental policy as restraint in depleting the earth's resources so that the livelihoods of future generations on earth would not be degraded on worse terms than the present generations.

Sustainability is not an unknown concept in business economics, which uses this concept to denote a company's long-term economic and social stability. However, as a basis for the theory of good corporate citizenship, the concept has been generalized so that it not only signifies narrow economic viability but also includes consideration of the company's social and environmental sustainability.

The sustainability ideal can be specified with the theory of the Triple Bottomline, according to which the company must not only be aware of the economic profit but also include the impact on the environment and the social relations to employees, customers, the local community or the state in the assessment of business success (Elkington, 1997). This consideration is thus aimed at realizing the company's social responsibility, as it integrates economization, ecologization and power increase into an overall whole (Frederick, 1995). The strategy acquires a temporal dimension when sustainability focuses on the company's obligations to the environment and future generations. Thus, business ethics not only has a social dimension but also is put into interaction with nature, according to which the ethics' goal of what the French philosopher Paul Ricoeur calls "the good life for and with the other in just institutions" (Ricœur, 1990, p. 202) does not make sense without being seen in relation to the living nature.

Sustainability is thus part of the company's social responsibility, which is central to dialogue with the company's internal and external constituents. This is based on the notion of the company as a moral actor, which, as Lynn Sharp Paine claims in *Value Shift: Why Companies Must Merge Social and Financial Imperative to Achieve Superior Performance* (2003), expresses a shift in value in the economy, where we no longer perceive the company as a neutral instrument for profit maximization or as a fictitious legal entity, but first and foremost as morally responsible with values and principles (Paine, 2003, p. 81). Here, we find a perception of the company's responsibility, which means that it must not only follow the law but also engage constructively in the social improvement of society.

The German philosopher Hans Jonas has in *Das Prinzip Verantwortung: Versuch einer Ethik der technischen Zivilisation* (1979) contributed with a basic definition of the concept of responsibility. He argues that technological and scientific developments have given humanity a far greater responsibility than earlier in history. As we have far greater power to destroy the earth, the responsibility of humanity has intensified (Jonas, 1979). According to Hans Jonas, the ethics of responsibility is not only about respect for contemporary people but there is also a very close connection between sustainability and responsibility in the sense that responsibility implies the obligation that there may be human life on the earth in the future. The concept of responsibility expresses an absolute categorical principle that we have a duty to ensure sustainable development.

This overarching categorical and ontological concept of responsibility can be described as the background to corporate social responsibility (Maccio, 2001, p. 17). CSR not only includes individual responsibility but also involves the institution's institutional responsibility as a moral actor. CSR depends on the company's capacity to be ethically responsible for its actions, strategies and policies. Ethics is the basis for a management structure that creates a culture of responsibility in the organization. With this, CSR must not be defined as "enlightened self-interest" only based on economic considerations in order to achieve higher returns but also based on the notion of the company as a good citizen with rights and duties to society.

The argument for the moral responsibility of the company is based on its great power in society. Here, a distinction can be made between the company's institutional responsibility and the individual responsibility of employees, directors and middle managers. As an expression of the company's institutional responsibility as an organization, the notion of the company's moral responsibility goes beyond the purely legal responsibility and includes a wide range of ethically defined areas of responsibility in relation to the company's various stakeholders. In this way, CSR is based on a moral conception of the economy, which is expressed by good citizenship, where the company assumes responsibility for the vulnerable and weak in society (Etzioni, 1988).

This implies a critique of those who claim that it has not been proven that companies as institutions can be held morally responsible, that only shareholders and the financial owners can have legitimate interests and claims on the company and that CSR entails an unacceptable restriction of the company opportunity to trade freely in the economic market. This widespread skeptical attitude has not understood that CSR is in the company's own interest because it can create a better environment for its own transactions by actively engaging in improving society (Buchholz & Rosenthanl, 2002, p. 304). Social responsibility will undoubtedly improve the company's image in the public, and thus, further bureaucratic regulation can be avoided if the company proactively engages with society. Social responsibility is an important contribution to the company's efforts to live up to society's expectations, and the private business community should engage socially because it has such a great responsibility that it can even help solve social problems by seeing new business opportunities.

In addition to such pragmatic arguments of wisdom, we can emphasize that CSR combines the enlightened self-interest with regard to the moral custom and the ethical principles of society (Frederick, 1994, p. 153). Here, CSR expresses respect for human rights and the need to treat the company's various stakeholders in a fair and equitable manner.

Based on these ontological and ethical definitions of corporate social responsibility, we can now differentiate between the various elements of social responsibility. In light of the ideal of corporate good citizenship, with Archie B. Carroll of the Business and Society movement (Carroll, 1979; Carrol & Buchholtz, 2000), a distinction can be made between (1) financial responsibility, (2) legal responsibility, (3) ethical responsibility and (4) philanthropic responsibility.

Financial responsibility can be defined in terms of the demand for profit maximization, as determined by Milton Friedman: "The social re-sponsorship of business is to increase its profits" (Friedman, 1970). But this responsibility also involves fair treatment of shareholders. Good management here involves a responsible and financial prioritization and use of resources, not least in relation to employees and customers. The financial responsibility also entails the management's technical and professional responsibility to find and exploit market opportunities. In this sense, economic responsibility is different from moral responsibility because it is about pursuing self-interest and exchanging goods and services in the market according to capitalist principles.

The French philosopher André Comte-Sponville speaks here up against a strict separation between economic rationality and moral responsibility. He argues that there is an ethical sphere, a legal sphere, a moral sphere, an economic sphere and a religious sphere that should not be confused. Therefore, he is critical of "La mode de l'éthique des Affaires," where one simply considers the company as a person and a moral subject. This distinction may have some resemblance to the divide between moral and economic responsibility, but it is exaggerated when Comte-Sponville believes that economics and morality can be kept separate. This is an old-fashioned view of the science of economics (Comte-Sponville, 2004).

Legal liability is about the obligation to follow the law and play the rules of the game without breaking the law. This also means that the company must not just move on the border of the law and always try to escape where the fence is lowest but also make a real effort to comply with the meaning of the law. Legal responsibility is expressed internally, where the company works to ensure that employees abide by the law, and it is expressed externally to ensure that the company's products and services do not contradict society's legal rules. This compliance requirement applies not only nationally but also when multinational and transnational corporations operate globally and locally in foreign countries. It is characteristic that CSR is regulated, in particular, with soft law instruments that encourage the company's self-regulation, while corporate governance in addition has also been sought to be implemented through ordinary legislation (Monks & Minow, 2004, p. 98).

In this tension between corporate governance and CSR, ethical responsibility is not only defined as an effort to do what is responsible and right in an economic and general legal sense, cf. the letter of the law, but also to go beyond the economic and legal requirements and voluntarily strive to be morally responsible. Ethics is about finding the right balance in the gray zone, where actions can create economic profit and be in accordance with the law but still contain ethical problems that make them unacceptable. In cases of conflict, the ethical obligation takes precedence over the economic and legal considerations. In this sense, ethical responsibility embodies broader considerations of justice and sustainability in the company and in society. Therefore, ethical responsibility goes beyond financial and legal responsibility. It can be defined as respect for justice and involves striving for fair treatment of all stakeholders. This means that ethical responsibility is central to the company's democratic legitimacy (Sedel, 1995, p. 79).

Corporate philanthropy is not just about the corporate philanthropic gift to the outside world but also about the responsibility to be philanthropic in a way that truly benefits society. There is a long tradition of corporate philanthropic responsibility, where companies give large gifts to society as a demonstration of power and wealth and because they want to do something for the local community (Sexty, 2001). Corporate philanthropy is in many cases closely linked to the effort to give the company a better public image in society. With Michael Porter, we can emphasize here the importance of integrating philanthropy into the strategic and economic core areas of the company (Porter & Kramer, 2002). Corporate philanthropy involves reflection on how the money can best be used for the common benefit of society and the company.

From these definitions of the concept of responsibility, it is clear that we must consider corporate governance as an integral part of CSR if we are to make sense of the notion of good corporate citizenship. This represents a concept of management that integrates ethics into management practice (Mattsson & Rendtorff, 2006; Pedersen & Rendtorff, 2004; Rendtorff, 2015b, 2016b, 2017b, 2019a, 2019b, 2019c; Rendtorff & Mattsson, 2012). In this perspective, rules of good management are a natural realization of the company's overall social responsibility. The ethical demand that manifests itself in the need for healthy markets, shareholder protection, transparency, value-based management, ethical accounting, requirements for auditing and reporting and for public relations expresses in a more or less formalized sense an enforcement of the overall connection between sustainability and social responsibility. This is the case whether it is the US initiatives with *The Federal Sentencing Guidelines for Organizations* (1991) and the transparency legislation, Sarbanes-Oxley, or the European initiatives on good governance and the *European Commission's Green Paper on Corporate Social Responsibility* (European Commission, 2001, 2002; Moon et al., 2012; United States Sentencing Commission, 1995), developed by the European Commission from 2014 into the definition of CSR as the company's impact on society. The rationale for corporate governance thus combines the pragmatic consideration of economic earnings in sound economic markets with overall ethical and democratic considerations of making companies more legitimate in society based on fundamental principles of sustainability as well as ethical and social responsibility. This can be seen as a development of research on business ethics in the perspective (Rendtorff, 2009a; 2009b; 2010b; 2011a; 2011b; 2011c; 2012; 2014c; 2017a; 2017b; 2017c). Thus, we integrate business ethics with corporate governance, corporate social responsibility and stakeholder theory.

7.2 Corporate governance, CSR and strategic management

The organization theorists Michel Capron and Françoise Quairel-Lanoizeelée have developed the basis for the strategic application of CSR and corporate governance. They emphasize that the United Nations (UN) has established that companies play an important role in sustainable development in the sense that in their work they can stimulate economic growth and social development by being aware of the environment and their social responsibility (Capron & Quairel-Lanoizeelée, 2004, p. 5). The company is a part of civil society, and environmental and social themes cannot be excluded from the company's strategic management.

At the international level, the company can contribute to solving important world political problems concerning the environment, for example, to avoid the destruction of the ecosphere, overconsumption of resources and deterioration of the environment; fight social poverty; and engage in mediation in wars and armed conflicts, and also by working for human rights. Concrete rights of particular relevance to companies include the so-called workers' rights, adopted by the International Labour Organization (ILO) (United Nations, 1958), which include Prohibition of child labor, Prohibition of forced labor, Prohibition discrimination of and freedom of association and the right to organize. Of course, these rights do not make sense if one does not first respect fundamental rights such as the right to life, the prohibition of slave, forced or other compulsory labor and not least the right to privacy, social security and the right to a family life that occurs in UN Conventions on Civil and Political Rights (CCPR) and on Economic Social and Cultural Rights (CESCR). Thus, CSR management does not go unnoticed by the company's responsible contribution to solving the problems of the world community in a broader sense, as described in the UN's various declarations, conventions and policy strategies.

The European Commission follows the UN's strategy for sustainable development when it emphasizes that CSR is not only about complying with the law but must also be understood as a voluntary commitment to do more than what is legally required to protect human rights, the environment and the company's relationships with various stakeholders. The EU Green Paper and subsequent "Communications" on corporate social responsibility have emphasized that there is a direct link between CSR and sustainability, as CSR must be seen as part of the company's contribution to sustainable development (European Commission, 2001, 2002; Moon et al., 2012). In this context, the triple bottom line is central to reporting and evaluating the company's societal benefits, which are oriented not only toward economic growth but also toward social development and environmental protection, which are included in the assessment of the company's activities.

This approach to CSR implies that companies and other private and public organizations are considered not only as economic entities but also as open systems that have different social obligations to society as a whole (Scott, 1998). This close connection between CSR and sustainable development forms the basis for a strategic reflection on the company's good citizenship, which may be perceived as particularly necessary at a time when international opinion puts increased pressure on companies that run a great risk if they do not comply with the standards of the international community for sustainable development. The pressure on companies to contribute to social responsibility has not least increased due to the emergence of the many aggressive and very active NGOs, the World Business Council for Sustainable Development, Transparency International, which monitor the companies' activities.

Here, international declarations such as the Rio Declaration of 1992 and the Johannesburg Declaration of 2001 from the UN Summits on Environmental Issues or other declarations such as the UNESCO Declaration on the Protection of the Human Genome from 1997 are important ethical and legal guidelines for companies' contributions toward the common good of mankind. But we can also mention codes of conduct for multinational companies or the principles of the Caux Roundtable Principles for Business Conduct from 1994, which were the result of talks between Western and Asian business leaders that went out to improve the world's social and economic situation, on finding common principles for ethical conduct in business across different cultures in the East and the West. Here, the Japanese concept of "koysei" ("living together and working for the common good"), combined with the Western concept of "human dignity," became the basis for a common code of conduct on responsible business morality (Enderle, 1999, p. 43).

In continuation of the overall strategy for sustainable development, the UN has created agreement on the Global Compact principles, which enforce CSR on the basis of the UN Declarations of Human Rights and Principles for Environmental Protection. These should be seen in the context of the ILO's guidelines for CSR (International Labour Organization, 2002). In addition, the OECD Guidelines for Multinational Contracts (OECD, 2002) can be mentioned. Most recently, the UN Commission on Human Rights has begun to formulate guidelines for companies' work with CSR and respect for human rights. These Guidelines for CSR and corporate governance can be seen as an attempt to define some general framework for healthy and responsible behavior in order to not only create positive growth and social change but also ensure fair treatment of all company stakeholders, including customers, employees, owners, investors, suppliers, local communities and more controversial competitors. The international codes of conduct can be said to orient themselves toward all the four dimensions of CSR that we have mentioned, namely, that companies in their activities consider the economic, legal, ethical and philanthropic dimensions of CSR as well.

The global process of formulating principles for sustainable development is based on the notion of the possibility of a global civil society, in which the company is considered a responsible participant. The requirements for companies from NGOs and trade unions contribute to the adoption of international Guidelines and codes of conduct for CSR and corporate governance, but also ethically, ecologically and socially conscious consumers in Europe and the United States have fought for Fair Trade and respect for the environment as criteria for responsible corporate governance. Consumer organizations have worked for the idea of organic or ethical labeling, as a basis for consumers to be sure that the products are produced with social responsibility. Products with the Max Havelaar brand should, for example, be products that are produced with organic quality and under socially acceptable working conditions. In this connection, efforts can be highlighted to develop rules for fair business conditions, for example, at the Ethical Trading Initiative. The movement for socially responsible investments (SRIs) is growing, and both among ordinary shareholders and institutional investors, there is greater interest in the triple bottom line and intangible factors in the evaluation of the company's sustainability. Furthermore, the need for protection of the company's brand and its good reputation is also of great importance for the co-thinking of CSR and strategic management.

CSR and corporate governance are not only the company's actual "license to operate the company," but these forms of management also express the prerequisite for the company's financial sustainability. The argument for this connection between responsibility and financial progress is based on a new institutional notion of the company's legitimacy. When the company is an actor integrated into the social community of society with its specific norms and values, and when economic markets cannot be separated from the social context, it is necessary to relate to the norms and values of society if there is to be a sustainable management strategy. Otherwise, the company will be excluded from society's sphere of social and political legitimacy, and this will most likely mean that the company's key stakeholders, employees, investors, customers and suppliers will be indifferent, reluctant or directly negative toward the company. In some cases, they may even turn away from the company and boycott its products and services.

Despite the strength of this argument of legitimacy, however, it has not been possible to determine a direct causal link between economic growth and the company's social commitment. There have been many empirical studies, but they have shown both a positive and a negative correlation between economic performance and ethical performance. It is quite difficult to measure oneself to a connection between the economic and the ethical, but it is both economically and socially problematic if we end up in a situation where everyone chooses to go freewheeling, that is, to be "Free Riders" in terms of being socially responsible and working for the common good. Conversely, if we assume that the company can make money from being immoral, for example, by producing defective products and so forth over time, it will not be a viable strategy. "Free Rider" actions cannot be repeated because other players will have become aware that the company has acted irresponsibly and therefore have been warned and will turn you away from the company. Thus, there are not only short-term microeconomic arguments for corporate social responsibility but also long-term macroeconomic arguments for sustainability and the company's work for the common good. However, these arguments are not only economic but they are also based on broader considerations of responsibility and societal affiliation, which place the company in the context of society of general social legitimacy, where the ethical values of not doing harm and work for the good as well as for taking care of the human person takes precedence.

In the strategic perspective, economic arguments are combined with normative business ethics arguments and with sociological arguments as a means of ensuring the company's legitimacy in society. The neo-institutional theory in sociology in combination with the stakeholder analysis helps to understand how the direct and indirect stakeholders affect the company. CSR and corporate governance need to include relationships not only with power stakeholders or explicit contracts with companies but also with other stakeholders who have an interest in the company from the point of view of social legitimacy (Mittchell, Agle, & Wood, 1997). Here we cannot get around the importance of CSR and corporate governance in relation to creating legitimate relationships with a focus on the good for the company's stakeholders (Argandona, 1998). According to the great German moral philosopher Immanuel Kant, we can consider the company a world citizen. What is important in CSR and corporate governance is the contribution to the common good of society in order to create more sustainability and protect the company's citizenship on a global level, which implies the company's responsibility to contribute to solving the problems of globalization.

Here, the economic growth of the company is combined with the consideration of its social legitimacy. The company is perceived as an integral part of society, and the company's values are created based on the stakeholders' different internal and external expectations of the company (Powell & DiMaggio, 1991). With the neo-institutional theory in sociology, it can be argued that legitimacy is determined by the institutional environment of the company. These environments represent the social and cultural expectations of the company that require a specific social and environmental presence in society. To deal with these expectations, it is necessary for the company to construct its image, brand and social appearance in accordance with the requirements and expectations of the institutional environment. This institutional legitimacy is not always directly visible and explicit but can be implicit and presupposed in norms and habits as the basis for the company's legitimate rational action in society. A number of important articles from the neo-institutional theory in sociology can be mentioned, which can be regarded as the basis for the institution's institutional legitimacy (Di Maggio & Powell, 1983; Oliver, 1991).

The neo-institutional theory in sociology also allows us to point out a number of different and perhaps even contradictory expectations of the companies of the various stakeholders that embody the possible economic, social and environmental expectations that may assert themselves in modern complex societies. Despite the fact that these expectations present themselves as ideals, they are often reflected in the real and factual demands of the stakeholders to the companies. We can mention the following: Shareholders and investors expect to get a reasonable return on their investments, safe risk and crisis management, financial transparency and possibly respect for the threefold bottom line in day-to-day business management. Banks and creditors expect professional crisis management and financial security, and environmental and social conditions cannot be avoided. Employees and trade unions want companies to ensure equality and promote good working conditions and create a social safety net in the workplace. They hope that the company will contribute to development work, improve motivation and prevent burnout and stress. They want not only respect for their privacy but also personal development and learning at work. It is also not least important that the company represents values that the employee can support.

Consumers, customers and clients expect a fair price and good product quality and environmentally friendly products and that companies respect society's ethical norms and basic legal rules. Suppliers expect stable business relationships, secure payments, respect for contracts and perhaps even help with ethical production control so that they do not violate basic codes of ethics and rules of law. Competitors want respect for the market's basic rules of the game, agreement on the industry's code of conduct, for example, by companies refraining from running on moral freewheels and thereby failing to respect basic norms for environmental and social ethics. The local community expects the company's social commitment and contribution to the common good, and they expect the companies to take a constructive part in the development of civil society. States and international organizations expect companies to create growth and jobs while contributing to the well-being of society, respecting the environment and behaving as good citizens who promote the wholeness and coherence of society's values. States want companies to be aware of the ethics and rules of the countries in which they operate and to act with integrity without using bribes or increasing corruption in the countries in which they operate. International, national and local NGOs and other interest groups expect transparency in companies' actions, respect for human rights and sustainability, and it is often emphasized that the company must contribute to society as a good citizen.

According to the neo-institutional theory in sociology, a company can consciously choose between different strategies to relate to these social expectations (Di Maggio & Powell, 1983; Oliver, 1991). Even those companies that do not take CSR seriously would of course like to have social acceptance. They just ignore the demand for legitimacy. They may even aggressively try to enforce themselves as a company that makes a virtue out of running on moral freewheeling and concentrating on what it finds most important, namely, making money. The company will here avoid being confronted directly with CSR, and it will reject CSR and business ethics as meaningless for financial success. This attitude is often seen by companies that do not perceive public communication as important and mistakenly believe that they can evade the game of legitimacy. Unfortunately, in crisis situations, they are harshly reminded that they have had a naive and reluctant view of their symbolic and dramaturgical relationships with the public and, through their arrogance toward ethics and social responsibility, have worsened their ability to secure lasting and stable social legitimacy.

Another strategy would be to attempt a proactive affirmation of social expectations. We can argue that strategic corporate governance and CSR are part of this proactive search for legitimacy. Here one is aware that the survival of the company depends on its ability to maintain its legitimacy in society. The company's work with value-based management can in continuation of this be regarded as conscious and rational efforts to respond to society's expectations through "Best Practice" and responsible behavior. This does not have to contradict the strategic perspective but can be seen as a symbolic response to society's social expectations in order to protect and develop the company's brand, image and reputation in the public (Grunig & Hunt, 1984).

In continuation of this importance of the legitimacy of the company's sustainability and operation, it can be maintained that there is a Business Case for CSR and corporate governance. Here we can refer to John Elkington's *Cannibals with Forks: The Triple Bottom Line of Twenty-First Century Business* (1999). In this book, the theory of the triple bottom line is developed on the basis of the international policy on sustainable development. The company must act in the field of tension among economic, social and environmental considerations if it wants to develop to the maximum in the long term. Although Elkington does not reject the tension between ethics and economics, he emphasizes that we must strive for the ideal situation where a convergence between corporate social responsibility and economic development is established. The ideal of the company's good citizenship implies a notion of a company that is at once capable of producing growth and value for shareholders, employees and customers and that, at the same time, through economic growth contributes to the development of society. Such a company does not only consider corporate governance and CSR as a matter of advertising, that is, to have a good brand or as a kind of risk and crisis management but considers the contribution to society as a fundamental part of the company's raison d'être. In this context, stakeholders are perceived as resources that help to create innovation, as well as increased learning and competitiveness, in the company.

This attempt to understand corporate governance and CSR as an integral part of the company's management strategy can be operationalized on the basis of a Balanced Scorecard, as it has been developed by R.S. Kaplan and D.P. Norton. As a management tool, the Balanced Scorecard is intended as a means of measuring financial, social and intellectual capital when integrating employees' services and the company's social conditions into general reporting (Kaplan & Norton, 1998). Here it is possible to extend the measurement of services to a much wider circle of stakeholders, which makes it possible to measure the effect of corporate governance and CSR. The Danish company Novo Nordisk is one of the companies that has worked on using the Balanced Scorecard as an instrument to operationalize the sustainability strategy and the threefold bottom line. This is a "Sustainability Scorecard," which includes the consideration of the stakeholders as well as the environmental elements of the company's services in the balancing and measuring of competitiveness and of the company's strategic behavior. Thus, corporate governance and CSR are not only expressions of risk management but also about developing proactive operational procedures that improve the legitimacy and social acceptance of the company.

7.3 The stakeholder model as an instrument for corporate governance and CSR

The approach to business ethics referred to as stakeholder or stakeholder theory can help us define the strategic basis for corporate governance and CSR (Freeman & Reed, 1983). According to this theory, ethical principles and values are the result of communication and dialogue between organizations and their stakeholders. Stakeholder-oriented business ethics perceives the communication between the company and its stakeholders analogously to a political democracy, where everyone is involved in the decision-making process through debates and consultations (Bonnafous-Boucher & Rendtorff, 2016a, 2016b, 2016c, 2016d, 2016e, 2016f). Stakeholder theory is based on the ideal of a possible constructive dialogue with stakeholders as a basis for deliberative reason, which, in addition to a critical dialogue, can provide good reasons for the company's strategic decisions. This is based on a communicative foundation of business ethics as embedded in a critical review of arguments in a space for open dialogue with the involvement of all stakeholders. This is based on Jürgen Habermas' theory of communicative action and of the foundation of legitimacy in communicative action as based on "the unforced compulsion of the better argument" (Habermas, 1981).

The starting point for the stakeholder theory is a critique of a corporate model that restricts the company's legitimate consideration for shareholders. The stakeholder theories redefine the company to be an entity within the economic, political and social sphere of society. The stakeholder model perceives the company as a network of several different participants (Clarkson, 1998). It is not only shareholders and investors who contribute to value creation in the company. Therefore, other considerations must be taken than just worrying about these groups. In fact, an interest-based management model is fundamental if the company is to have real sustainability and survive in the long run in a complex, globalized economy. Here, with Edward Freeman, it can be emphasized that the stakeholder model is in fact the most developed "pro-shareholder theory," because the involvement of a wide range of stakeholders will ultimately provide the greatest return for the company.

Therefore, Freeman also emphasizes in a polemical critique of CSR that we should not primarily talk about corporate social responsibility but rather about "Corporate Stakeholder Responsibility," that is, define CSR and corporate governance as a broad responsibility in relation to the stakeholders if we really want to place corporate governance and CSR at the center of strategic management (Freeman, Velamuri, & Moriarty, 2006). According to this stakeholder model, it is emphasized that it is in the company's stated self-interest to realize that economic efficiency and competitive advantages can only be ensured if the company involves stakeholders in the strategic planning and formulation of the company's vision and mission. The basis of the interest model here is a critique of the neoclassical belief in the existence of an economically clean market independent of social conditions. The stakeholder model is also critical of the notion that companies can act as economic agents without also dealing with political and social issues (Bonnafous-Boucher & Rendtorff, 2016a, 2016b, 2016c, 2016d, 2016e, 2016f).

The stakeholder theory criticizes an economic view of business based on the ideal of free competition and rational utility calculation. We must admit that in many cases the market is not characterized by fair competition but rather by Darwinian principles of the survival of the fittest. Contrary to Milton Friedman's abovementioned ideal notion that "social responsibility of business is to increase its profits," the stakeholder theory emphasizes that large companies will benefit from their economic superiority to achieve greater power (Wheeler & Sillanpää, 1997, p. 33). The big companies have gained enormous power over the economy and society and, therefore, cannot escape being also responsible according to their political and social influence. Furthermore, legislation on modern companies, with the potential separation of management and owners and limited liability for shareholders, means that investors and shareholders no longer have great power over their actions. Instead, management has gained more power over the company, not least because they possess maximum information and make most daily decisions. This power becomes especially conspicuous if one examines the size of their wages. The consequence of these skewed power relations and a lack of understanding of the company's other stakeholders is negative impact on employees, customers, suppliers and society as a whole.

In their theory of the stakeholder business, David Wheeler and Maria Sillanpää emphasize that in the complex risk society, the company is exposed to intensified pressure from various groups and stakeholders in society, which means that the company can no longer perceive itself as a purely economic agent in a perfect market. The company cannot be content with production, marketing and financial management but must involve the stakeholders in management and strategic planning and public relations and enter an open dialogue with these stakeholders if the company wants to survive in an international climate with intensified competition and vigilance concerning the activities of the company. Against this background, the stakeholder model can be seen as a concretization of the neo-institutional analysis of the company's position as an open system in a larger societal whole.

This implies that the neoclassical theories, the Taylor-inspired notions of Scientific Management or the production-oriented theories of strategic management such as Michael Porter's theory of competitive strategy in industrial analysis are not sufficient to understand the requirement of corporate governance and CSR. This is because traditional management theories are primarily based on production-oriented perceptions of efficiency and sustainability. In his early works on strategy and competition, Porter describes the company on the basis of a rational structure based on efficient utilization of the division of labor. In this context, his view of organization can be regarded as a Darwinian theory of "Survival of the fittest."

David Wheeler and Maria Sillanpää apply a similar critique to the School of Human Relations and the Human Resources paradigm of corporate governance, as they emphasize that this approach focuses on employee needs and interpersonal relationships by aiming to integrate employees into the company in such a way that he or she feels loyalty and commitment in providing the utmost to the production. This view can be described as the theory of adaptation to the outside world, that is, as a "Survival of the fitting view" (Wheeler & Sillanpää, 1997, p. 114). Although the School of Human Relations or the Human Resources School has been extremely important to companies' contributions to human prosperity and personal development in the workplace, their approach is not without problems. It is especially the implicit incapacitation, alienation and oppression of not only employees but also customers through the psychological marketing paradigm that has been criticized, and that is why there are increasing problems in making human relations theories work, as employees and customers become more and more aware of their political and social rights and thus have increasing expectations for the honesty and integrity of companies.

In this situation, a more complex view of the organization is needed. The stakeholder theory must therefore be based on a cybernetic and systems theory view of organizations. Cybernetics comes from Greek and means governing art. Knowing cybernetics can thus be seen as part of CSR and corporate governance. According to such a theory of communication and systems, organizations engage in constant interaction with their surroundings (Walther-Busch, 1996, p. 208). The cybernetic conception of organization is based on the fact that organizations enter into a complex interaction with their surroundings. If organizations are to survive and achieve long-term stability, they must constantly pay attention to the interaction with their environment in order to observe and control the company's interactions with other actors. This can give the organization a better basis for reflexive and considered action when it discovers problems or contradictions in relation to the economic, political or social environment.

In this systems theory perspective, which functions as a concretization of the neo-institutional approach to organizational theory, the stakeholder perspective on the company can be regarded as an organizational ecology, where the organization instead of functioning as a bureaucratic and hierarchical structure with rigid order and control systems appears as an "inclusive company" that is in constant interaction with its surroundings (Bonnafous-Boucher & Rendtorff, 2016a, 2016b, 2016c, 2016d, 2016e, 2016f). This interaction contributes to the company's self-observation in order to ensure its growth and survival. Considering the company as an open communication system in sustained interaction with the environment, the stakeholder dialogue can be described as a progressive reflective learning process with a view to improving and developing the organization's self-observation. Thus, the involvement of the stakeholders in the company's learning process contributes to the organization's development and is therefore a fundamental condition for the company's continuous learning "Learn how to learn" (Wheeler & Sillanpää, 1997, p. 133). Therefore, it is also fundamental to the company's sustainability and ability to act in relation to its surroundings that it can integrate a formalized stakeholder dialogue in its daily practice as a basis for management and decisions.

This means that the stakeholders can not only be defined strategically as objects or causes that, as an expression of the advantages and disadvantages of the strategy, do good to or harm the company. We cannot settle for the instrumental stakeholder theory (Jones, 1995). In the light of the concepts of CSR and corporate governance and the company's work for sustainability and the good life at the societal level, the stakeholders' demands are evaluated based on the vision of the common good that is implied in the company's values. Despite some skepticism about the idea of the common good built into the pragmatic and liberal view of the stakeholder theory, it can thus be argued that the stakeholder perspective implies a view of the common good, as it is claimed by Edward Freeman, that stakeholder interests converge over time and are therefore based on the interplay between the individual and the common interest as essential to the dynamics of stakeholder theory.

This is evident from Freeman's definition of a stakeholder who, as a universal person, ultimately cannot escape a consideration for the common in society that goes beyond the individual interests (Argandonã, 1998). Freeman argues that a stakeholder in an organization (by definition) is any group or individual who can influence or is influenced by the achievement of the organization's goals (a stakeholder in an organization is [by definition] any group or individual who can affect or is affected by the achievements of the organization's objectives) (Freeman, 1984, 1994). Everyone, even those who do not shout out loud about their rights, in principle have a right to be heard and involved in the company's strategic decision-making process, if they are influenced by or influence the company's decisions. In other words, anyone who is a victim or benefits from the activities of an organization should be considered a stakeholder. Stakeholders are defined as any group of individuals or organizations that can benefit or be affected by and whose rights are violated or served by the actions of the company (Freeman, 1998, p. 250).

Against this background, Freeman has significantly summarized the stakeholder theory in ten basic principles, which read as follows: (1) We need to generalize the marketing approach. (2) Everything that we do serves stakeholders. We never trade off the interests of one versus the other continuously over time. (3) We negotiate with primary and secondary stakeholders. (4) We constantly monitor and redesign processes to make them better serve our stakeholders. (5) We act with purpose that fulfills our commitment to stakeholders. We act with aspiration toward fulfilling our dreams. (6) Stakeholder interests go together over time. (7) Stakeholder consists of real people with names and faces and children. People are complex. (8) We need solutions to issues that satisfy multiple stakeholders simultaneously. (9) We need intensive communication and dialogue with stakeholders – not just those who are friendly. (10) We need to have a philosophy of voluntarism, to manage stakeholder relationships ourselves rather than third parties such as governments (Freeman et al., 2006).

These ten principles clearly show how the stakeholder theory can be regarded as a network-based, communicatively oriented theory that works toward placing the company in a societal context with the aim of promoting both the interests of the individual and the interests of the community without compromising understanding of the company's business economic basis (Bonnafous-Boucher & Rendtorff, 2016a, 2016b, 2016c, 2016d, 2016e, 2016f). Moreover, these principles are very important as the foundation for democratic management of hospitals and other health care organizations.

7.4 How to prioritize between different stakeholders?

Despite the strategic gain of this formulation of the stakeholder approach, we are still left with a number of problems in figuring out the relationship between the various stakeholders. Determining who counts as stakeholders and defining what status they then have are extremely complicated. For this, we need a theory that builds on Freeman's basic definition of the stakeholder concept. In this connection, we can distinguish between (1) voluntary versus involuntary stakeholders, for example, owners versus nonowners, and (2) primary and secondary stakeholders, that is, stakeholders who have a direct and real connection to the company, for example, owners or employees and stakeholders whose relationship to the company is more peripheral, for instance, occasional customers. This is closely linked to the distinction between external and internal stakeholders, for example, employees and customers. This provides a limited definition of relevant stakeholders in an organization that is able to distinguish between the importance of the company's various stakeholders. In this perspective, a stakeholder is defined as (1) any group or person who is indispensable for the company's survival, success and well-being (2) or is important for the definition of the organization, its mission and purpose and/or is influenced by the organization and its activities. Stakeholders occupy more or less different roles and positions inside and outside the company (Mittchell et al., 1997).

Thus, stakeholder theory as a basis for CSR and corporate governance is based on the active involvement of the company's various stakeholders in the decision-making process. This definition is symmetrical as it engages in dialogue with stakeholders and not only strategically, because it incorporates potential changes in the company's strategy in the calculation, which also includes commitments to new stakeholder groups, and because it also takes a position on broader policy objectives in the evaluation of the company's stakeholders. In this neo-institutional perspective, stakeholders are seen as participants in a communicative process aimed at stabilizing the company's societal legitimacy. Therefore, stakeholders should have status as an end and not just as a means.

Today, property rights of the company do not entitle the owners to do as they please in relation to the company and its other stakeholders. It is in the stakeholder theory that the company should not be regarded as an abstract economic unit but that it is placed in a social context with specific duties and responsibilities. Therefore, property rights cannot give the right to disregard the required respect for individuals and for the company's overall stakeholders. In the light of neo-institutional sociology, management with a focus on stakeholders contributes to the institutionalization of ethical norms of concern and respect for the rights of stakeholders as fundamental to corporate culture.

However, the question of the definition of stakeholder status in relation to reflections on corporate governance and CSR is further complicated when we must analyze the various dimensions of stakeholder status. The problem is whether one can distinguish among instrumental, normative and descriptive elements of stakeholder theories when relevant stakeholders need to be identified (Donaldson & Preston, 1995). Instrumental stakeholder theory does not necessarily go beyond the traditional business model but makes the company's interest in profit maximization the basis of the analysis (Jones, 1995). Descriptive stakeholder theory merely identifies groups or individuals that can actually be termed stakeholders based on the current definition, without making any ethical prioritization of those stakeholders. However, the normative theory goes further and includes beyond the description of the actual stakeholders the question of why certain people or groups should be considered by the company for the purpose of CSR and corporate governance, and the normative theory also seeks to answer the question, about who really counts as the company's stakeholders.

Mitchell, Agle and Wood have in a very important article "Toward a Theory of Stakeholder Identification and Salience: Defining the Principle of Who and What Really Counts" offered a proposal for both a descriptive and a normative determination of stakeholder status, which in my opinion can very well be used as a basis for integrating stakeholder theory into CSR and corporate governance. This approach is about how managers should relate and prioritize between different stakeholder requirements. Mitchell, Agle and Wood try to come up with a definition of "Stakeholder Salience" ("The degree to which managers give priority to competing stakeholder claims"), that is, how the company should formulate its strategy in relation to stakeholders and concretely prioritize between different stakeholders. The theory is not only descriptive but also instrumental and normative to the extent that it goes beyond just determining the relevant stakeholders. It is argued that there are three perceptions of prioritization between stakeholders (Stakeholder Salience), which are pervasive in the stakeholder theory, and which must be perceived as relevant to include in the definition of stakeholders: (1) The stakeholder's power to influence the company, (2) the legitimacy of the stakeholder's relationship with the company and (3) the urgent nature of the stakeholder's claims against the company (Urgency). Mitchell, Agle and Wood emphasize that the differences in stakeholder theory do not so much concern the determination of actual stakeholders. There is broad agreement on the distinction between a limited and extended determination of relevant stakeholders, and most admit that it is difficult to establish once and for all who the company's stakeholders are. It is in CSR and corporate governance in a complex globalized society that many different and often unexpected individuals, groups and institutions can become relevant as stakeholders (Mitchell et al., 1997, p. 855). A company that acts inclusively in relation to its stakeholders works to define its stakeholders in order to improve its activities and its relationships with the environment.

In continuation of this attempt to define relevant prerequisites for prioritization between stakeholders in corporate governance, we can highlight the following groups that should be involved in CSR and corporate governance in the company: (1) Investors and shareholders who contribute to the company's financial activities; (2) managers who are responsible for the company's strategy and day-to-day management; (3) employees who contribute to production with their labor; (4) business partners that the company works with; (5) customers who guarantee the company's existence; (6) the local community, which supports and benefits from the company's activities; (7) civil society, including NGOs and political organizations in the local community; and (8) the environment, including consideration for future generations, animals and nature and their representatives between different lobby groups and organizations. Based on this broad definition of the company's potential stakeholders, it can be argued that it is impossible to take into account so many different groups and that it is, therefore, impossible to define a broad area of responsibility for the company. In addition, the interests of the various groups pose a potential conflict, making it impossible to reach agreement between these groups because they represent different and conflicting interests.

In response to this objection, it can be emphasized that reports and evaluation of strategic management in relation to stakeholders must be included in good corporate governance. Stakeholder dialogue is about the company's increasing self-observation and reflectivity, but this does not necessarily imply respect for the interests of all stakeholder groups. It is an unfinished process that strives to involve all the interests represented by the various groups that make up the company's stakeholders. Thus, we have not yet fully answered the question of what is important to include when managers have to choose between different stakeholder requirements. Here we can detect an initial vagueness in the stakeholder concept, which also lies in Freeman's definition. This broad definition leaves many things to the decision of the individual companies. This was perhaps to a lesser extent the case with the original Stanford Institute definition of the stakeholder concept of 1963, which defined stakeholders as the groups as an "[o]rganization is dependent on its continued survival." Here again, we encounter the dilemma between working with a broad or a narrow definition of the company's stakeholders. But perhaps this distinction between broad and limited stakeholders forms the basis of the divide between primary and secondary stakeholders, which helps to make Freeman's definition of the stakeholder concept applicable to strategic management. It can be argued here that a narrow definition of stakeholders is important, because then only stakeholders who have a direct connection with the company are included. This approach is based first and foremost on the company's basic economic interests, and only then comes the social and political definition of the stakeholders.

A further issue that Mitchell, Agle and Wood highlight as an element that complicates the discussion of the stakeholder concept is the problem of the relationship between those who demand something of the company without having any particular power and those who influence the company as important to determine how to prioritize between stakeholders (Claimants versus Influencers). Signing up with requirements in relation to the company does not necessarily mean that you have an important influence in the company. Therefore, many companies tend to highlight stakeholders by force rather than those who believe that they have legitimate demands that the company must take certain considerations into account. Furthermore, the distinction between current and potential stakeholders can be mentioned as something that should be considered. Here we must not forget the meaning of the so-called sleeping stakeholders. Current stakeholders may be less important than potential stakeholders because potential stakeholders have far more power and influence over the company. In this context, both common power and common influence of the interests must be mentioned as part of the determination of their status as stakeholders. When choosing between these different considerations, power and legitimacy become the most important criteria for prioritization between stakeholders (Mittchell et al., 1997, p. 862).

Identifying the relevant stakeholders is thus one of the most important aspects of strategic management in CSR and corporate governance. In this context, economic and political power is an extremely important criterion for choosing between relevant stakeholders. This is in line with a transaction cost theory about companies (Williamson). The behaviorist conceptions of the company do not emphasize so much the formal economic conditions as the real political conditions as determining the understanding of the power of the stakeholders (March). The neo-institutional theory goes further in this context when it considers organizations as open systems, which means that greater emphasis is placed on legitimacy in determining stakeholder status. Therefore, it can be argued that "[l]egitimate stakeholders are the one that really counts" because leaders operate in a socially constructed world where illegitimacy leads to "isomorfish pressure" on organizations operating outside the established norms (Mittchell et al., 1997, p. 864). Stakeholders gain importance based on the company's organizational ecology. But according to Mitchell, Agle and Wood, this is also one of the reasons why Urgency (urgent work on the organization) becomes central as part of the definition of stakeholder status. When a stakeholder becomes intrusive, it becomes particularly important for corporate governance and CSR.

The consideration for the power of the stakeholders can be justified based on the company's search for influence, which is based on the company's utilitarian interest in survival, which makes it necessary to deal with external coercion. Legitimacy is also associated with power but, at the same time, expresses a broader consideration that refers to the groups and people who are important to society as a whole. Legitimate stakeholders are thus central to the authority of the company. Here, Mitchell, Agle and Wood refer to Suchman's definition of legitimacy, which determines legitimacy as a generalized ability to respond to the expectations of the outside world: "Perception or assumption that the actions of an entity are desirable, proper, or appropriate within some socially constructed system of norms, values, beliefs, and definitions." But it also means that the legitimacy of the stakeholders is difficult to define, and it must be determined based on various individual and organizational considerations. The same applies to the definition of the urgent stakeholders. Here it is important to point out that the intensity of different stakeholder requirements varies over time, and this necessarily affects the prioritization of the different stakeholders. Different stakeholder requirements mean that a well-founded strategy for CSR and corporate governance must always be able to analyze the relationship between relevant stakeholders and thus continuously ask the question of "[t]he principles of who and what really counts depend on the interests and perceptions of managers" (Mittchell et al., 1997, p. 872).

The tension among the stakeholders' power, legitimacy and pressure on the company forms the basis for Mitchell, Agle and Wood's bid for a typology of relevant stakeholders: (1) Dormant stakeholders, (2) discretionary stakeholders, (3) demanding stakeholders, (4) dominant stakeholders, (5) dangerous stakeholders, (6) dependent stakeholders, (7) definitive stakeholders; but we can also mention (8) nonstakeholders and not least (9) latent stakeholders (Latent Stakeholders), which are not currently considered important for the company but not least can be important in the future.

This typology expresses an important systematization of the relevant stakeholder requirements for stakeholders who must decide who and what should mean something to the company. It is a good idea to integrate CSR and corporate governance in relation to stakeholder theory as an expression of the company's ability to respond to societal issues (Corporate Performance and Corporate Social Responsiveness) (Frederick, 1994). The consequence is that a normative core can be pointed out in stakeholder theory, as has been emphasized by various theorists prominent in the stakeholder approach. According to Mitchell, Agle and Wood, this normative core can be defined as follows: "Power and urgency must be attended to if managers are to serve the legal and moral interests of legitimate stakeholders" (Mitchell et al., 1997).

There is thus a close connection between legitimacy, influence and power and the pressure that the individual stakeholders put on the company when it comes to prioritizing between considerations. Therefore, stakeholder theory is an important tool for improving CSR and corporate governance because it helps to make decisions much more strategically sound. In addition to this, however, as already mentioned, it is important to emphasize that the stakeholder theory also needs a direction that goes beyond the isolated prioritization of individual interests. Strategic management with a focus on stakeholders is also about finding a solution that everyone can vouch for. With this, we can arrive at a justice-oriented element of the stakeholder theory that combines its instrumental, descriptive and normative elements as a basis for CSR and corporate governance.

7.5 Fairness as a basic principle of justice in CSR and corporate governance

The ultimate benchmark for a prioritization between stakeholders who influence and are influenced by the organization can, in the ethical normative sense, be determined as reasonableness in the treatment of their requirements. Reasonableness can be conceptualized by the Fairness principle, which helps to establish a close connection among CSR, corporate governance and the good citizenship of the company. The principle of fairness means that the stakeholder analysis is based on a fair and impartial treatment of the company's stakeholders. But what does Fairness and Reason mean concretely in an organizational context? Here we can find important insights from Robert Philips in *Stakeholder Theory and Organizational Ethics* (2003) (Philips, 2003).

John Rawls' political theory provides a good basis for understanding business as a good citizen of an orderly democratic society. Rawls' theory of Justice as Fairness was first and foremost developed in *A Theory of Justice* (1971). In this book, Rawls defends a conception of Justice as Fairness based on two principles of justice that underlie the basic structure of society. These two principles are (1) political freedom for all citizens. (2) The principle of difference, which states that social inequality can only be justified if it is in favor of the most disadvantaged in society. The principle of difference can serve as Rawls' justification of freedom and equality in a free market economy, because it can be said to contribute to the welfare and rising income of the most disadvantaged. In the context of the present presentation, we share Rawls' view that, although it is quite difficult to determine in what circumstances inequality can be justified, we cannot avoid the fact that the free-market economy contributes to the disadvantaged up from the wave of prosperity. Following the communitarian critique, however, it can be emphasized that Rawls cannot work with an isolated free-floating subject but has to integrate his principles of justice into a broader understanding of the self as a participant in society. This is the basis on which Rawls can justify his principles of justice. There is also reason why Rawls in *Political Liberalism* (1992) has reformulated his theory of justice with concepts of "Overlapping Consensus" between "Comprehensive Doctrines" and as "A Political View on Justice," which is not completely determined by a rational metaphysics. When we argue here for "Justice as Fairness" as a basis for stakeholder dialogue, we let ourselves be determined first and foremost by the late Rawls' new interpretation of justice as in Rawls (2001): *Justice as Fairness: A Restatement,* Harvard University Press, Cambridge, Massachusetts. In this work, Rawls defines Justice as Fairness as a political concept for a democratic society (p. 21), which develops a "System of Fair Cooperation," which is based on "A Reasonable Overlapping Consensus" (p. 33). The two principles of justice thus serve as the basis for background institutions in an orderly society.

Philips combines stakeholder theory with Harvard professor John Rawls' moral philosophy and political theory in his effort to define the foundation of organizational ethics. It is an effort to transfer the principle of fairness from political philosophy and democracy theory to organizational theory. The concept of Justice as Fairness contributes to the foundation of CSR and corporate governance as a fundamental management principle for the legitimate treatment of stakeholders. As an ideal for justice in the organization, Fairness helps to choose among the normative constitutive stakeholders, that is, the narrowly defined core stakeholders, on the one hand, and the derived and more broadly defined stakeholders, on the other. In addition, the company's openness to nonstakeholders and new potential stakeholders is very important to take into account (Philips, 2003).

In the light of considerations of CSR and corporate governance, we can emphasize that stakeholder theory must be part of the effort to seek convergence over time for all stakeholder requirements, which are expressed in the concept of sustainable development. Arguing for Fairness as a basis for fair treatment of stakeholders in the light of CSR and corporate governance does not necessarily mean that all stakeholders should be treated equally, but rather that there should be a minimum of Fairness in decision-making procedures for corporate decisions. In continuation of Philips, it can, therefore, be emphasized that a simple egalitarian interpretation of Fairness would be wrong.

Fairness as a basis for prioritization between stakeholders is based on equal and fair treatment in the decision-making process and not primarily on equality in the distribution of services and goods from the company. We, therefore, agree with Philips when he argues that radical changes in business law and in the place of the company in society are not necessary for a stakeholder theory that forms the basis of good corporate governance. However, we do not agree with Philips when he says that the concept of stakeholder should not be interpreted as broadly as is sometimes done in politics, for example, when Tony Blair, inspired by Anthony Giddens, had started talking about a "Stakeholder Economy" (Philips, 2003, p. 32). Why, however, be so reluctant with a broad application of the stakeholder concept? Why not create as broad a legitimacy basis as possible for the company's actions by considering a wide range of stakeholders? The broad horizon for stakeholder theory is precisely one of the strengths of a theory that strives to describe the company's position in a comprehensive social network.

Conversely, it is important to state that stakeholder theory is in principle open to various substantial moral beliefs. Following on from Rawls and Freeman, we can emphasize with Philips that stakeholder theory should definitely not be considered as a Comprehensive Moral Doctrine but as a procedure by which the company can address legitimate claims from stakeholders with different degrees of power and urgency (Goodpaster, 1991). Openness to stakeholders is therefore a way of considering the obligations of organizations toward various agents and constituents in society. In the light of Rawls' political philosophy, an organization is a voluntary association (Voluntary Association) and as such is not part of the basic structure of society (Rawls, 1971). This perspective implies that it is not the whole of society that is interested, even though the company has social obligations that go beyond the obligations to their shareholders. This combines business ethics and political theory. By applying the wisdom of Rawls' theory of justice to the theory of organization and in relation to business, it becomes possible to make sense of Rawls' concepts of "The Original Position," "The Veil of Ignorance" and the Difference Principle within organizational theory (Philips, 2003, p. 49).

In continuation of Freeman, Philips and Rawls, we can, therefore, argue that the moral core of stakeholder theory, which follows from the principle of difference, is that Justice as Fairness in organizational theory implies that constitutive stakeholders such as shareholders, customers, suppliers, employees and the local community must be treated equally and fairly and that inequality can only be justified if it demonstrably improves the conditions of the most disadvantaged in society (Freeman, 1994). Philips argues against Freeman, which does not make a distinction between "Organizational Membership" and "Citizenship" and, at the same time, claims that we can justify a greater internal inequality in the organization than we would normally recognize as acceptable in political matters in society. In contrast to this position, we can maintain that if we apply the Rawlsian concept of Justice as Fairness to organizations, we can only justify a large degree of inequality on the basis of the "principle of difference." This is the consequence of the realization of CSR and corporate governance in relation to the company understood as a moral agent. We agree with those who claim that it is in fact possible to apply the principle of difference in relation to economic markets and that Fairness also applies directly in relation to the company's stakeholders.

This means that a company's constitutive stakeholders must be perceived as participants in an "Original Position," where by rational consideration behind the veil of ignorance (they do not know their personal position in the future company), they are thought to have chosen the principles and the fundamental freedoms and the principle of difference as the basis for organizational justice defined on the basis of Fairness (Rawls, 1971). This perspective implies that themes concerning political and moral rights are introduced as a basis for understanding the company's constituents. This raises the difficult question of justifying the absence of political democracy in the company, which is often led by professional leaders with top-down management of the company's strategy and values. This inequality can be justified on the basis of the principle of difference, which expresses the need for economic efficiency for growth and prosperity in society. At the same time, this expresses an argument against the so-called Stakeholder paradox, which states that an organization cannot have priority duties (Fiduciary Duties) to constituents other than shareholders and owners, because it would make the concept about "Fiduciary Duty" meaningless. If we look at the organization in the light of Rawls' theory of rational determination of fundamental principles of justice behind the veil of ignorance, it becomes possible to perceive the company's obligations in a broader perspective, where it is necessary to relate to a plurality of priority duties (Multitude of Fiduciary Duties) if we are to realize Justice as Fairness through CSR and corporate governance.

This means that the application of the principle of Justice as Fairness as a basis for ethically correct action in organizations and in economic markets can be concretized by means of the concept of orderliness in business or "Fair Play." Philips explores the roots of the concept of "Fair Play," which goes back to John Stuart Mill, and expresses a cooperative interaction with other people, which creates new obligations for cooperation and moral responsibility. In an ethical sense, the consideration for "Fair Play" thus expresses an ethical response to the challenge of opportunism. According to Philips, the concept of "Fair Play" was already developed in John Rawls' early articles when he argued that "Fair Play" is a common advantage and creates a basis for fair competition and cooperation between persons who allow their freedom to be restricted by organizations or by economic markets. Under these conditions, an obligation arises to cooperate for the benefit of all. We can thus claim that Justice as Fairness is expressed in a duty to "Fair Play" and implies a responsibility to cooperate for the common good and for equality when dealing with the demands of the various stakeholders. Justice as Fairness, therefore, implies a mutual commitment to work for the common interests, and this is central to the use of stakeholder management as a basis for corporate governance and CSR.

On this basis, management with a focus on stakeholders can be seen as an attempt to address social expectations of the company's good citizenship and as an expression of the company's efforts to contribute to promoting the common good in society. But stakeholder theory also becomes legitimate in the perspective of strategic management because stakeholders have legitimate demands to be treated fairly and equitably by their organizations and companies. Different groups of stakeholders are legitimate stakeholders if they have well-founded rights to be treated fairly and equitably by the organization. In accordance with the company's good citizenship, it is necessary that the considerations of sustainability, CSR and corporate governance are recognized as a basis for fair treatment of all interests. It may be that stakeholders who do not have a direct affiliation with the company and therefore do not have an obvious normative legitimacy and obligation of the company as core constituents, nevertheless, have a clearly formulated requirement to be taken into account. Therefore, in continuation of Philips, we can emphasize that civil society organizations and social activists may have legitimate demands in relation to the company, provided that they can at some point assert themselves as the company's core constituents, for example, employees, customers or representatives of the local community (Philips, 2003, p. 152).

7.6 Toward fairness governance in organizations

When we apply the stakeholder theory's principles of fairness and fair play in relation to stakeholders, they become expressions of the realization of CSR and corporate governance. Capitalist economic markets depend on responsibility and justice as external determinants to the same extent as they can be determined by economic morality, the rule of law and ethical principles. In this context, company ethics guidelines and codes of conduct will constitute an important framework for "Fair Play" in the economic market. The task is to make them normative standards of conduct in institutions and organizations so that we can justify the legitimacy of economic markets. This constitutes the market institutional realization of CSR and corporate governance.

In this context, we have emphasized that Justice as Fairness provides the necessary framework for making CSR responsible management with a focus on stakeholders, which is the background for an increased ability to relate to society's expectations of the company. This is an important way of turning the debate on CSR away from abstract discussions toward specifically meeting the societal challenges for the company. This is the background for realizing CSR and corporate governance in the company's daily context. Here, stakeholder theory concretizes the company's ability to enter into dialogue with society and thus prove itself as a good citizen through ethical principles, respect for human rights and professional business ethics. Thus, an interest-based approach to CSR and corporate governance provides a case-oriented focus on the company's ability to deal with actual societal issues. Against this background, the stakeholder theory can be used as a basis for an actual realization of CSR and corporate governance in strategic management. This approach to CSR can be considered practical and action oriented, because it is about the company's practical contribution to society in its core strategy instead of just talking about it (Walk the Talk). Everything must be left not only to governments and legislators but also to the concrete responsibility of companies to contribute to social improvements.

This theoretical discussion of the relationship among CSR, corporate governance and stakeholder theory should have helped to clarify the basis for analysis and decision-making in concrete matters. Here it is important to state that principles of justice are applied differently in relation to different organizational aspects. Here, the stakeholder analysis contributes to the creation of legitimacy when crises arise in the company both internally and externally in relation to external expectations of companies. The stakeholder analysis comes with a specification of various requirements in relation to the company's specific problems with a view to improving strategy and implementing values through CSR and corporate governance.

In order to explain how to communicate between different stakeholder considerations, we can finally highlight the leader's judgment, practical reason and wisdom as a basis for joint action as well as good and right decisions (Paine, 1994). The importance of judgment in management with a focus on stakeholders contributes to realizing the various stakeholder requirements in the best possible way, which converges over time toward a common notion of the good for the company. Thus, good leadership is an expression of an ability to ensure that stakeholders' interests converge over time, cf. the quote from Freeman that "[s]takeholder concerns go together over time." The leader's ability to reflect and take a critical stance is an essential part of strategic management. This can help to implement the ethics of CSR and corporate governance through the stakeholder dialogue (Bonnafous-Boucher & Rendtorff, 2016a, 2016b, 2016c, 2016d, 2016e, 2016f). The concepts of sustainability, responsibility and fairness, and also the consideration for the community, thus become practical guidelines for leadership in complex societies. Thus, Justice as Fairness as a basis for strategic management, based on stakeholder dialogue, is of central importance for the realization of corporate governance and CSR in modern companies. This is also essential for management of hospitals and other health care organizations.

8 Health care organization ethics and ethical values in hospital management

8.1 Toward a system of bioethics and biolaw in hospital organizations

On the basis of the bioethics and biolaw of principles in relation to the theory of corporate social responsibility, sustainability and stakeholder management, we can propose a system of hospital ethics in hospital organizations (Jørgensen & Rendtorff, 2018; Jørgensen, Rendtorff, & Holen, 2018; Rendtorff, 1998, 2002a, 2003, 2008, 2014a, 2015c; Rendtorff & Kemp, 2009). This system is based on the principles of sustainability, respect for human autonomy, dignity, integrity and vulnerability in the context of business ethics and corporate social responsibility (CSR). The argument is that it is necessary to focus on the concept of organization in health care ethics if we want to have a comprehensive and holistic understanding of ethical problems in hospitals (Spencer, Mills, Rorty, & Werhane, 2000). Accordingly, we will later also need to work out the institutional implications of major ethical theories like consequentialism, deontology and virtue ethics. Research on ethics committees needs to investigate the organizational implications of these committees. Moreover, ethical practice has been restricted to clinical dimensions centered around interpersonal physician-patient encounters. The possible influences of ethics committees on organizational behavior and institutional structures need to be analyzed in the perspective of bioethics and biolaw. In order to clarify these relations, it is necessary to analyze the function of ethics committees in health care organizations with theoretical and practical focus on stakeholder management (Bonnafous-Boucher & Rendtorff, 2016a, 2016b, 2016c, 2016d, 2016e, 2016f).

Indeed, general organization theory and practice have emphasized the need for organizational ethics (French, 1984; Paine, 1994). Ethics programs and ethical leadership are promoted by many hospital organizations. Sometimes, clinical ethics committees have been involved in these programs. But, in many cases, initiatives do not involve ethics committees, and there is no collaboration between different ethics groups. In order to prevent this lack of communication, we will argue that ethics committees represent important instances for improving and institutionalizing bioethics and biolaw in hospital

DOI: 10.4324/9781003147848-8

organizations. We should not forget the importance of ethics committees for efficient ethics programs in hospitals. However, it is not always clear how we can integrate the different dimensions of ethics.

Therefore, this chapter discusses the place of ethics committees in relation to different kinds of compliance programs and organizational ethics initiatives in hospitals (Rendtorff, 2001, 2002a, 2002b, 2002c). The problem is how we can give meaning to ethics committees within the dominating theories of organizational management in hospitals, including systems management, total quality management, behavioral management, benchmarking or different initiatives for values-driven management in hospital organizations. We think that the function of ethics committees should not be restricted to clinical issues but should include the institutional and organizational dimensions of ethics (Spencer et al., 2000). In order to develop this argument, we will first define the relation between health care and organization theory. Then we will show how recent changes and problems in modern hospital organizations have increased the need for bioethics and biolaw and values to improve quality of care in health care organizations. Moreover, different types and positions of ethics committees in hospital organizations are discussed. Thus, we will investigate the relation between ethics committees and hospital management. We think that ethics committees are good models for different kinds of compliance and quality- and values-driven management. In fact, ethics programs may not be efficient without ethics committees. These contain the ideals of ethical competence and reflection that are needed in organization ethics programs. In shaping values-driven management on the model of ethics committees, we can increase communication and dialog at many levels of hospital organizations.

Clinical ethics in hospital organizations relates to the norms and values that guide physicians, nurses and other health care personnel when dealing with patients in the daily clinical work. The norms of clinical ethics guide medical practice and health care. This includes protective responsibility of physicians toward patients where respect of a patient's human dignity cannot be ignored. Thus, there are significant organizational factors that influence the formation of clinical ethics in hospital organizations (Rendtorff, 2001, 2002a, 2002b, 2002c). The effort to integrate ethics in teaching and professional education of health personnel is very important. Here, we might consider the hospital staff of members of a learning organization and reflect on how the learning potential of the hospital organization might be used more efficiently. In many contexts nurses and physicians have set up systems for teaching ethics and developing ethical awareness in the daily practice of the hospital organizations. This contributes to the awareness of ethics problems and dimensions, both at the collective and at the individual levels in hospital organizations.

Moreover, clinical ethics should not only be understood in the framework of the physician-patient relation but also be considered as an organizational problem of leadership and hospital management. Today, most hospitals around are aware of the necessity of values-driven management, stakeholder management and the need for values at the high executive level of hospital management. Many hospitals have worked with different models of values-driven management in order to improve their organization. This work cannot ignore the problems of bioethics and medical ethics. Therefore, hospital management contributes to some of the functions that should have been filled out by a system of hospital ethics committees.

Thus, when we discuss the different clinical aspects of hospital management, we should not ignore this informal ethics of protective responsibility of physicians, nurses and health care personnel (Hildebrandt & Schultz, 1997). This is very important as a basis for a more official system of ethics committees in hospitals, including ethics councils, research ethics committees and other official ethics bodies, to develop ethics policies, monitor ethical decision-making, implement guidelines and work for general awareness of ethics in the hospitals and health care organizations. In different parts of the world, it is important that we maintain respect for patient autonomy, dignity, integrity and vulnerability through informed consent and concern for hospital ethics. Here, we can emphasize the importance of the ethical integrity of health care personnel in relation to treatment of a patient. Thus, such an informal culture of ethics development in hospitals and health care organizations is very important.

8.2 Ethics structures supporting ethics in hospitals and health care organizations

Nevertheless, in order to develop bioethics and biolaw in hospitals, it is important to set up a system of ethics structures that supports ethics in hospitals and health care organizations (Spencer et al., 2000). Here, it is necessary to focus on more or less formal and informal institutional and organizational structures that are important for developing ethics structures and systems in hospitals. Important sources for developing bioethics and biolaw are in this context national and international ethics bodies, like national and international ethics councils, like the ethics councils in different countries, of the EU or UNESCO, and the development of different systems of research ethics committees in different countries. In countries where there is a national council of ethics, such a council is very important for creating structured debates and initiatives on bioethics and biolaw. The national councils of ethics integrate bioethics and biolaw with clinical and organization ethics. Together with research ethics committees and clinical ethics committees, national councils of ethics contribute to the development of ethics for physicians, nurses and other workers and professionals in hospital organizations. In many cases this contributes to the dissemination of ethics to the different professional groups of the hospital with integration of ethics in work and education of nurses, physicians and other hospital employees.

Thus, with these formal structures of ethics councils and ethics committees in health care, it is possible to introduce the major positions on ethics into the formulation of ethical principles of hospital work (Rendtorff, 2001, 2002a, 2002b, 2002c). Many professionals argue for a somewhat utilitarian view on ethics facilitating scientific progress and treatment of patients in hospitals. Others focus on a deontological position being critical toward new technologies and caring for human dignity and integrity. In addition, a phenomenological understanding of ethics based on a communicative view of treatment in close connection with an ethics of care can also be found in the work of the ethics councils and ethics committees. Indeed, it is important that ethics councils and ethics committees also have a case-oriented and casuistic approach based on the analysis of different particular bioethical problems in order to develop proposals for action, rules and legislation for development of bioethics and biolaw in hospitals. In these case studies, there are no definite ethical views, but they are dependent on the analysis and decision-making in particular cases. In many cases, the mandates of ethics councils and ethics committees are open, and they help formulating laws and regulations on ethical problems and issues. In this context, it is important that ethics councils and ethics committees contribute to democratization and stakeholder dialog in relation to employees, patients and the general public.

It has been argued that it is important that ethics councils and committees contribute to create debate and awareness in society and hospitals about ethical issues (Rendtorff, 2001, 2002a, 2002b, 2002c). Here, ethics councils have a double function of creating awareness and debate, on the one hand, and contribute to new norms and consensus, on the other hand. In bioethics and biolaw, it is important that ethics councils contribute to find ethical solutions and principles to new problems of medicine and medical technology. In this context, ethics councils and committees create greater awareness about ethical questions, and they contribute to regulate ethics in health care organizations and new technological developments.

The role of ethics committees and councils in society and hospitals has been considered as a way of creating awareness about bioethics and biolaw as an independent topic. It has helped a professional to get awareness about ethics independently of their specific professional orientation. This creates personal awareness and understanding of the role of personal integrity in ethical decision-making. Thus, ethics councils and committees have great impact on clinical ethics in hospital and health care organizations in different ways. Ethics is introduced as a new kind of regulation of medical and clinical ethics. The process has resulted in an awareness of the many different stakeholders in debates on clinical ethics. It involves both users/clients/patients of hospitals and health care systems, workers and professionals and a number of laypeople who are concerned with the developments of medical technologies. When ethics committees create meetings and conferences, they involve different stakeholders. This means that agreements and disagreements among stakeholders are revealed in the activities by ethics councils and ethics committees.

Thus, ethics councils and committees contribute to define different positions on ethics that are relevant for health care organizations. Of particular importance for health care organizations, we can mention respect for autonomy and informed consent, concern for care for the vulnerable patients prioritizing those who really need treatment, a utilitarian and pragmatic outlook ensuring efficiency and equality in treatment, focus on community and protection and respect for the dignity of human life. These ethical values are important in many different fields of clinical ethics. In many countries there are ethical councils, clinical ethics committees and research ethics committees in hospitals and health care organizations. These committees deal with particularly difficult topics of bioethics and biolaw, for example, hospital care for patients, hospital policies, specific procedures in hospitals and health care organizations, new research proposals, new technology, genetics, reproductive technology, genetic manipulation, organ transplantation, euthanasia, pain treatment, general health care ethics and ethics of treatment of patients.

These different understandings of ethics are related to concrete decision-making about cases. This is a matter of reflective judgment. Judgment relates to decision in bioethics and biolaw in hospitals and health care organizations. In this context different dimensions of medical treatment are evaluated in the light of the basic ethical positions. Reflective judgment considers clinical realities in order to formulate a clear connection among diagnosis, therapy, prognosis and treatment. It considers the patient in the tension between person and object in order to formulate the right connection between ethics and medical treatment. This need for reflective judgment is stressed by the lack of ethics committees in the hospitals. In this situation, physicians have greater personal responsibility with reflective judgment for making correct decisions.

The need for ethics council and ethics committees in hospital and health care organizations is often debated critically in many countries. It is emphasized that there is an important need for protection of patients in clinical realities. In addition, many people stress problems of communication between physicians and patients. The arrogance of the medical profession contributed to larger distance between medical professionals and health care workers as well as health care professionals. The need for ethical education at both individual and organizational levels is mentioned by many as a way of improving the role of clinical ethics in hospital decision-making.

In addition to ethics councils and ethics committees, the framework for bioethics and biolaw in many countries around the globe suggests emphasizing research ethics committees as important for the development of ethics. The global need for research ethics committees in medical systems was established by the Helsinki Declaration on protection of human beings in biomedical research. A system of research ethics committees is proposed in order to make a deontological respect for patients' rights and autonomy an important part of ethics in hospital. Such a system of research ethics committees proposes informed consent as a primary tool for protection of research subjects in medical research. It is important that a system of research ethics committees is well organized with participation of physicians, other professionals and laypeople. The system is based on a judicial understanding of review of research protocols, and it follows general legal requirements when looking at research proposals. With such a system of ethics committees, the law can be said to be a move toward integrating ethical considerations in clinical considerations of medical research. The framework of the law contributes to procedural installation of autonomy and "informed consent" as key terms for clinical ethics. The establishment of a system of research ethics committees will have an important influence on general protection of informed consent in clinical reality. Nevertheless, there is also a possible danger of such a system of research ethics committees with regard to the concept of ethics. The isolation of research ethics committees from the clinical reality in their form of legal instruments in the framework of the legal system can paradoxically be said to open up for a lack of formalized ethics in the clinical reality because ethics is dealt with in the research ethics committee.

8.3 Professional and organizational learning

Ethics councils and ethics committees are examples of external systems influencing the formation of clinical ethics in hospitals and health care organizations. Such formalized systems do not exist internally as a part of the organizational structure of the hospital (Hounsgaard & Eriksen, 2000). The ethics discourse has, however, had an impact on organization of hospitals and health care institutions. A very striking feature of this is the increased significance of professional and organizational learning in different hospitals. Professional caregivers are in many cases aware of the necessity of integrating education in ethics in the curricula for health personnel. Nurses, physicians and other members of the care- giving team are getting knowledge of ethics in their basic education and in education offered to increase their professional competence once they are working in the hospitals.

Ethics education is today integrated in theoretical and practical teaching and development of competencies of action and judgment of health care professionals, nurses and therapists. But there is also an understanding of the need to educate and teach the patient/clients or users of the hospitals. It is very important to conceive the acquirement of ethics competencies as a matter of organizational learning. Here, it is not only health care professionals but also all members of the organization who participate in the organization's learning practices in order to improve different practices and functions.

Conceiving the hospital as a learning organization can be done in the framework of a number of different theories of learning. The necessity of teamwork in a highly technically sophisticated environment makes organizational learning a matter of increased reflection (Easterby-Smith, Snell, & Gherardi, 1998). Theories of knowledge management emphasize the social character of knowledge. The emergence of ethics is a part of the social construction of knowledge in organization. Theories of knowledge management state that creation of knowledge happens in an interaction between individuals and organizations. A hospital is a knowledge-intensive organization, and ethics can be understood as an important kind of practical knowledge, which should be generated in organizational interaction.

In the perspective of theories of knowledge management, the informal ethics of protective responsibility and respect for patient dignity can be conceived as unspoken tacit knowledge related to particular individuals in organizations. It can be argued that it is the aim of organizational learning and knowledge creation to make such tacit ethical knowledge explicit in order to use it in the treatment and care processes. The discussions of ethical learning aim at institutionalizing ethical reflection as a part of organizational behavior reflection (Easterby-Smith et al., 1998).

In this process of developing a reflective and organizational perspective on ethics, the great variety of practically oriented theories of organizational learning can be used to understand the importance of education for developing clinical ethics in hospitals. The education in ethics improves organizational culture. Organizational learning is a process that relies on the collective dimensions of the organization (Spencer et al., 2000). We can distinguish between different levels of reflections on organizational practice. "Single loop" learning evaluates possibilities of action in perspectives of already-existing structures. "Double loop" learning represents a deeper perspective of change that questions the structures in themselves. In the education and development of clinical ethics based on reflective judgment, as well "single loop" and "double loop learning," putting both daily practices and whole organizational settings into reflective analysis are relevant dimensions in order to increase ethical understandings and collaborations among members of the organization (Hounsgaard & Eriksen, 2000).

The necessity of considering learning of ethics competencies on the organizational level becomes clear by the fact that the professional health care worker does not only need a personal intellectual competence. Organizational learning is linked to knowledge management of advanced knowledge organizations (Nonaka, 1994). He or she should also be able to take part in social groups or communities of practice in a hospital setting, which requires many different competencies. The individual learning process placed in the organizational context is a situated learning, in which personal development takes place in interaction with environment. In this context the social group works at developing common intellectual capacities at the organizational level.

Leading members of health care teams have important responsibilities for developing the capacities of ethical reasoning and ethical competencies among the members of the health care teams. In a changing health care system, ethical competence is rather an ability to exercise judgment with accuracy and to act rightly in new and unforeseen situations (Hounsgaard & Eriksen, 2000). Competencies in ethics are closely related to professional abilities of caregivers of both intellectual and care related dimensions. The leader of the health care team should help to increase the ethical learning of the professionals in order to develop these competencies. The specific character of the ethics of learning how to care has been less emphasized in most literature of education of nurses and physicians. Education has centered on acquirement of specific professional and scientific knowledge. In order to improve clinical ethics, many nursing schools and universities have recently been aware of specific dimensions of learning how to care. Caring requires several emotional, intellectual and practical competencies that should be acquired in a specific learning process. The ethical dimensions of care are dependent on knowledge and experience of health care professionals. But care also requires its own reality, and this should be made clear in the teaching of clinical ethics to health care personnel.

At the same time, teaching clinical ethics should focus on reasons and issues rather than on motives, morals and emotions of individuals. This is due to the sensible character of the issues of the problems of clinical ethics. A key value in clinical ethics is respect for integrity of patients. There is an "untouchable" zone of wholeness constituting the personality of individuals. The educator should teach health care professionals to make respect for integrity basic to treatment. But education itself is also committed to respect for what is untouchable in each individual. Education cannot violate this strong moral principle of respect for integrity. Therefore, the educator should focus on integrity in the process of learning clinical ethics.

Respect for integrity is very important when patients are included in the learning process (Paine, 1994). Clinical ethics also plays a part in patient education. In the treatment process, health care professionals should inform, guide and educate patients. Patient education and information about ethical issues are very important. Patient education should be involved in all the dimensions of clinical treatment and care. This does not exclude that there is a specific logic and argumentation in patient education. We should not forget that the patient is a weak situation that has a special demand on the teachers' and caregivers' responsibilities. A further part of patient education concerns preventive medicine in order to make citizens work with their own protection of their health.

Education in clinical ethics differs from scientific learning in medicine and nursing sciences by using ordinary language rather than highly scientific terms. Ordinary language is close to the phenomenological experience of clinical reality and helps revealing the many dimensions of this context for ethical reflection. In order to make clinical ethics a part of care education in ordinary language, it is directed toward the improvement of the judgmental capacities of individuals. The humanistic ideal of enlightenment, which is "general education," is of major significance in order to increase the ethical competence of health care professionals. General education and will to learn about ethics are ideals for clinical ethics in the hospital. Teaching of ethics is based on a general will to acquire knowledge of other than the purely scientific aspects of hospital practice.

Learning of clinical ethics in hospital is not only a matter of theoretical learning by external educators or team discussions among health care professionals. It is important not to forget informal transmission of knowledge among older, experienced caregivers and younger, inexperienced workers. Modern institutions seem to ignore the irreplaceable function of the transmission of ethical knowledge in an individualized learning process where the learner learns everything from the close relation to the master in the field

(Nonaka, 1994). New theories of education stress the significance of this way of learning. Capacities to exercise judgment and openness for the many aspects of tacit knowledge are learned in this process, which goes on in many practices and working communities in hospitals. Many practical capacities are exclusively transmitted to new professionals in close relations to experienced health care workers, nurses or physicians. Ethical competencies in clinical settings in hospitals are, therefore, not only functions of theoretical knowledge but also consequences of practice. It involves the capacity to react to very different social situations. There might be a conflict between theoretical presuppositions and practical knowledge. Reflection and judgmental exercise include capacity of developing professional knowledge. In this way, ethics is an integral part of health care workers' professional capacities.

8.4 From organizational learning to health care organization ethics

Ethics committees and organizational learning provide us with the basis for organization ethics in health care as the basis for responsible governance of hospitals and health care organizations in the framework of bioethics and biolaw. Research on governance and organization in health care organizations focuses on ethical problems and immoral behavior in both public and private hospitals and health care organizations. Organizational governance in health care deals with general ethical issues of responsible governance that is broader than legal ethics restricted to problems of compliance with the law (Spencer et al., 2000). The need for organizational governance of health care organizations is combined with ethics programs and values-driven management in many public and private organizations around the world. Organizational governance ethics aims at ensuring compliance and development of ethics programs in order to ensure ethical responsibility in hospitals and health care organizations in order to show their willingness to collaborate with the authorities and to be good and responsible citizens.

In this context, the organizational ethics in hospitals and health care organizations is combined with business ethics and professional ethics (Rendtorff, 2001, 2002a, 2002b, 2002c). Many countries have established procedures and structures to deal with organizational wrongdoing. In the United States, the 1991 Federal Sentencing Guidelines for Organizations define conditions for organizational responsibility and how criminal organizations can be prosecuted. These guidelines specify that organizations should set up compliance and ethics programs in order to avoid criminal actions. If organizations follow these conditions, they show their willingness to collaborate with the authorities and to be good and responsible citizens. Therefore, organizations with ethics programs may have a change of a reduction of their punishment in case of being prosecuted and sentenced for a criminal offense. Indeed, the U.S. Federal Sentencing Guidelines consider the organization as a "moral person" (French, 1984; Paine, 1994).

In Europe, different forms of political pressure have increased awareness of organizational social responsibility and challenges of organizations to act like good and virtuous citizens. Many governments want businesses to take their part of social responsibility in society. Private and public companies cannot be neutral with regard to the problems of community, and they have to contribute to general social welfare. The need for organization ethics is indeed very urgent in biomedicine and, in particular, necessary in relation to development of bioethics and biolaw in hospitals. Because these organizations deal with individual human beings, vulnerable patients, eventual immoral actions may have very harmful consequences. Moreover, in the case of legal prosecutions by patients, hospitals may, if they are declared responsible, have to contribute with huge economic compensation for damage. Therefore, ethical guidelines have been proposed in both European and U.S. health care organizations. This also happens in other parts of the world. What is important about these proposals is that they make a bridge among clinical ethics, biomedical ethics, organization ethics and professional ethics.

Such values-driven management contributes to formulate and clarify ethical principles and values of hospital organizations. Different value statements, mission statements or codes of ethics in hospitals can help to determine issues of administration of hospitals, specific ethical issues in the physician-patient relation and ethical problems among health care professionals – physicians, nurses and other members of the health care teams. Value statements reflect different ethical cultures in particular health care context according to the place of hospitals in society. Private health care organizations in the United States in a profit-based market economy deal with different problems than public state-financed hospitals in Europe. However, in increased complex environments of work, the need for reflective awareness of ethical values is as necessary in public as in private health care organizations. Moreover, many questions of professional ethics depend on the organizational culture and institutional dimensions of the work.

As representatives of an organizational bureaucracy, professionals inhabit roles that structure their treatment of patients that also are ascribed a place in the structure of the organization (Spencer et al., 2000). These role-relationships reflect culture, values and goals of the organization, and people act as members of organizations determined by their structures. Organizations are intentional systems with purposes and goals that, even though they are nothing but the sum of individuals and something more, as a unity are capable of doing good and harm in society. Organizational action reflects a collective decision-making. This influences patient-care decisions and individual actions of professionals. Therefore, because of these actions, which are like intentional actions, it may be argued that organizations are moral agents that can be held accountable and responsible for their actions.

Thus, even though organizations are very different than individuals, they have responsibility like individuals because they are capable of acting intentionally and as agents in community. Organizations acting as a totality develop an institutional practice that, as all other webs of actions, must be able to be evaluated from an ethical point of view. Consequently, integration of organization ethics, patient care ethics and professional ethics in a totality of bioethics and biolaw is very important for developing a responsive, learning and ethical culture in modern hospital organizations. In this perspective, the ultimate goal of organization ethics may be determined as being "integrity" at the organizational level. Organizational integrity should include both clinical ethics dimensions of correct patient-physician relations and professional ethics dimensions of professionalism in daily practice in hospital work. We need to focus on the moral personhood of organizations to ensure ethical responsibility (French, 1984). This increases orientation of health care professionals toward values and rules of professional understanding of good working practice. Rather than being only an individual virtue, organizational integrity characterizes the ability of the organization to act with moral responsibility and honesty at all levels of the organizations. Organizational integrity defines the "wholeness" and coherence of organizational behavior based on codes and values constituting mission and goals of the hospital.

8.5 Organizational complexity in health care organizations

Due to the increasing complexity, health care organizations face a number of challenges. In many countries focus has been put on the organizational structure and leadership of hospitals. Such a quest for ethical hospital management may be documented by describing some of the problems facing modern hospital organizations (Hildebrandt & Schultz, 1997). Indeed, ethical problems in hospitals are not restricted to the one area of the organization. Macro-issues of administration and economic dimensions of organizations influence micro-issues of how patients are treated by physicians and nurses in the hospital. Ethics problems cannot be sufficiently dealt with by focusing exclusively on patient-physician relations of informed consent, truth-telling or treatment decision because many concrete problems are caused by organizational structures. Moreover, conflicts between different professional groups in hospital organizations, concerning work time, quality of work, conflicts of interests, productivity and so forth, cannot be considered in isolation from patient care ethics and hospital organization ethics. Therefore, professional ethics research has been proposed in order to define the best practice of health care professionals. In addition, there is a need to discuss the structure of hospital organizations in order to increase the efficiency and quality of care.

In this context, ethical issues are getting high priority because of a number of ethical problems facing modern health care organizations. In the United States, values-driven management in hospitals faces quite particular problems (Spencer et al., 2000). After years of strong physician paternalism and power over employees and patients, the increased commercialization of health care organizations has changed the picture. Increased costs of health care in private institutions and demands for protection of the weakest citizens have led to proposals for reforms of the health care system. The government has been trying to establish cost efficiency and universal coverage. After the death of these reform proposals, U.S. hospitals are still confronted with problems of how to improve the existing hospital organizations. In this context, a number of management tools, like total quality management, have been proposed. Such a need for values-driven management and compliance programs in hospitals is largely due to the reality of a society with a high degree of litigation. This may be the reason why some programs have been dominated by legal measures being compliance-oriented rather than values-oriented programs of ethics. The situation in European hospitals has been very different due to the traditional public financing of health care organizations. Many hospitals have had a bureaucratic and hierarchical organizational structure with a strict separation between administration and health care units. Moreover, the health care units have been strictly separated according to scientific specialization. In addition, many hospitals have been responsible for similar task without having any sort of formalized collaboration.

These structures do not work very well in a situation with increased pressure on hospital organizations. Organizational problems in hospital management reflect some immanent structures of the organization of health care organizations (Spencer et al., 2000). Many hospitals have experienced different problems in coping with new situations. The challenges reflect very deep changes among different parts of the hospital system. Patients are becoming more demanding. They are aware of their rights, and they consider themselves as consumers or customers rather than thankful subordinates to the charity of the health care personnel. Moreover, patients require treatment for many defects that few years ago would be considered as destiny, for example, fertility problems, cosmetics or sophisticated organ transplants. In addition, hospital employees no longer consider their work as a vocation, and they want better conditions. This can indeed be analyzed as changed demands of legitimacy by society. Therefore, different new forms of management have been proposed.

Requirements of institutional change are responses to new problems of organization in society. Health care organizations experience conflicts among different stakeholders, administration, health care team, patients and others (Spencer et al., 2000). Sincere collaboration between these groups should include open dialog and realistic communication about economic budgets and ethical values. So, hospital organizations are unfortunately full of different and opposing views on this matter. Thus, hospital management is confronted with many paradoxes. In addition, many health care organizations are confronted with a transition process toward modern and more complex, technologically based hospitals. Increased economic pressure on efficient use of resources in hospitals influences the work and the opinions of the health personnel. One of the paradoxes of hospital management can be defined as a "vicious circle" of the oppositions between limited resources and increased demands of efficiency. But we can also mention the high degree of complexity of medical work. Such work requires flexibility, timing, rationality, know-how and intelligence. At the same time, this work should be performed in an efficient organization. In addition, public hospital management is determined by political decision-makers' opinions about adequate resources for the institutions. Moreover, hospital organizations contain several isolated systems of action. Different groups have different responsibilities, and they do not necessarily communicate with one another. Physicians and nurses care about treatment or research, while administrators are concerned about economics and efficient use of resources. Political leaders are only interested in money. At the same time, they want to be respected among their voters, potential patients who would like to stay in good hospitals. Moreover, politicians argue rhetorically for better hospitals while underestimating necessary economic resources. Consequently, the crisis in hospital management is determined by confrontations between very different rationales. We are indeed in search for new structures of leadership that are able to handle these problems. Many different kinds of reforms of hospital management have been proposed in order to avoid the bureaucratic structure of traditional hospitals. In order to succeed, all these forms of management should bridge the gap between different work cultures of the hospital, for example, the opposition between administration, patient culture and the work culture of health care teams. It is required that hospital management increases quality of treatment, efficient use of resources and indeed the human values of hospital treatment. In order to promote these goals, close collaboration among management, administrators and employees is needed. All stakeholders have duties for the improvement of the organization. To enforce such responsibility, management should be based on common values and reinforcement of organizational integrity. Indeed, capacities of dialog with stakeholders, increased organizational learning, capacity of combining service, respect for human dignity and improvement of efficiency without diminishing quality are among the capacities that are requested for modern hospital management.

8.6 From clinical ethics committees to organizational ethics committees

We will now analyze how ethics committees can be very important for developing new ideas for hospital management responding to the crisis of traditional health care organizations (Hildebrandt & Schultz, 1997). A number of different kinds of ethics councils and committees have been set up in hospitals in the United States and Europe and in other parts of the world. Looking at the different kind of ethics committees, we realize that they have had little concern for considering ethical problems in the perspective of organization ethics (Rendtorff, 2001, 2002a, 2002b, 2002c). This is very sad because the evolution of hospital organization requires that ethics committees at different levels are more aware of ethical problems in the framework of hospitals and health care organizations. In most cases there been a strict divide between the work of ethics committees and hospital management. Most committees have not been interested in organizational ethics. The center of focus of clinical ethics committees has been problems of physician-patient relationships. At the level of professional ethics, ethics committees have been committed to find excellence that is the good and virtuous practice of health care professions. As in clinical ethics, issues of professional ethics have been discussed mostly on the model of interpersonal ethics based on the intimate personal encounter.

This lack of perspective is sometimes due to ignorance and inadequate knowledge of organizational problems or even hostility to organization theory among members of ethics committees. Because of little interest in such issues, ethics committees have not been able to understand complicated matters of hospital administration or issues of interaction of hospitals with their social and political environments. The work of ethics committees has, therefore, been rather invisible on the organizational level, and the committees have little influence on management decision-making. However, few reports about interest and work on issues of hospital management in ethics committees do exist. In France, in the system of ethics committees in the Paris region, there has been awareness about organizational dimensions of ethics in order to improve the quality of treatment, but in general public authorities have been responsible for hospital management. In Great Britain, hospital management has in general not been including patients or physicians and other health care personnel. This situation is very similar in many European countries.

In the lack of direct preoccupation with organization ethics, one might still maintain that ethics committees have implicit organizational significance (Rendtorff, 2001, 2002a, 2002b, 2002c). This cannot be denied. Ethics committees as governance and management institutions are important facilitators for developing ethical cultures of hospitals and health care organizations. Patient care ethics committees have already for some time helped to point to the awareness of ethical problems in the patient-physician relation. Research ethics committees contribute to make physicians and researchers reflect on the ethical dimensions of their activities in a way that opens for responsible action. Professional ethics committees should be more frequent in health care organizations because they would indeed be able to focus more deliberately on organizational issues and thereby help to create a culture of communication in the organization.

On this basis, fostering ethics committees in the framework of hospital management might be able to contribute to many different practices in the health care organization. The committees would be able to evaluate decision-making and help to develop management tools for the responsible administrators in health care organizations. They could focus on the importance of having continuing attention to the ethical values of the organization. Ethics committees may also be important for pointing out ethical problems all over the organization. They could help to establish interdisciplinary dialog among different groups of employees in hospitals about values and ethical problems. This includes promotion of respect for patients' rights and awareness of organizational impact on conditions for patients in hospitals.

Thus, ethics committees are very important for good hospital organization. Given this fact, it is paradoxical that they have restricted their activities to interpersonal relations when there are many ethical issues in organization ethics that need to be addressed. Ethics committees, therefore, should focus more on these problems, and administrators should understand that there are many ideas developed within clinical ethics that should be further promoted for the health care organization. The future of ethics committees is a broader scope of application of their activities. This change of perspective does not have to ignore the insights of clinical ethics and different analysis of ethical principles governing patient-physicians' relations. Rather, we need to transform the insights of clinical ethics, so they meaningfully can be applied at the organizational level. We cannot ignore that all ethical problems have organizational dimensions. These should be clarified in order to understand all the dimensions of ethics in health care. Decisions about informed consent, truth, ethical principles and good medical practice in ethics committees have an impact on the structure and culture of the hospital organization. At the same time, many administrative issues of the organization, financial policies, resource allocation, public relations, relations to political decision-makers and so forth cannot avoid to have an impact on the clinical reality of the organization.

Consequently, clinical ethics can no longer be limited to patient-physician ethics nor be considered as a problem among physicians or nurses. Many problems of modern hospitals must be considered at many different levels, and this is only possible if we take the perspective of organizational ethics. However, this perspective does not leave the institution of ethics committees. We should rather give ethics committees a greater significance of the organizational and institutional level. There should be close link communication between ethics committees and hospital management. Ethics committees should be integrated in frameworks of values-driven management in health care organizations.

8.7 Ethics committees, governance and values-driven management

In order to develop the right relation between clinical ethics and organization ethics, we would, therefore, have to find an organizational structure for decision-making and ethical reflection, which could address both clinical and organizational issues. In this context, we would propose an integration of clinical ethics committees in a framework of governance, business ethics and values-driven management of hospital organizations (Rendtorff, 2001, 2002a, 2002b, 2002c). Values-driven management is developed within business ethics research traditions. These are a framework of organizational decision-making. This kind of research looks at the organization in its social and moral environment. In this way, business ethics is also based on institutional organization theory. Business ethics can, as we have seen in the discussion of corporate governance and stakeholder management, be defined in many different ways, but in some respects, it is concerned with the formulation of the just relation among the different stakeholders of the organization.

In a Kantian approach to stakeholder theory, stakeholders are defined as "groups and individuals who benefit from or who are harmed by, and whose rights are violated or respected by, corporate actions." A criticism of this definition is that it is too wide and includes too many groups among relevant stakeholders and that the theory does not include any measure for deciding among the relevant stakeholders (Bonnafous-Boucher & Rendtorff, 2016a, 2016b, 2016c, 2016d, 2016e, 2016f). Therefore, a narrower definition of stakeholders has been delineated, for example, groups that are vital for the organization or groups that help to define the organization, its mission, purpose and goals and/or are most affected by the activities of the organization. This approach has the advantage of being a tool for determining the moral foundations of values-driven management. In a Kantian and communicative approach to stakeholder management, we might say that fair and just treatment of all stakeholders is one of the main purposes of ethics and values-driven management in organizations. In this way, stakeholder theory marks an important framework for mediating in conflicts among different groups in the hospital. This goes for oppositions among administrators, patients, physicians and other groups.

Stakeholder management should be regarded as an initiative to integrate interaction among different stakeholders in the health care organization. Moreover, stakeholder management as the basis for values-driven management contributes to the improvement of the ethical climate and culture of hospital organizations. In order to develop such an ethical climate in the organization, it is important to make the sense of values and ethics a part of the policy of the organization. In order to be effective, values must be visible and play an important part for the relation between the organization and its stakeholders. Organizations have to work with the formulation of the values and make them publicly available so that everyone can become aware of the vision, mission and values of this particular organization. This articulation of the core values of the organization should be done in order to have an impact of basic strategies and decisions of the organization. These core values can be institutionalized in the development of an ethics and values program for the hospital and the health care organization. The program should involve administrative, patient-oriented and professional ethics dimensions. It should indeed set up authorities for evaluation, decision-making and advice.

An ethics program in hospital organizations should include possibilities for organizational learning and training of different members of the organization (Rendtorff, 2001, 2002a, 2002b, 2002c). It is in this context of formulating, sanctioning, training and developing values programs for health care organizations that ethics committees may have important functions and possibilities. To the extent that ethics committees already exist in hospitals, they are excellent places of beginning a process of setting up values-driven management in hospitals. In this way, the ethics committees could overcome their traditional limitations to the physician-patient relationship. When no such committee exists or when it cannot be made responsible for having a central role in developing values-driven management, it would however be a good idea to make ethics committees a part of programs for values-driven management in organizations. Such a committee would help to improve the quality of health care. Moreover, it would be important to help developing training in ethics and formulation of ethics.

Nevertheless, it must be noted that this would expand the area of ethics committees to organizational ethics, and it would be necessary to work with dimensions of organizational ethics in the committee. It is very important that programs of ethics or values-driven management include possibilities of evaluation and auditing. The ethics committees in the organization might also be responsible for this. The different legal situations in United States and Europe with regard to hospital organizations constitute very different environments for the implementation of values-driven management in these different countries. The legal requirements of the Federal Sentencing Guidelines in the United States imply that organizations are legally pushed to establish ethics programs in order to detect and avoid violations of law. The guidelines develop specific criteria for a meaningful compliance program, and these must be followed by establishing ethics programs in health care organizations. Indeed, a specific set of guidelines has been made for such organizations.

Therefore, establishment of values-driven management in the United States is at the outset directed at compliance, even though they in many cases have gone far beyond the legal requirements and established values-centered ethics programs or Total Quality Management programs. Institutionalization of ethics programs implies the development of formal structures in the organization. These structures may involve as many stakeholders as possible of the organization. On the basis of our analysis of the importance of ethics committees, such a program may also involve the setup of such committees at all different levels of the organization. These committees may have an advisory function, but they may also have authority in relation to specific decisions about mission or policy statements.

The ethics program may include evaluation procedures, and it should involve measures for training and education of members of the organization. In order to give ethics committees greater impact on hospital organizations, it is necessary to operate with a kind of "open system morality," where ethics committees also have the possibility to respond to problems of hospital management. In the framework of institutionalization of ethics programs, ethics committees could have an advisory function reporting directly to hospital management. Even if ethics committees are not a direct part of a given ethics program, their advisory function to hospital management is very important. In this way, ethics committees contribute to the different aims of organization ethics integrating patient ethics, professional ethics, general organizational issues as well as relations to external stakeholders in society.

The basis for implementing ethics programs should indeed be dialog and communication with the different stakeholders. In order to mediate between the different rationales of different hospital groups, dialog-based management aims at confronting the different positions between each other in order to lay open implicit power structures and models of legitimacy in the organization. Dialog-based management seeks to include different groups in communication about important decisions and basic values of the organization. This includes discussions about economic priorities and allocation of resources. Dialog with stakeholders is an important instrument in order to have efficient values-driven management in hospital organizations. Dialog has a great symbolic function of inclusion of different stakeholders as parts of organizational culture. Values-driven management can be seen in the perspective of theories of organizational culture. At issue is improvement of organizational culture in formulating new values for the organization. Values-driven management can be related to organizational learning and change of organizational behavior.

To work with values is a major contribution to change and improve the ethical values of the organization. It is a way of constituting communities of professional organizational reflection in a very similar way to hospital ethics committees. Values-driven management in hospital organizations in order to improve the level of profession and quality therefore involves (1) a vision of human well-being; (2) a vision of organizational well-being; (3) open communication about daily practices; (4) continuous dialog, learning and conversation about the organization; and (5) a process of formulating long-term visions of the future of the organization. A particular model of values-driven management, which has been used in Danish hospitals, is the management model DIALOGOS.

DIALOGOS was developed by Torbjørn Meyer from Copenhagen Business School. He has used this model at two Danish hospitals as research examples in a Ph.D. dissertation in 1996. He has done pioneer research on such an installation of ethics in hospitals (Hildebrandt & Schultz, 1997, p. 345). This model of management considers dialog as essential to hospital management. Management is a communicative process where all stakeholders are heard in the process. DIALOGOS is closely related to organizational learning. Identifying basic values aims at organizational improvement. Finally, learned experiences are measured in a process of reporting. This is written in a final report. On this basis the process of dialog is determined by the following steps: (1) Identification of values. In this phase basic values of the organization are identified. This includes determination and questioning of basic values from different stakeholders. Especially, the prejudices of different professional groups are discussed. (2) Analysis. On the basis of the preliminary identification, the possible scenarios of collaboration are identified. In addition, possible scenarios of conflict are identified. (3) Dialog with stakeholders. Based on the analysis, meetings with all stakeholders are prepared. Basic schemes of interpretations of interests are described. Furthermore, possible solutions to conflicts and different problems are proposed. (4) Coordination. Finally, representatives of different stakeholders are included in a process of coordination in order to define the best possible outcome of the process. Experiences from the process are collected. On this basis proposals for organizational change are put forward to the executive board of the organization in order to improve the organization. In this view, values-driven management based on dialog with all stakeholders is systematized organizational intervention, aiming at learning and flexibility in considering all stakeholders, creating the foundations for organizational improvement. It is an important aspect of this model of dialog that it includes all stakeholders of the organization. This opens for a wider understanding of problems and possibilities of the organization. Therefore, values-driven management is an important manner of improving clinical ethics in the hospital. With this, we combine governance, ethics and stakeholder management in the management of modern hospitals and health care organizations.

8.8 Legitimacy models for ethics committees in hospital and health care organization ethics

In conclusion, we can say that we, in this chapter, have proposed a governance model for hospital management in the framework of clinical ethics and organization ethics (Rendtorff, 2020a, 2020b, 2020c, 2020d, 2020e). This was based on an integrated approach to hospital ethics considering ethics committees from different angles of bioethics, biolaw, business ethics and professional ethics. This corresponds to increasing demands to consider clinical ethics from individual as well as institutional perspectives. The argument is that it is necessary to focus on the concept of organization in health care ethics if we want to have a comprehensive and holistic understanding of ethical problems in hospitals. This also includes focus on the institutional implications of major ethical theories like consequentialism, deontology and virtue ethics. Moreover, ethical practice has been restricted to clinical dimensions centered around interpersonal physician-patient encounters. Organization theory and practice have emphasized the need for organizational ethics. Ethics programs and ethical leadership are promoted by many hospital organizations. Sometimes, clinical ethics committees have been involved in these programs. But, in many cases, initiatives do not involve ethics committees, and there is no collaboration between different ethics groups. Thus, we have argued for the importance of ethics committees for efficient ethics programs in hospitals. The problem is how we can give meaning to ethics committees within total quality management, benchmarking or different initiatives for values-driven management in hospital organizations. Thus, the function of ethics committees should not be restricted to clinical issues but should include the institutional and organizational dimensions of ethics.

Finally, in order to illustrate the legitimacy requirements of hospital management through ethics committees, we would like to propose three figures for hospital ethics committees. These figures are the following: (1) The discursive, procedural model, (2) the substantialist model and (3) the reflective judgmental model. We want to argue that the third model is the one that fits most adequately to the integration of ethics committees in the governance and management of health care organizations.

1. *The Discursive, Procedural Model.* This model can be said to be based on the philosophy of communicative action of Jürgen Habermas. The model proposes the idea of hospital ethics committees to look at situations of conflict of values, and it proposes the argumentative confrontation between different sorts of values as the basis for solving such conflicts of values. The model does not stand for the fact that hospital ethics committees could impose values. Rather they are spaces of mixture ethics and of the confrontation between different sorts of rationalities. This model may have the problem of being too formalist and not contributing with a particular content of the specific biomedical situation. The model is very good to regulate hospital ethics in a pluralist society with many different viewpoints on moral issues. The problem is, however, that the approach does not deliver any specific solution to the specific ethical problems in society. The limits of this model are that it fundamentally has an advisory function without giving specific directives for decision-making.
2. *The Substantialist Model.* This model argues that it is possible to formulate substantial values as the basis of the function of the hospital ethics committee. It is argued that this committee should come up with particular well-defined values in order to put an emphasis on the particularities of what to do in the committee. The substantialist model says that these values should be the foundation of the policy of the hospital personnel in the particular situation. This model is difficult to impose in hospitals and health care organizations where a particular rationality of value cannot be formulated as the foundation of a pluralist hospital ethics. It is very difficult to argue for such a substantial model of ethics in a pluralist society with many different conceptions. This model is aiming at a guiding function, but this is also the limit of the model, because in a pluralistic society with respect for patient autonomy, it is in danger of imposing its views on the patient's points of view.
3. *The Reflective Judgmental Model.* This model is to my view the most important function of a hospital ethics committee. Judgment is referred to the capacity of reflective judgment of the physician. It is the capacity to apply rules to new cases and to analyze these cases in the light of these rules. Hospital ethics committees can help to lay open the concept of the patient as a whole human being, which is implied in such an analysis of medical judgment in relation to the hospital ethics committees. In this play of reflective judgment, new cases are seen in the perspective of hermeneutical reflective judgment. This model relies on the view of judgment as the bridging function between many visions of the good in the formulation of ethical decision-making in concrete cases. It is the aim

to find good solutions for tragical dilemmas and unusual cases where it is difficult to find given rules to apply. It is the problem of the relation between problems that do not fit into the traditional ways of solving problems. The approach does not go so far as to build on a substantialist model, but it aims at finding durable solutions to the problems related to the specific cases. This model should aim at having an innovative and reflecting function while judging specific cases in bioethics.

Part IV

Biolaw, governance and sustainability

9 Universal principles for governance in an ever-changing world

9.1 Why universal principles?

Dealing with global challenges encompasses to rethink which criteria economic, social and environmental decisions are made from. As multilateralism claims its place in global agenda, emerging countries demand a greater incidence in the international debate. New frameworks for global decision-making need to be made. This points to creating a new form of global governance and designing new cooperation mechanisms to favor developing countries.

Global governance in a post-pandemic world should ensure the provision of global public goods, such as timely and free access to vaccine and health care resources. As other interests are also very important, such as mitigation of climate change, and social and environmental goals that the United Nations has set in the past decades, global health seems to be a critical issue that must be urgently considered.

Universal principles of cosmopolitan biolaw are needed for the optimization of international cooperation systems as well as the realization of a new interjurisdictional development agenda adapted to a multifactorial and interdependent world ever exposed to disaster and disease. In this scenario, we propose intercultural guidelines to build policies in a development cooperation system, which otherwise may erode the expansion of an effective cooperation agenda between developed and developing countries. The normative content of cosmopolitan principles must be aimed at transforming the world economic system into a cooperative and solidarity space moving toward a fully integrated world to foster and preserve international aid as a focused global policy.

When saying "universal principles," we mean "shared" ones, understood as complementary and interrelated to one another, with no pre-established hierarchy among them, and that are observed by most human beings committed to morality and law. As international biolaw's principles do not enjoy a legally binding force because of their naturalistic configuration, cosmopolitan biolaw's principles are able to tolerate a denser content that allows the coincidence and agreement on their meaning at a material level, which would enable them to adopt a legally binding scope.

DOI: 10.4324/9781003147848-9

In this order of ideas, we assert that universal principles for governance in an ever-changing world can build a framework for the protection of human and nonhuman beings from biomedical and biotechnological perils as well as from risky environments raised by current pandemics and other global threats. Therefore, we need to justify how and why such principles are significant in building frameworks for global governance in pandemic and post-pandemic times. This implies to be aware of that the principles are interdependent as they reciprocally presuppose one another as guides for the ethical and legal protection of persons and extra-human entities. However, universal principles can fall into tensions, dilemmas and even contradictions. Therefore, their epistemological configuration must be carried out within the framework of social solidarity and responsibility as meta-principles that shape legal systems aimed at protecting the weak and vulnerable.

The principles are flexible and ductile enough to work simultaneously in very specific fields of application in relation to different global governance issues, and therefore, they contribute to the development of human persons' protection in an interjurisdictional context. Thus, cosmopolitan principles entail a protecting role of both individual and social dimensions of human rights.

The principles are also normative criteria to improve humans' protection in risky global scenarios. In this way, the principles have a cultural importance, both for public debate and for legislative processes on diverse matters related to governance and sustainability as we will see soon. In this way, unlike other principlist conceptions of biolaw, they encompass a normative connection between ethics and law, while the principles are ductile enough to be applied both in ethical and legal contexts.

On the other hand, universal principles are not only formal and theoretical concepts but rather they are also practical guidelines. In this sense, they are not reduced into one another so that any normative tyranny is avoided. However, as this is not a completely done model, the internal coherence between the principles should be deepened.

Moreover, the relationship between the principles and specific cases must be understood as a hermeneutical dynamic, namely, as belonging to a circle of interpretation. The principles cannot be defined in a purely abstract way, but rather, they must be considered in the light of specific applications and very precise factual scenarios of diverse scale. In this way, cosmopolitan biolaw cannot be understood without a hermeneutical reflection aimed at applying deliberative general rules on specific cases. Therefore, as universal principles can be developed in a framework of common morality norms, they also re-present a model of reflexive judgment to understand the relationship between general norms and cases. In this way, we think that from our proposal, both casuistry and extreme principlism can be overcome.

According to the aforementioned discussion, it would be a mistake to read the principles from axiological hierarchies. Rather, they articulate different decisive normative dimensions for governance and sustainability. This means that the hermeneutical analysis of the principles' meaning in different legal and ethical systems should include a prescriptive vision of how they work and should work in multicultural societies. Therefore, the principles must be taken as an expression of all legal and moral values that most countries share.

From an hermeneutical and phenomenological approach, it is important to distinguish between the broad meaning of being human and the more specific meaning of being a person. In the first sense, every human being is morally significant insofar as it deserves rights and protection. In the second sense, person is a dynamic political and social entity whose interactions with the lifeworld entail moral importance. In this way, having personality means freedom and identity, which enable personal dimensions' development. Therefore, a person is able to embrace its own and others' existence, being the only entity able to care for itself and other creatures in a legal and moral sense.

Every person is involved in a teleological process, meaning it is not predetermined but in a permanent construction molded by will and capacities as well as by social and environmental events. Thus, a person is a self-conscious and free entity, turning into a moral agent for secular, multicultural and plural societies. Thus, a person is a rational being who is aware of itself and its capacities for moral judgment, which distinguishes it from other entities in the world.

Cosmopolitan biolaw's vision of personality goes beyond a minimalist understanding, because it is not exclusively focused on autonomy but also on equivalent conditions, such as dignity, integrity and vulnerability. Universal principles for governance are related to limits of human existence and lead to a vision of development of a civilized society that seeks the realization of human beings from key values, including solidarity and responsibility. Thus, a human individual cannot be understood without taking into account its relationships with other people in society. Universal principles make visible how important social dynamics are for governance, sustainability and biomedicine's regulation and oversight. For this reason, the principles find their essential realization in the sympathy and solidarity that must exist between all social agents. In other words, cosmopolitan biolaw's principles are made to work in deliberative and pluralistic societies where a democratic culture exists, which recognizes every human being by including respect and care for human entities according to how close to a person they are.

Therefore, the ideas of human and nonhuman persons, understood as ontological realities rather than legal conventions, are key criteria to identify, define and configure universal principles for governance in an ever-changing world.

9.2 Dignity and inter-species policy

We do not assert that this is an overriding principle of cosmopolitan biolaw. Undoubtedly, dignity is a diffuse and controversial principle, whose epistemological content is rather ambiguous. Also, its traditional configuration fossilized within international biolaw's instruments never reached a legally binding status probably due to its conceptual thinness as well as its anthropocentric and speciesist understanding. However, neglecting dignity as a principle for governance would lead us to counterintuitive scenarios because while its theoretical and normative content are not compelling enough, it is also undeniable that, at least from a procedural point of view, dignity can be helpful to clarify some priorities in ruling conflictive global scenarios where human and nonhuman entities' autonomy and integrity are at stake.

From a nontraditional perspective, the concept of dignity has three important dimensions. Originally, it has expressed an intersubjective recognition of distinctive aspects of personality. Dignity represents the quality of being and the spirit of a valuable and honorable person in society. It is then understood as a virtue that has public recognition in a community essentially concerned for the other. Therefore, dignity means something that the individual can acquire by itself, through its conscience, responsibility and freedom, because it refers to the way the person undertakes his or her existence and unfolds his or her moral decisions. In a second sense, dignity becomes an ontological or natural aspect of every human being and, as such, requires the respect for fundamental rights. Thus, dignity means a substantial and intrinsically valuable aspect of the person's humanity. Therefore, as a member of the human species, each individual possesses an inalienable dignity. These two dimensions are anthropocentric and also speciesist. The third dimension we propose is beyond anthropocentrism and speciesism, and it displays itself as an ontological condition (subject to juridification) shared by human and nonhuman entities at different levels of normative intensity. The ability to suffer and experiment pain and the capacity to show interests and preferences make humans and nonhumans equal from an ethical point of view. Thus, violating dignity means to reify and instrumentalize any sentient entity, that is, treat it as mere means to ends with no other justification than moral and juridical arbitrariness.

Therefore, dignity can also be understood as a political concept that is justified by democratic and interspecies thinking. This is also a formulation of dignity, understood as an intersubjective and interspecies virtue. Indeed, the recognition of others' dignity as independent moral entities is the basic condition for the public sphere's development and flourishing. Tolerance and mutual respect among humans and from humans to nonhumans are crucial to establish and institutionalize the notion of dignity under this intellection.

Even though there are important disagreements on a unique interpretation of dignity, some substantial ideas can be exposed as follows. First, dignity emerges as a virtue of recognition of the other, in an intersubjective and interspecies relationship. This recognition would be based on social constructions, and as a social construct, dignity would point to a capacity to sympathize with others that any person has by virtue of his or her position and behavior in the public space. Second, dignity is universal and shows the intrinsic value and moral responsibility of each human being to one another and to nonhuman creatures. Third, the person must, as a result of his or her intersubjective and interspecies understanding of dignity, be considered an invaluable entity. Therefore, no human being, independent from its condition, can and should be subject to any action that implies materializing and reifying his or her existence. In most cases, we should analogically extend this idea toward nonhuman settings Fourth, dignity is based on relationships between the Self and the Other, which prevents individual and social human degradation. Fifth, it is noted that dignity defines certain taboo situations and emotions as limits of a civilized behavior. This means that there are certain attitudes against humans and nonhumans a society must reject. Sixth, dignity emerges, consequently, in a civilizing process of humanity as a social entity. And finally, as a seventh idea, dignity includes an openness of the individual to the metaphysical dimensions of life that refer to dignifying behaviors in extreme situations of existence, such as existential risk, suffering and death, among others.

However, a status of degradation or decrease of dignity could be considered in very specific situations and scenarios, which would rather be focused on an individual's bodily aspects. Dignity, in this sense, could be considered degraded in conditions of extreme suffering, torture, loss of self-respect or arbitrary abuse, among others. The loss of dignity would then be the loss of a dignified body. Indeed, the body can be degraded into levels of radical damage, destruction and monstrous deformation, because the individual can lose his or her dignity by decaying and degrading by virtue of face and body's changes.

This body's degradation may also involve an important dependence on the others, for example, in cases of dementia or Alzheimer. In situations of extreme sickness and in relation to people whose body or physical-psychological dimension has been fractured, the loss of dignity will lead to the feeling of repulsion toward the body itself. The same can happen in cases of post-torture or in some types of treatment being degrading for a patient. However, in a context of global governance and sustainability, degrading dignity also means to abuse the innocent and defenseless, whether it is human or not. As falling into a state of unworthiness does not merit being excluded from the human community, that also means that other nonhuman entities historically neglected must be considered as part of a sustainable world.

A compelling definition of dignity should reject all types of discriminatory or degrading treatment, such as cruel punishment, torture, discrimination, racism, male chauvinism and speciesism. Defending human dignity means defending nonhuman dignity too, as a way of providing protection to individuals in multiple dimensions, even when confronted with power structures and species marginalization. Thus, proclaiming dignity in international declarations is, finally, to claim nondiscrimination, equity and social justice at an interjurisdictional and interspecies level. These demands would be involved in solidarity and responsibility, understood beyond a mere anthropocentric point of view.

A contemporary global governance cannot accept an anthropocentric and speciesist conception of dignity. Affirming the inalienability of human dignity implies begging the question, because we ourselves, the humans, are who claim having that condition, and it is not possible to sustain the truth of that assertion without resorting to arbitrariness, religion or metaphysics. When international instruments emphasize dignity as "human dignity," they are saying that this condition belongs to our species, but affirming, thinking or even assuming that dignity is an exclusively human attribute, put there by someone or something before we appeared in existence, turns out to be an implausible idea. Therefore, the human assertion that dignity is an attribute only inherent to human beings lacks compelling solidity and is ideologically speciesist and totalitarian.

9.3 Autonomy and global responsibility

Autonomy is also a controversial concept. While many defend self-determination with religious devotion, others consider it to be a dangerous value, which has been overrated especially in political and bioethical settings. Both positions are not pacific, and their evaluation necessarily entails deepening into contradictory and competing conceptions on personal liberty. Understanding autonomy as an absolute principle can engender a bizarre addiction to individualism, which seems not to be the course human actions should take in a globalized world. However, stringing the ability of self-determination can be as pernicious as fostering a society without community, that is, a global village where each one lives encapsulated in its own individualism. A society only made of a sum of atomized particles living in a kind of collective solipsism is not sustainable. Yet, a society with no room enough to display substantial levels of autonomy is not sustainable either.

A principle of autonomy for global governance must be situated in an intersection with personal rights and public responsibility. Historically, there have been painful collisions between the strong tradition of personal freedom and privacy and ideals of minorities' sacrifice in pursuing the social order. As a matter of fact, a so successful epistemology as utilitarianism is essentially grounded on this controversial idea. Thus, a defense of autonomy seems to hide a disturbing palimpsest: Championing the autonomy of the most encompasses sacrificing the least.

If we consider the enlightened understanding of rationality as a motivation for human conduct, we should accept that autonomy cannot be vindicated at expenses of social responsibility. Otherwise, all public life would fall into counterintuitive scenarios. However, people are not simply rational creatures. We often appeal to emotions as a way far more effective than logical arguments in changing our behavior and obtaining what we expect. Assuming a lexical pre-eminence of autonomy over public responsibility is dangerous, but it is also inconducive for sustainability and global governance.

Gaylin and Jennings (2003) analyze a central dilemma of our time: The balance in a liberal society between individual autonomy and social responsibility. They ask themselves what level of autonomy should be sacrificed by individuals and groups for the sake of the greater good. The authors argue against increased interference by the state in everyday life instead of pushing for advancing in public policies that engender a "moral compass" in which a supportive environment is created for children to be more inclined to learn the social value of self-discipline and rational decision-making. In this fashion, autonomous individuals hardly realize the importance of more basic moral emotions like shame, guilt and pride, and the influence of communities, family and traditions on human conduct and social order. This has engendered a "culture of autonomy," meaning a "predominant sensibility" of our society that makes us unwilling to control people unless they are explicitly harming others.

What they call "the perversion of autonomy" implies that social order and intersubjective cooperation depend not only on the enforcement of law by state power but also on a citizenry that has internalized both self-discipline and moral instincts. As the ability to make rational choices depends on an evolved capacity of self-determination, that is also contingent to the development of responsible individuals able to balance their personal expectations with their social obligations.

Rendtorff and Kemp (2000: 25–31) argue that, in a modern, pluralistic and liberal society, individual autonomy is the right everyone has to live his or her life according to his or her own inclinations and preferences. In this sense, autonomy is considered in liberal societies an overriding value. As autonomy is a principle of freedom, it points to self-government. Therefore, people are considered autonomous when they are able to govern their own lives and decisions from their capacity for self-legislation, which analogically extends itself to the civil space as a public policy. This means that moral agents who are free and able to decide by themselves, even if their choices are wrong or go against the mainstream opinion, have the prerogative of exercising their autonomy.

However, autonomy must be understood in light of social responsibility, as self- determination means (i) the ability to create ideas and goals in life; (ii) the capacity for moral self-legislation and privacy; (iii) the ability to make rational decisions and act without external coercion; (iv) the ability to get involved politically in the public space, which implies not only social responsibility but also a personal one; and (v) the ability to consent, which is often displayed in clinical, biomedical and political surroundings.

Autonomy for global governance implies free moral choices but in tune with a set of values that individuals consider to be correct and fair for themselves and for the public sphere. Being morally autonomous is, then, related to rational choices and personal decision-making rather than to the invention of contingent personal values. If autonomy entails a substantial and procedural interdependence with shared values in a legal, moral and religious system, it must be backed by specific authorities and jurisdictions aimed at ensuring social cohesion. A cosmopolitan autonomy means the ability to act autonomously in situations strongly characterized by an important degree of exogenous determinations, which demands not only self-determination but also social compromise.

The political origins of autonomy indicate that there is a very close relationship between individual autonomy and society's political organization. In modern democratic societies, the idea of justice presupposes that citizens are free and equal, meaning freedom and equity should be guaranteed for all equally. Hence, a fair society evolves in a construction process where autonomous agents have rationally agreed to the identification, definition and acceptance of common principles of justice. In that context, it would be important to emphasize that any society grounded upon autonomous and responsible decisions of its citizens is, at the same time, a community structured from argumentative agreements on common values.

Global governance must be based upon autonomy understood as a multifactorial value that recognizes political societies as deliberative communities able to respect the public sphere's dynamics and the democratic exchange of opinions among citizens as a basis for building common and interjurisdictional ideals. Therefore, a legitimate global governance should be built on individuals' self-determination insofar as it encompasses social responsibility. In this fashion, autonomy is crucial for the development of moral agencies, willing to foster the respect for individuality and social cohesion at the same level of intensity.

This is very clear in new technologies' environments. The vertiginous developments in science and technology, which affect the understanding of life, demand from humanity a global response to ethical implications of such empowerment beyond a mere liberal intellection of autonomy. The international community must accept some universal principles to guide, oversight, reflect and resolve the emerging and growing dilemmas caused by the unprecedented bioscientific practices.

In fact, human health does not depend solely on the development of scientific and technological research but also on psychosocial and cultural factors. This means that persons' identity is a synthesis of multiple determinations, including biological, psychological, social, cultural and spiritual ones. In this way, new approaches to social responsibility to ensure that progress in science and technology contributes to justice, equity and global governance need to be made. Moral sensitivity and ethical reflection must be an integral part in any process of scientific and technological developments, and therefore, cosmopolitan biolaw must play a predominant role in the reflection, deepening and eventual solution of dilemmatic issues emerging from bioscientific settings.

Consequently, a universal principle of autonomy should:

a. Provide a universal framework to guide states in formulating interjurisdictional policies for governance and sustainability when facing with biotechnological advances.
b. Guide positive actions of individuals, groups, communities, institutions and public and private corporations in such context.

c. Promote respect for the lives of human beings and their fundamental freedoms.
d. Recognize the importance of the freedom of scientific research and the benefits derived from scientific and technological developments but always respecting fundamental freedoms.
e. Foster multidisciplinary and pluralist dialogue on bioethical and biojuridical issues among all stakeholders and pluralistic societies in general.
f. Promote equitable access to medical, scientific and technological developments; the rapid exchange of knowledge of those advances; and the exchange of benefits, with special attention to the needs of developing countries.
g. Safeguard and promote the autonomous interests of present and future generations.
h. Emphasize the importance of biodiversity and its conservation as a common concern of humanity.

In addition, professionalism, honesty, integrity and transparency in decision-making must be promoted, in particular, when international conflicts of interest emerge. This should be taken as an opportunity for informed, pluralistic and public debate within local orders and between diverse international jurisdictions. However, debate must be independent, multidisciplinary and pluralistic and intended to (i) evaluate relevant ethical, legal, scientific and social issues related to risks involving human and nonhuman beings; (ii) give advice on ethical problems in international clinical scenarios, such as pandemics; (iii) evaluate scientific and technological developments; (iv) make recommendations and contribute to the preparation of guidelines for international governance; and (v) encourage debate, education and public responsibility.

A proper assessment and management of risk related to life sciences and associated technologies should also be promoted. For this reason, transnational practices should be fostered to ensure that any activity included within the scope of cosmopolitan biolaw is compatible with its universal principles. In this fashion, the role played by states in implementing, applying and promoting universal principles for governance must be aimed at taking appropriate measures, whether legislative or administrative, to power education, training and public information about scopes and limits of autonomy in the framework of social and global responsibility.

As personal freedom and social responsibility are not competing values, community life is grounded on shared ideals as a necessary condition for self-determination. Autonomy supposes an institutional and cultural framework founded on the common value of respect for social diversity and personal freedom. Therefore, understanding autonomy can not only raise liberal ideas but it should also recognize that individuals are situated in complex and multifactorial environments of a large number of social practices and intersubjective relationships. Moreover, focusing governance only on the principle of autonomy leads to forget human condition's fragility. Therefore, autonomy for global governance must be understood as closely interrelated to integrity and vulnerability.

9.4 Integrity and the raise of bioscientific empowerment

In various instruments of international biolaw, this principle seeks to protect human identity and integrity, by prohibiting human cloning (identity) and germline genetic interventions that alter the genotype (integrity). In the same way, it introduces a suggestive obligation that is justified by the spatial-temporal expansion that human action has undergone in the bioscientific era, which points to the extension of responsibility for the consequences of present humans' acts toward future generations.

While governance and sustainability can also be understood as intergenerational concepts, this idea of intergenerational integrity is key to configure a universal standard for bioscientific practices' ruling and oversight. Important epistemological roots of intergenerational integrity can be found in Hans Jonas' (2003) works. He proposes to extend responsibility, in accordance with the technological extension of human actions' scope. His imperative of responsibility encompasses integrity to complement traditional ethics' categories. Therefore, although individual actions require only traditional ethics and law norms to be governed, Jonas' ethics aims to fit better into contemporary nomenclatures of existence, where human action is modified by technoscientific advances. In that order of ideas, Jonas proposes a further-reaching imperative, where moral (and, also juridical) norms must refer to a predictable real future as a dimension open to our responsibility.

To configure his project, Jonas proposes a new imperative, which in one of his formulations says: "Act so that the effects of your action are compatible with the presence of genuine human life on earth." Authentic human life supposes two cardinal elements. First, the conservation of the environment and biodiversity. Second, the preservation of the human genetic identity. For Jonas – a conservative philosopher – it is essential that both ethics and law be built on the paradigm of respecting natural human characteristics, because only in this way, autonomy can be championed, as its consecration lies on the possibility that any self-determined agency has to discern between good and evil. Therefore, as the biosciences have the permanent temptation to enhance and perfect the human being, namely, to determine it and deprive it from that freedom, it is necessary to articulate contemporary existence in tune with the imperative of responsibility that underlies the obligation of protecting human integrity and identity.

In this sense, both cloning and germline genetic interventions (although they are practiced for therapeutic purposes) undermine an archetype of "a genuine human life." Cloning does so because it fractures human identity and promotes the gradual fossilization of a society with "given" and "produced" individuals, that is, with originals and copies of different ontological status.

Also, germinal manipulations impact an authentic human life because their effects are transferable to offspring, and as there is not enough evidence about their scope, they represent a potential risk for future generations.

The epistemological density of a universal principle of integrity can be boosted by appealing to the precautionary principle. This is an international biolaw's instrument, designed by UNESCO's World Commission on the Ethics of Scientific Knowledge and Technology. According to the normative content of the document, the precautionary principle generally defines actions on topics related to the application of knowledge or practices of new technologies that are considered uncertain regarding their effects and consequences and aftermaths. In other words, as there is not enough reliable information to carry out an assessment of risks and benefits associated with a specific biotechnological practice, as well as we have not enough evidence to determine a precise equation between beneficence and nonmaleficence, the precautionary principle orders to abstain from acting.

Therefore, if technoscientific assessments of hazards associated with the consequences of technological actions are not entirely compelling, that is, they are not conclusive regarding contemporary actions' aftermaths, the evaluation must be done, not only based on available empirical data but also from a rational estimation that allows to determine reasonable levels of minimization of risks. The intrinsic fallibility in accurately predicting certain consequences of technological actions obliges, and, at the same time, encourages to prevent risks, by taking certain measures in relation to possible dangers that new technologies may entail. In this way, it is each individual who decides which risks he or she is willing to accept, rationally assessing possible consequences of his or her acts. Only then, technology is a tolerable event, that is, it acquires viability when a reasonable balance is generated between costs and benefits emerging from performing technological and biotechnological actions.

Integrity is adjacent to the precautionary principle (*Vorsorgeprinzip*), which gives the individual sufficient power to decide responsibly to excuse himself or herself from actions that may be harmful to self or to others. This principle is currently indicated as an element of judgment at the moment of assessing the consequences that contemporary technoscientific events imply, by progressively establishing itself as an ethical, political and juridical criterion to deal with the possibility of an irreparable catastrophe underlying present and future life.

The precautionary principle points out that in the face of the progressive increase of uncertainty regarding the scope and power of technological inventions, the awareness of risks associated with them has also proliferated. This phenomenon has finally confronted human beings with their destiny and with their responsibility to engender a predictive and anticipatory model to protect humanity and extra-human entities from the pernicious scopes of human action itself.

In this order of ideas, the precautionary principle works as an integral norm of sustainable development that meets the needs of present individuals without compromising those of future generations. From this relevant feature of the principle and its growing presence in different international instruments, as well as in different epistemologies that analyze different threats new technologies pose to life as a whole, we think it is important to standardize the reception of the principle and foster an interjurisdictional understanding of it.

Some criteria to achieve an internationally shared intellection of the principle can be the following:

i. The precautionary principle must apply when there is considerable scientific uncertainty about the causality, magnitude, probability and nature of global threats.
ii. Some forms of scientific analysis should be mandatory in global risk settings. This means that a mere fantasy or speculation is not enough to activate the precautionary principle device.
iii. Because the precautionary principle is designed for risk contexts with little-known outcomes and probabilities, the possibility of a certain peril, even if it is unquantifiable, can be sufficient to consider the application of the principle.
iv. The application of the principle must be limited to those risks that are unacceptable, such as possible threats to the lives of future generations or vulnerable groups in the global context.
v. The intervention of the precautionary principle must be required before the possible disaster occurs, not once it has occurred.
vi. The intensity of the application of the precautionary principle must be proportional to the magnitude of the possible risk. Therefore, and although in many cases the only answer to a possible negative impact of new technologies is a total prohibition, it must be considered that an absolute moratorium may not always be the best response to a latent risk.

Thus, when human activities lead to morally unacceptable damages caused by possible but uncertain technoscientific performances, certain actions must be taken to avoid or mitigate such negative impact. In this context, "morally unacceptable" means a damage to humans and the environment that violates integrity of life, health and the existence of future generations.

We can also take the concept of precaution as an ethical responsibility and a legal norm. As an ethical responsibility, the precautionary principle has, in its normative content, a moral scope. In the same way, its applications require axiological evaluations that are sensitive to morals. In this sense, a problematic element arises because of the great variety of ethical approaches the principle seems to tolerate. As this diversity of approaches seems to be contradictory with the claim of universality of ethics, we think it is necessary to consider that people who tend to disagree on abstract principles of common morality often have the ability to reach agreements on policies created for specific risk scenarios. This is because moral judgments often rest on firmer axiological platform than abstract ethical theories we can eventually agree with.

The precautionary principle understood as an epistemological basis for the principle of integrity must be considered from a moral symmetry between actions and omissions. There are relevant epistemologies that can reinforce this idea. In a classic text, James Rachels (1975) analyzes the moral status of action and omission in the context of killing or letting die, namely, active and passive euthanasia. Rachels exposes two consubstantial examples to show that there is no difference between killing and letting a person die. In the first, he tells us the case of a subject, named Smith, who surreptitiously enters the bathroom and drowns his nephew in the bathtub to collect a large inheritance. In the second scenario, another subject, named Jones, who can also get a succulent inheritance if his nephew dies, enters the bathroom with the intention of drowning the child, but just before doing so, the child slips, hits his head and begins to drown. Jones, doing nothing, just observes the scene and hopes that his nephew ends up drowning by himself. The problem lies in discerning whether Smith's behavior is morally worse than that of Jones. Certainly, by an innate tendency, most people would answer yes, that indeed, it is much worse to have drowned a child than simply to let him drown by himself. However, Rachels argues that both behaviors are morally equivalent, specifically for two reasons: (i) Both conducts have the same motivation, and (ii) both behaviors pursue the same purpose. We would add a third reason: (iii) Both conducts had the same consequence. Therefore, as a principle of coherence, inherent in moral deliberation, requires that morally equivalent actions must be evaluated in an equivalent way, it would be arbitrary and whimsical to affirm that Smith acted worse way than Jones.

On the other hand, Singer (2011) considers the distinction between a direct intentional effect and a secondary effect to be artificial, as it is not possible to become independent from responsibility by arbitrarily placing our intention on one object instead of another. By foreseeing both effects, we must, then, accept responsibility for the possible effects of what we do. Thus, he affirms that accepting the distinction between intentional and unintentional consequences would lead us to tolerate, as morally plausible, practices that our common sense would reject. Would it be morally acceptable to release the directors of a company who decide to dispose of toxic waste, in the least expensive way, by throwing it into the nearest river?

In the same way, Singer rejects the distinction of the moral statute of an action and an omission. According to such axiological disproportion, there would be a moral differentiation between acting and causing certain consequences and omitting to do something that provokes exactly the same results. Therefore, for Singer, the classic understanding of moral responsibility presupposes the doctrine of acts and omissions, because, otherwise, a differentiated moral perception of them could not be justified.

In this way, the "acts and omissions doctrine" rests on a legalistic understanding of moral normativity, by virtue of which it can be followed that insofar as people do not violate certain mandates that point out explicit moral obligations, they can do everything that the prescriptive universe permits. In this way, the respect of such mandatory constellation is guaranteed by simply abstaining from doing the opposite of the legal standard, namely, avoiding perpetrating legally forbidden actions. The normative nature of these mandates is similar to those contained in the Ten Commandments and are stated as categorical obligations of nonmaleficence, namely, as negative or prohibitive duties: You shall not kill, you shall not lie, and you shall not steal, among others.

It seems, then, that radically distinguishing the normative value of acts and omissions strategically simplifies the mental process that leads us to adhere to a mandate. Thus, it is much easier to satisfy the obligation not to kill than to avoid the death of innocent people who perish from hunger every day. Therefore, the distinction between the moral status of acts and omissions makes a less demanding public morality emerge.

Being responsible for our actions also encompasses being responsible for our omissions. In this sense, in many scenarios linked to new technological practices, responsibilities derived from the scope and consequences of those inventions may not be individual but shared. In fact, large-scale industrial accidents do not usually occur because of a well-determined individual failure but because of a complete constellation of interrelated acts under a systemic chain of technological design.

The protection of integrity demands to analyze costs and benefits of new technoscience's applications. In this context, a precautionary principle must be applied when the following conditions are met: (i) There is considerable uncertainty and scientific insecurity; (ii) there are scenarios or models of possible harm that are scientifically reasonable, namely, whose prediction is based on plausible scientific reasoning; (iii) the uncertainties cannot be reduced in the short term without increasing, at the same time, ignorance about other relevant factors of more intense levels of abstraction and idealization; (iv) the potential risk is sufficiently serious or even irreversible for present and future generations or, at least, is morally unacceptable; and (v) there is a pressing need to act now, as procrastination can engender the exacerbation of risks, as well as increase the costs involved in solving it.

Regarding the implications of integrity for science, a sustainable governance implies to build a science capable of better reflecting on uncertainty and complexity of technological practices. In this sense, both the quantitative and qualitative dimensions of uncertainty require an explicit and differentiated treatment.

Among the tasks that should be specially considered in this context are as follows:

i. Optimize the role of a science of integrity that displays a systematic search for possible surprises and ways to deal with them.
ii. Improve oversight of empirical research.
iii. Be more realistic in the reception of the role and potential of science when evaluating complex risks.

iv. Increase knowledge and transdisciplinary approaches for sustainable development.
v. Increase the protection of life as a whole.
vi. Harmonize the work of different actors and sectors linked to the application of the precautionary principle.
vii. Use more participatory instruments as a strategy to increase the effectiveness of interjurisdictional deliberation and governance.
viii. Give responsibility to governments in the reception and application of measures to mitigate global harm.
ix. Develop individual and collective capacities, as well as monitor technological systems.
x. Increase transparency and shared knowledge.
xi. Promote not only freedom but also equity and impartiality in international technological trade.
xii. Recognize on equal terms all different cultural contexts involved in some complex and problematic scenarios.
xiii. Allow and promote that each country determines and chooses its own standard acceptability of risks as long as it does not put at risk global safety.

In short, a universal principle of integrity protects human beings, animals and the environment against the uncertain but predictable risks associated with human actions, already modified by contemporary technological enhancement. In this sense, integrity points to a rational approach and an ethically and satisfactorily justified management of risks for present and future life as a whole. Therefore, it is also intended to use and apply, in the best way possible, key categories of systemic sciences of complexity to make wiser and more plausible decisions in highly conflictive scenarios.

9.5 Vulnerability and the future of life

We understand vulnerability as mainly associated with the impossibility of self-determination, namely, those people unable to give voluntary consent or actively participate in decision-making processes deserve special protection in that context. Consequently, a principle ordering the special protection of vulnerable people demands the respect and protection of the intrinsically feeble condition of the human being, which, conceived as a biological and psychological individual, is vulnerable and, as such, is exposed to damages, risks and threats. The procedural extension of this principle is greater than that of any other, because, in material terms, it subordinates autonomy, dignity and integrity, among others, to the finite and mortal condition of human beings. Therefore, respect for vulnerability would assume an ontological priority over other mandates.

In this sense, and although it is a statement that deserves further analysis and debate, vulnerability can be considered as a key basis for an interjurisdictional order, as the feeble and fallible condition of the human being is perhaps the real ontological substrate for the configuration of a sustainable global governance. In fact, the legal organization of local and international institutions, as well as the principles and rules of any system, is aimed at protecting life, intrinsically vulnerable, as a way of preventing sustainability from being threatened by the risk of destruction and global catastrophic harms.

Moreover, any governance model should have the purpose of protecting the weakest and most vulnerable against discrimination and eventual destruction operated by social and natural threats. Thus, a democratic and pluralistic society considers, in its legal framework, the punishment for those who, making use of their eventual position, power or possibilities, abuse others arbitrarily and disproportionately.

However, international instruments do not seem to consider that in the current era of genetics, other forms of discrimination, stigmatization, marginalization and human exploitation may emerge. In other words, vulnerability, currently, assumes another ontological facet that is only visible when human life collides with the whole plexus of bioscientific practices that can subject it to a constant risk of intergenerational scope. In this sense, while dysgenic practices represent the most controversial face of genetics, eugenic techniques also point to intense dilemmas for governance and challenge it to understand vulnerability beyond the traditional meaning of human rights.

In fact, eugenic genome edition is based on the search for a stereotype of human being, which obeys patterns defined by Western scientists. This unbridled search for perfection encloses a palimpsest: The persistent exploration of bioscience to find the key for human perfection and thereby homogenize our nature making species genetic diversity disappear. Once this goal is consolidated, it is not difficult to imagine new forms of exclusion, exploitation and discrimination coming into the social structure.

From a global and intergenerational understanding, the principle of vulnerability refers to three key concepts: (i) The maintenance and perpetuation of humanity, (ii) the protection of biodiversity and the environment and (iii) the protection of the human genome. These ideas are consubstantial to one another. Let us see.

Vulnerability encompasses the responsibility that present generations have in providing the sufficient and necessary conditions, to ensure the satisfaction of the needs and interests of future generations. This does not mean that current human beings should predict the needs and interests that future human beings will have, assuming that those will be equivalent to ours in the current era. Assuming this would lead us to accept counterintuitive scenarios as we cannot know that our interests and needs should be perpetuated and received by the new generations. In a terrain as marshy as that of the genetic practices, whose nature and scope are not completely and definitely sanctioned, it is dangerous to think that way.

What is easy to predict is that the future world will be a highly technological one, and its ontological aspects will have mutated, probably, in a critical way, so that the reception, understanding and meaning of existence will be quite different from the current one. The stimuli, advances, conflicts, institutions and society in general will be so different from the current one that the needs and interests will also have changed in relation to the present world. Therefore, we argue that it is plausible and desirable that current human beings acquire responsibilities regarding future ones. However, these cannot be either supererogatory or implausible in terms of rational prediction.

Vulnerability also points to the importance of self-imposing the duty to ensure that future generations will enjoy sufficient autonomy to dispose of their favorite political, economic and social systems, as well as preserve their cultural and religious diversity, always respecting human rights and fundamental freedoms. While we are not certain that the autonomy of future people will not lead to self-destruction, it is very tolerable to reason that trying to configure the necessary means and instruments for future human beings can enjoy substantial degrees of autonomy, but understanding and even expecting that those generations will not do with their freedom what we do today with ours.

The principle of vulnerability also orders to respect biodiversity, being emphatic enough to impose the obligation to protect and ensure the survival of other nonhuman species. Vulnerability avoids an anthropocentric, speciesist and reductionist imperative as if the mere fact of respecting and preserving human life was the only condition to ensure its subsistence and sustainability on the earth. In addition, the principle of vulnerability recognizes the importance of nonhuman species' sustainability as an irrevocable factor for human sustainability.

However, and as biolaw has already recognized (Valdés & Lecaros, 2019), the era of gene and biotechnology is not only a time molded by the technical domain of the world, but it represents the breeding ground for a well-determined way of how reality happens under a virtual structure that does not refer only to the Industrial Revolution but also and, above all, to the splendor of instrumental reason and metaphysics. Indeed, the metaphysics of the contemporary subject has its basis in Cartesian thought, in which the human being is reduced to being the only reason of all certainties. Reason governs and dominates all the broad and problematic horizons of human endeavor, reducing it to being a rational subject, which represents a world as an object, an image and also a system.

Vulnerability should not be understood from a Cartesian perspective. And this is not a trivial matter. A sustained and devastating intervention of the environment dictated by economic imperatives, tenaciously adhered to bioscientific advances, has been operated by technological actions since the second half of the twentieth century. That constitutes the most radical transformation of nature we can remember. The certain possibility of reaching levels of knowledge and action, unimaginable in the past, encourages the human of globalization to distort its intellection of goods and impulses it to the irrational task of the superfluous possession of instruments and devices created by virtue of the technological hatching. In this insane race to capture life on the planet, most human beings do not even question the possibility of extending certain rights to nature and animals. No international instrument says anything about the indiscriminate killing of 100 billion cows a year caused by the meat industry or the unspeakable suffering of those animals in tenebrous factory farms. Nor do they notice the extreme environmental damage that the production and breeding of this exorbitant amount of livestock perpetrate on the ecosystem. Therefore, if an international governance is really intended to recommend the states the preservation of environment and biodiversity, it must emphasize the protection of nonhuman beings as a key element for global sustainability.

On the other hand, respecting vulnerability implies that current generations should ensure the preservation of the cultural diversity of humanity, by championing human rights and fundamental freedoms. In the same way, present human beings have the responsibility to identify, protect and conserve the material and immaterial cultural heritage, as well as to transmit it to future generations. It is important to say something else about this point, because it makes clear the importance of biolaw to build new models of hermeneutical approach to rule bioscientific practices that threaten the common heritage of humanity. If we understand that the human genome represents the common heritage of humanity, it can only be altered by germinal interventions, because those perpetrated by somatic line do not pass the genetic condition to the offspring. Most, of jurisdictions in the world, when regulating genetic manipulation, do not distinguish between germline and somatic manipulations. Therefore, any somatic alteration is not included into the criminal type, no matter how horrible it may be. New hermeneutical models have been already developed to perfect international regulation in this context (Valdés, 2021).

A universal principle of vulnerability is also related to education so that it has a didactic and, at the same time, therapeutic purpose. The current generations must ensure that they and future generations learn to live together in an atmosphere of peace, security and respect for international law, human rights and fundamental freedoms. In addition, current generations must protect future generations from the scourge of war. In this sense, future generations should inherit from the present one the conditions for an equitable, sustainable and universal socioeconomic development. Education is also an important factor. It must be used to promote peace, justice, understanding, tolerance and equality for the benefit of current and future generations. Thus, current generation must prevent itself from carrying out actions that may cause or perpetuate any form of discrimination for future generations.

In configuring the principle of vulnerability, the reminiscence of Jonas' (2003) ethic is indisputable too. We already advanced something in this regard when we analyzed the principle of integrity, especially highlighting the concept of genuine life, which represents the articulating nucleus of his imperative of responsibility. It is pertinent at this time to delve a little deeper into Jonas' ideas that underlie vulnerability.

Jonas conceives an ethics for the technological civilization (ethics of responsibility) as a true criterion of moral imputation for human acts, as well as a categorical duty to limit the technological intervention of the world. His ethics establishes a causal relationship between contemporary technological empowerment, permeated and determined by the ideas of innovation and progress, and the modified scope of human action, which can now affect the future as well as all extra-human nature (environment and animals).

His reasoning is simple but very original and ahead of his time. If the scope, that is, the possible consequences of human action, has spread, horizontally in space and vertically in time, there is no reason to continue to avoid extending, in time and space, the moral responsibility for that action's aftermaths. This extension will complement traditional ethics. Jonas (2003: 32–33) proposes a new mandate, which, in opposition to the Kantian categorical imperative, seeks a principle of objective responsibility aimed at engendering public policy to govern and oversight biotechnology. Therefore, although individual actions require only the norms of traditional ethics, Jonas' ethics is intended to understand more accurately current conditions of existence, as human action is modified by technoscientific advances. In this fashion, Jonas' imperative surpasses enlightened moral subjectivity as it points to a concrete and objective future as a new horizon for human responsibility. The imperative of responsibility considers the real and concrete consequences of human action, as well as a futuristic factor that seeks to be placed as a moral foundation of universal value. Therefore, as the risks associated with technological practices also include the initiatives of genetics, the possibility of devastating the environment is related to altering, modifying, fracturing and perverting the genetic configuration of humanity.

Finally, respecting a global principle of vulnerability implies the ability to project its moral correction in time, as it protects upcoming generations, that is, those individuals who do not yet exist. This can only be justified in order to rationally predict possible present actions' aftermaths for future individuals. In this way, a global governance grounded on vulnerability is a governance for present and future generations. In this way, international policy for those who do not exist yet can only be legitimized as plausible and effective by virtue of rationally predicting future consequences of present acts.

9.6 Justice and resource allocation in pandemics

This principle points out equitable access to health, especially regarding the access to timely and appropriate medical care and the availability of basic and fundamental medicines required during treatment. As justice refers to an adequate distribution of benefits and burdens in society, it also encompasses the obligation of governments to provide citizens a minimum standard of health care. As the obligation to guarantee the right to health is progressive, it is understood that the state must implement policies and develop initiatives intended to provide the maximum possible health (access, opportunity, quality) with available resources.

Since the fulfilment of this obligation is mediated by resources availability and the economic solidity of the state, certain rules or criteria must be defined and established to optimize the distribution of benefits when availability is precarious or insufficient. The identification and definition of these rules are quite relevant, as it implies establishing distribution criteria, which are usually competitive and mutually exclusive, such as need, merit or effort. International instruments are not explicit on this matter, so their binding effect is diluted.

International biolaw is also unspecific regarding which model of health system is better to be adopted in order to guarantee the maximum realization of health. The issue is not easy to be approached, but at least we must now try to clarify some conflicting points so as not to leave this principle in the dark.

Costs restrict, sometimes dramatically, how much health a state can deliver and guarantee and how much benefit can be obtained from institutional actions. In the same way, costs can quickly tear down the best initiatives to ensure a fair and equitable health. In addition, resources – always finite – must be optimized to meet many other needs parallel to health, such as education, defense, transportation and security, among others. Therefore, some questions arise: Are inequities and costs really a problem of justice in health? If so, does the problem of inequities and costs threaten access to health and a fair distribution of benefits? If the answer, again, is affirmative: How should benefits be allocated?

It is evident that a principle of distributive justice is in tune with a public health system that guarantees, at least, equal and timely access to health. However, these benefits are limited by other components of multifactorial nature, such as resources availability, existing public health policies, possible inequities in distribution and the rationing of goods and services. In this way, a principle of distributive justice for health care environments should be based, at least, on two premises: (i) Access, coverage and equal quality in health is a right, and (ii) the state has the obligation to implement a system that, at least, comply with the minimum required in that context. In this sense, the right to a decent minimum of health can be specified as an expedited access to specific goods and services that all persons need equally, which implies to ensure universal access to *fundamental* health.

From a procedural point of view, we think that a mixed health system is tolerable only if a minimum standard of health can be satisfied. If so, the health system could work at two levels: (i) A level of mandatory social coverage for basic, critical and catastrophic health needs (preventive health, primary health, high complexity health, special services for the disabled and pandemics, among others), and (ii) a second level of private coverage to satisfy other needs and desires. From this perspective, such model shows that the state's obligations regarding the right to health are not unlimited and that the basic and critical needs are not inexhaustible either. With this certainty, there seems to be a greater consistency in the reciprocity between citizens' rights and the administration's duties.

Therefore, the proposed model points to a convergence between several theories of justice, as it incorporates moral premises supposed to be transversal to all of them, because, on the one hand, it guarantees basic health for all and, on the other hand, it allows an uneven access depending on personal initiative and purchasing power. From an egalitarian theory, a principle of equal access to good is proposed, as well as a principle of equity in the distribution system. From the utilitarian theory, we see criteria such as minimizing public dissatisfaction, maximizing social utility and promoting decision-making about resources allocation grounded upon a cost-effectiveness analysis. And based on a libertarian theory, the model allows distribution according to market fluctuations, as the second level of coverage entirely depends on the capability to access the private health system.

Obviously, the model is not exempt from difficulties because the principle of justice's hermeneutics is always conflicting and, sometimes, equivocal. Probably the crucial task is to clear up and obtain certainty about how a society could devise, fairly and unambiguously, a public policy to recognize the right to satisfy basic and critical needs, without creating a right to very expensive and expansive forms of treatment and therapy that would reduce resources that, in other circumstances, could be used more effectively. While there are paradigmatic theories about this, the problem is far from being definitively closed.

However, in pandemic times the conflictive scenario of scarce resources allocation is crossed, at least, by four types of moral disagreement, which can be analogically extended to the legal sphere, by engendering relativism in deliberation: (1) Disagreement on facts, (2) disagreement due to lack of information or data, (3) disagreement on rules and their applicability and (4) conceptual disagreements on crucial moral notions. As we have already stated in this book, common morality means prima facie principles, so these vague and general rules must be specified to gain more precise content.

If there are competing specifications, one must apply models of moral balance to determine which norms should prevail. Identifying and taking courses of action within a process of moral deliberation are not related to common sense or prima facie principles, as these are only formally shared. Rather, any deliberative process is related to the relative weight and binding force of norms. Furthermore, as an eventual balance could also be intuitive, partial or arbitrary, it is possible to build criteria to reduce intuition, partiality and arbitrariness by defining procedural rules for resources allocation.

In this complex atmosphere, a critical conflict has arisen: How to fairly deal with large numbers of patients who fall into a critical health condition. This has provoked that, in both developed and developing countries, health systems started to work in scenarios where demand for intensive medical care exceeds resources availability.

There is a need for ethical and legal (binding) guidelines to allocate treatment and scarce resources when many people compete for them. However, such guidelines are potentially controversial and obscure. We will propose a method to guide resource allocation in difficult cases. We intend to liberate reasoning and decision-making from abstract procedures exclusively based on dignity. Therefore, our proposal does not have a paralyzing effect on deliberation as occurs with natural law positions. Epistemologically, it is built on a predictive or utilitarian component and a consensual or contractual component. The predictive element is necessary, that is, it must always be present in the equation, while the consensual one is contingent, as it should be applied only in some cases.

Even though biolaw essentially addresses legal conflicts in biomedical surroundings, its hermeneutical possibilities, such as the ability to identify new possibilities of damages, new individual subjective rights and new legal interests, are extensible to extreme clinical situations, that is, those borderline scenarios whose resolution calls for more decisive criteria, denser than simple prima facie bioethical principles. In this way, by starting from a specification of traditional biolaw principles, we configure a decision-making model based on rationally demonstrable and legally plausible rules.

9.6.1 First rule: Informed competence

When a substantially competent patient presents a critical condition, he or she must be fully and objectively informed about available treatments and their expected efficacy. In the case of an unpromising prognosis, a space must be opened for the patient to express his or her wishes, priorities and personal values in a scenario that may be definitive. Many patients, faced with an evident and proven futility of a ventilator, for example, will have the possibility of refusing, informedly, voluntarily and consciously, the resource, which might work better in other patients. As other models have already shown (Savulescu, Vergano, Craxi, & Wilkinson, 2020), refusal may not be necessarily contemporaneous, but rather, it can be displayed through a valid advance directive or eve through a surrogate decision. In order to optimize scarce resources allocation, it is essential to give decisional room enough to the patient, who can judge the expected quality of life after intensive treatment close to futility. The procedural effect of this rule is optimizing not only resources allocation but also time and opportunity of distribution.

Specifying the principle of respect for autonomy into a rule of informed competence reinforces the methodological power of self-determination, as well as it optimizes decision-making's aftermaths in pandemic clinical settings. This means that applying autonomy as a general principle in decision-making can tyrannize the process, because understanding it as a common morality norm dwindles the odds of achieving agreement on its epistemological density, which opens a hermeneutical abyss that prevents decision-makers from reaching consensus on its content and scope. Therefore, autonomy, understood as a common morality norm, can turn into a harmful component for any model aimed at building an efficient decision-making framework for resource allocation in pandemic times.

9.6.2 Second rule: Priority (to the most urgent cases)

This rule points to prioritize urgent cases, which clearly reduces demand in hospitals. For this, health centers must design a clinical protocol to evaluate mild, serious and urgent cases, by giving priority to the latter. Applying this rule refines demand for treatment in the waiting rooms, whereas the need-attention relationship is mathematically perfected. Indeed, as it is quickly determined who has the worst symptomatology, clinical efforts are optimized insofar as accurate procedures to identify which patients should be treated first are implemented, without impacting the mortality rate. Thus, there is no fatal effect in delaying attention for noncritical patients, which would certainly happen when urgent care would be postponed if any protocol to identify the most critical cases is established.

Therefore, the probability ratio used to calculate the expected utility when delaying treatment of less urgent cases is considered a representation of decision-makers' degree of rationality conditioned to the total information available. Thereby, (i) the real variables (and events) considered may depend on a particular action already foreseen, (ii) the available information already includes the initial information together and (iii) the degrees of prediction of potential events are understood as conditionals of a specific action so that decision-maker's possible impacts on the real world are taken into account as relevant calculation factors.

Thus, for any action it is preferable to ensure the clarity of the rational proof, to describe the relevant events sequentially. For example, to consider whether the mortality rate will decrease and the use of scarce resources will be optimized, one must first think about whether the most seriously ill patient will survive and then, conditioned to data, whether the survival rate and resources allocation will be optimized or not.

However, this is just one of the elements to consider in the equation to determine which patients to see first. There are cases in which not only severity but also resources availability plays a critical role in decision-making. Therefore, we need to configure another rule.

9.6.3 Third rule: Effectiveness

When resources availability is exceeded by demand, this rule requires determining if ventilator treatment is an equally effective resource for all clinically relevant patients, that is, we need to check out whether ventilators cause the same outcome for the entire universe of patients who urgently claim for them.

If this scenario is consolidated, it is recommend using a rule of equal treatment for the same need, namely, applying the rule of queuing, that is, first-come, first-served. Theoretically, this criterion would be objective and, therefore, legally defensible, as there would be no other axiological elements of judgment to determine ventilators' allocation. However, we consider that this idea presents a significant fissure. While the "same resource-same need" equation points to real scenarios, it also has an important hypothetical content, so the "first-come, first-served" criterion becomes fickle and arbitrary. Strictly speaking, it means that patients with a poor prognosis, who require long periods of treatment, receive care at the expense of patients who arrive later but with a much better prognosis. This will inevitably mean a reduction in the number of lives saved.

Clarifying this provides a robust basis to conclude the need to complement the model, as it can be reasonably assumed that otherwise the error probabilities will increase with a marginal ratio of success. Indeed, for this expression, it is evident that, the number of times the uncomplemented model is applied, the chances of failure grow logarithmically. Therefore, the fact that someone gets sick sooner or later is the highest criterion for deciding resources allocation when they are equally effective for all those in need seems to be an arbitrary criterion. In this order of ideas, the rule of effectiveness must be complemented with another that we call maximization.

9.6.4 Fourth rule: Maximization

This is a utilitarian but also innate element to compute probabilities, as its content is justified not only in theory but also in popular intuition. However, this rule also works from a contractualist perspective. Indeed, if we choose behind a "veil of ignorance" (Rawls, 1999), that is, if we do so as deliberators who ignore who we are and will be in society, it would happen that rational self-interest would lead us to choose a course of action that gives us the best chance of survival. In this way, reflective equilibrium, which is a notion of epistemic justification, would make us decide to save more lives, instead of fewer, on equal terms.

In fact, a set of principles and intuitions is in reflective equilibrium when principles and intuitions coincide and decision-makers know how judgments that intuitions encode can be derived from principles. As reflective equilibrium is not a permanent state of stability, a set of principles and intuitions can be derived from equilibrium by reconsidering new information, new principles and/or intuitions about new cases. Therefore, a rational agreement on a principle (or a rule) that is fruitful in promoting criteria to save lives in emergencies would encompass the aspiration to save as many lives as possible.

In practice, saving the greatest number of lives logically implies saving those patients with the highest probability of survival. Let us imagine that one group, A, has a 90% chance of surviving with treatment, and another group, B, has a 10% chance. For ten people treated in group A, nine will survive, but only one will survive in group B. Therefore, maximizing lives saved should be a universal decision-making requirement in pandemic or analogous scenarios.

However, saving the greatest number of lives also requires estimating the duration of treatment and the use of resources, as a longer therapy means that fewer patients can be treated. Let us consider that patients in group A take 1 week to recover and patients in group B take 2 weeks. We can save two patients in group A for one patient in group B. Therefore, group A patients, being those with the highest probability of survival, should have priority. Following this criterion, the survival rate is increased by 100%.

Therefore, any factor that reduces the probability of survival and, at the same time, optimizes the use of resources is relevant at this stage. We think that this model also provides a plausible legal justification as it considers not providing intensive care to patients with high morbidity scores and low chances of survival. This means that the final stage must first be solved, maximizing the expected utility; then such stage must be addressed, maximizing the conditional expected utility, looking for the optimal choice in first stage. Thus, we continue progressively backward, until the first optimal choice stage has been obtained, through a procedure known as dynamic programming (Bernardo & Smith, 2000).

This procedure, which is ultimately a reverse induction event, satisfies the requirement that, at any stage, its continuation must be identical to the optimal procedure started with the available information. Therefore, it is not necessary to consider expected utility maximization as a "principle" of this formulation, as it is simply a consequence of another tacit principle, which we could call quantitative coherence.

Therefore:

i. We should continue if at least the best options have been analyzed.
ii. We should stop if a doubtful option is the best so far.
iii. Otherwise, we should continue until the option analyzed is the best option so far; then we should stop in any case the best option has been reached.

Is it discriminatory to apply the maximization rule? No. It would be discriminatory to include not legally relevant criteria for allocation (i.e. age, race, sexuality, religion or political beliefs). However, it is not discriminatory to use clinical data to estimate prognosis, unless this is used to systematically harm a certain group. This would not only be discriminatory but also illegal and unconstitutional. Therefore, using the probability of survival versus the expected demand for resources as the content for maximization is legally defensible.

9.6.5 Fifth rule: Selection

The maximization rule is very efficient at the first level of allocation where the goal is to save the greatest number of lives. It is clear that, in these cases, patients with high survival rate must first receive the resource. However, there may be more patients with high survival probabilities than number of ventilators. In this case, a different allocation procedure is required for this group. The selection rule must then conform to a legally defensible criterion.

There are several possible policy options. They are not all legally defensible, nor are they equally competitive.

Option 1 Lottery (Savulescu et al., 2020)

The "first come, first served" criterion may work in less complex scenarios. However, we have already shown that, in more complex cases, it becomes arbitrary. Furthermore, as high-priority patients have already been selected for treatment, to the detriment of low-priority ones, such a lottery would have a marginal impact on overall survival.

Option 2 Desert (Savulescu et al., 2020)

This criterion, which considers merit for resources allocation, is based on an idea of poetic justice. It would be plausible, then, to destinate resources to those who most deserve it. However, who deserves more and who deserves less? Does the one who needs more deserve more? Does the one who contributes the most to society deserve more? Does the younger deserve to live because he or she has a greater desert of life than the older? Clearly, this criterion can lead to arbitrary decisions, such as prioritizing the young over the old without considering other important elements of calculation.

Option 3 Utility

This criterion implies the expected duration of posttreatment life and the expected quality of life. If applied correctly, as the reader has been able to appreciate in the probabilistic demonstrations that we have deployed before, this option can maximize the quality of life and, in turn, optimize decision-making and resources allocation.

Therefore, and as a first conclusion, it seems that the most efficient criterion for scarce resource allocation in pandemics is the utilitarian one, above egalitarian and contractualist ones, as well as over the normative concept of desert. And within the utilitarian universe, it also seems that the most objective decisional criterion is the possibility of survival, considering years and quality of life.

Second, a proper decision-making process is more effective if it employs objective criteria and is not distracted by personal values, intuition, moral conscience, religion, tradition or idiosyncrasy.

Third, efficiency does not only refer to resource optimization, which is central in this scenario. But also, it is aimed at improving the ability to decide, in the most effective and least onerous way possible, who lives and who dies.

Fourth, our synoptic proposal implies an explicit defense of a non-naturalistic form of legal realism. It is committed to, what we would call, a legal cognitivism. In other words, legal language is solidly suitable to the truth, as long as moral categories of law (and, in this case, biolaw) are not reducible to any natural property.

Finally, when dealing with life and death scenarios, there is no need to conjecture moral differences where there are only factual ones.

10 Global sustainability and cosmopolitan biolaw

10.1 Economy and sustainability

The concept of economic sustainability is binary. As economy grows, an important part of natural environment is intervened, often in a pernicious way. This means that while we need economic growth, we have to deal with the erosion of the ecosystem, which, at the same time, makes economy subsystem possible. This leads us to a disturbing conclusion: In the long term, economic growth is not sustainable. As Daly (1996) announced several years ago, the term "sustainable growth" (if by growth we mean an economic one) seems to be "a bad oxymoron," because economic progress is then possible by virtue of boosting poverty and causing environmental degradation.

Economic growth does not necessarily mean sustainable development. Economy is a subsystem of natural ecosystem, so this can stop being sustainable, whereas economy continues to grow. Sustainability is a qualitative concept; instead, economic growth is a quantitative one. In this way, a sustainable ecosystem encompasses a qualitative evolution toward holistic stability and harmony between several components of multifactorial nature, such as people, technology, policy, nature, governments, international regulations and so forth. Thus, economic growth implies to increase market transactions and accumulation of wealth. Therefore, while sustainability and economics should be convergent, reciprocal and collaborative goals, they are not.

Sustainability gets meaning then if it is only understood as development instead of growth. In this fashion, an alleged sustainable global society evolves toward nothing, which means that today sustainability, in terms of global economy patterns, is an empty concept but very useful to ensure economic growth. In fact, this is a tricky conjecture because nowadays economic progress does not mean qualitative improvement but a quantitative one. That is the reason why one of the most relevant indicators for economic development is technology. No matter how many poor a country has, technological growth marks its power in global economy. Most technologized countries are supposed to be the most developed ones, because technology also means economic and political power at a global scale. This has entailed that an undesirable confusion comes into play: To believe that sustainability

DOI: 10.4324/9781003147848-10

presupposes economic growth. However, sustainable development and economic growth should not be belligerent to each other.

If we agree that, according to contemporary understanding of economy, economic growth is not sustainable as it precisely implies to erode a sustainable development, the world could go forward in implementing efficient policy for global governance to, at least, stop devastating ecosystem, which as time goes by, seems to be more and more unable to regenerate itself. Therefore, concrete measures are needed. There is a whole mythical story about some tips to achieve a sustainable development. This story is cultural and, therefore, rhetoric. We have been bombed with the idea of green sustainability, so we have to save energy, take shorter showers, not littering and so forth. However, these actions, being desirable, advisable and, ultimately, moral, are still far from being able to reach sustainability. In global terms, it would be much more sustainable to stop eating meat, for example. But this is not advised by governments, agencies or even NGOs. Why? Because doing that would be counterproductive with economic growth.

We argued that economic growth is not sustainable. This means that it is impossible to economically grow forever. Nevertheless, the more economy grows, the more sustainability is eroded. In other words, as economy gets closer to its peak of growth, let us say, its 100%, global sustainability's odds dwindle to near 0%. This does not seem to be a promising future for humanity. In fact, it implies a disturbing idea that there is no future other than an agonic extinction. We will analyze this scenario at the end of this chapter. For now, let us take one more step in deepening in the dichotomy of global sustainability-economic growth.

As the threat of existential risk escalates in contemporary times, insisting on pursuing sustainability seems to be, at best, cynical and, at worst, useless. How can we talk on sustainability being aware of the great number of starving children in Africa? Is it a sustainable world with a critical level of large, desertified areas that once were exuberant but will not be anymore? Is climate change a signal of sustainability or degradation? Certainly, it is rather baffling to witness how governments talk about seeking and fostering sustainability at the time they multiply meat industry, mining and glyphosate rains. Why do we keep seeking economic growth and "sustainable" development as if the ecosystem was infinite? Can we fight poverty and famine outside a traditional economic growth? Do we really need "economic growth" to remedy misery and suffering in the world? Is global economic growth making us richer?

Nowadays, the pursuit of happiness means, more than ever, the quest for wealth. This is not a necessarily wrong attitude, but it may be imprecise. Most problems of life can be solved with money. However, this is not an absolute truth but the result of market structure. We need goods to survive, and to get them, we have to pay for. The more money we have, the more goods we enjoy. But, while the premise "problems are easier to solve if we are richer" works very well at a micro and local scale, its efficiency at a macroeconomic level is becoming rather marginal in terms of justice and distribution of goods.

As a matter of fact, while richer countries are getting richer, poorer ones are getting poorer. The same happens at a local scale where developing countries, with a notorious unfair distribution of benefits and burdens, shows that very rich small economic groups increase their wealth, many times, at expenses of large portions of poor population.

Already in 1995, there was evidence enough that in the United States, growth made Americans poorer by increasing costs faster than benefits (Daly, 1996). Currently, some developing countries, such as Colombia, are increasing taxes for lower middle class under the predicament that the country needs money to struggle with extreme poverty and that very few citizens pay taxes. However, this measure, grounded upon a traditional idea of economic growth, seems to be counterintuitive, at least for two reasons: (i) Lower middle class will become poorer, whereas the lowest class will obtain no relevant (rather marginal) benefits. The final outcome surely will be that the total number of poor in Colombia will increase dramatically. (ii) A better measure would be to engender strong policy to stop high levels of corruption historically installed in Colombia. Channeling that enormous amount of money, which the state would obtain if corruption was significantly broken down, to combat poverty would probably impact on improving the quality of life of the lowest and lower middle class without collecting taxes from them whatsoever.

Therefore, the idea of sustainable economy relative to the ecosystem has not been considered in any calculus of macroeconomic theory. In this fashion, an optimal scale of the aggregate economy is supposed to grow ad infinitum. This is not trivial as Daly (1996: 195) says, microeconomics is intended to establish an optimal scale of each micro activity, but at the same time, it fails in defining an optimal scale for "the aggregate of all micro activities." Given this scenario, economic growth means either many people are consuming little or fewer people are consuming a lot.

A sustainable economy is not possible that way. At least, not at the present. In this book, we have proposed some models for sustainable corporate governance and organizational economics in health care and hospital management. By doing so, we have emphasized that organizational improvement is not only financial growth. We also, and very especially, need values, knowledge, intelligence, efficiency, ethics and practical wisdom. We can extend these requirements to global economy too. In that case, we will also need some guidelines and principles configured in their normative content far from the fake paradigm of sustainable growth. Such a thing is literature, unless we think ecosystem to be endless and natural resources to be unlimited. Also, following Daly (1996: 196), we only obtain real income when capital remains intact. In this order of ideas, if our capital is ecosystem and our income is sustainability, clearly there is something wrong in current global economy.

We have some doubts regarding the concept of "global" economy. At the end of the day, it may be pernicious to think of contemporary economy as a "global" one. The problem is not the term "global" but its concept, that is, the content given to it by the current market and interconnected systems of production. If, in this sense, "global" is intended to mean an alleged sustainable growth of nations, thanks to a shared and interactive economy system aimed at treating life as it was a stock, we do not buy such a thing. We believe that "global" economy needs to be understood from a cosmopolitan perspective. Yet, "cosmopolitan" does not necessarily mean "global." "Global" is essentially an economic concept, that is, quantitative, pointing to economically colonize physical parts of the world. "Cosmopolitan" instead is an ethical concept, namely, qualitative, intended to engender a sustainable attitude toward the economic fragmentation of the world.

There may be other ways to reach sustainability (the income) without sacrificing the ecosystem and its subsystems (the capital). While those initiatives are not free from criticisms and controversies, they seem to be compelling enough for reason. We will address one of them now, which is considered to be very efficient and promising for sustainability.

10.2 Effective altruism: Individual and cosmopolitan action for sustainability

As we write these lines, a child dies from hunger every 10 seconds in the world, meaning more than 3 million per year (www.worldhunger.org). At the same time, while the rate of environmental damage increases across the planet, 100 billion cows were killed in 2020 to supply the world meat industry. Just for those who think that killing cows is not related to sustainability, we recommend reading a 2020 report by Carbon Brief (https://interactive.carbonbrief.org) where, upon trustable evidence, it is exposed that meat production accounts for one-quarter of the world's greenhouse gas emissions and takes up half of the planet's habitable surface.

Certainly, poverty and pain experimented by large portions of humans and animals all over the world is a significant issue for sustainability (for now, we will not talk about animals). No international policy has been able so far to end suffering and misery on the globe. Leaving the possibility to improve the conditions of existence of those who suffer to personal choices and initiatives, initially it does not seem to be the solution. However, individual choices can significantly help the world reach sustainability.

Peter Singer (2016a: 14) argues that if we can prevent famine and misery from happening without sacrificing anything of similar moral relevance, we ought to do it. He also states that if many people acted that way, not only our lives and society but also the world would be substantially changed. Why then to wait for state or government's policies to start changing the world and make it a better place to live? If as Singer (2016a: 5–14) does, we assume some premises as valid, we could give more compelling content to that position:

Premise 1. Suffering, poverty and starvation are bad things.

Premise 2. If benefits caused by helping others in need overcome by far eventual costs of our actions and these do not also entail a real sacrifice to us, we ought to help others.

Premise 3. If we can change a life for better without changing ours for worse, we ought to do it.

Singer's ideas displayed in his influential article "Famine, Affluence and Morality" (originally published in 1972) are the ground where these premises are justified upon and represent the philosophical foundations for effective altruism, which is a philosophical idea as it has been primarily developed by philosophers. However, they have not been the only ones responsible for the planetary spread of the movement this concept produced. Once the philosophical idea became a social movement, other people, from different backgrounds and disciplines, contributed to shaping an epistemology for it, not only in terms of its philosophical foundations but also regarding its predictive methodologies and specific procedures to achieve and guarantee the greatest effectiveness of altruistic actions.

While Singer's paper played a very important role in stimulating other thinkers, scholars and activists to deliberate about the moral importance of doing our best to help others, and it was discussed in some philosophical circles, it did not have a great epistemological impact. It was not, until about 2007, that Toby Ord and William MacAskill, at the University of Oxford, created the Giving What We Can organization, precisely influenced by Singer's work. Since that moment on, the movement gained a quite concrete configuration, until it became what it is today, involving many people and organizations in the world.

Effective altruism is not really very interested in motivations but rather in adding good to others through the real and objective consequences of actions. Of course, this requires this motivation even seeking a personal interest, to cause very concrete benefits for others, without engendering harm to them. Therefore, effective altruism is an idea consisting in two different but consubstantial elements: (i) Altruism: The idea that we should do our best to make the world a better place to live by helping others. This does not mean that everything we do must be altruistic but that we should live knowing that our actions impact others both positively and negatively. A meaningful life, therefore, must be intended to constellate systematic and permanent actions aimed at alleviating lives of those who are in poverty, pain and misery. (ii) Effectiveness: When helping others, we should use and allocate our resources in the most effective way possible. This point encompasses a radical difference between effective altruism and the traditional concept of altruism, understood as simple philanthropy. While this one means simply to do good, effective altruism implies to do the most good you can do (Singer, 2016a) according to our possibilities, rationality and will.

Effective altruism is based on that living a completely ethical life means using part of our economic, material and intellectual resources, to do the greatest possible good to others. The central argument is that we can do much more to help others (i.e. save many more lives) if we simply take a more objective and rational approach to what we do with our skills, time and money (Singer, 2016a).

If the goal is to do the greatest possible good, effective altruism holds that we must dispense with sentimentality and only give to organizations that are highly effective. Thus, instead of allowing emotion, intuition or loyalty to dictate our giving behavior, we must think more scientifically, about who and which social cause we should contribute to (Skelton, 2016: 137–146).

While effective altruism seems to point to an entirely advisable way of living, it is not difficult to find arguments in favor of all those who become effective altruists. However, we can also find some criticisms. First, effective altruism seems to have a counterintuitive component, as it is not concerned with the purity of motivations but rather with consequences. In this sense, the agent's selfish or altruistic intention would make no difference if the consequence was beneficial to others. Second, effective altruism essentially affirms that there is only one correct action to take in a given situation. Thus, it presents decision-making as a process reduced to white or black, when the world is much more complex and multifactorial than that. Third, as it is often impossible to know in advance the true impact of a donation, effective altruism is supported by a predictive theoretical calculation that may fail. Fourth, effective altruism does not address critical scenarios from an axiological point of view, such as the foreign debt of poor countries, imperialism, corruption and inequality of power. Therefore, at the end of the day, effective altruism does not change the status quo and does not demand radical advances on a global level. In this way, its true impact in global change is rather marginal. As many people are motivated by emotion when they donate to charity, pressuring them to be more rational could be counterproductive. In this way, overly analytical givers could act on a vertical hyper-rationalist logic that could nullify or at least inhibit the generous spirit that effective altruism seeks to foster. Sixth, human cognition has its limits, and an explicit attempt to do the greatest good can sometimes go wrong. A thoughtless application of effective altruism can, for example, lead to disregard important interpersonal values, poor life choices, psychological damage, unbalanced views and, at worst, several forms of bigotry. Seventh, effective altruism is a kind of charitable imperialism as it claims for itself the moral ground to make decisions, pondering, evaluating and ranking social causes and also the potential beneficiaries of donations. As such, it incites a rather perverse and also a highly concentrated way of giving, where the "experts" decide where the money goes rather than the individual donors.

We think that effective altruism can tolerate these criticisms as there is enough evidence, even though it is always open to discussion, to prove the efficiency of utilitarian moral theories to reach benefits for the most in society. In addition, none of the critiques is completely true because they express a high level of hermeneutics, which, in this case, is very probably grounded on ideological factors. Finally, there are several reasons (instead of interpretations) to think that effective altruism is a recommendable initiative and a good way of living. Some of them speak by themselves: First, if we donate only to charities that dramatically improve large numbers of lives and create a measurable difference, effective altruism will incentivize organizations to be more transparent and demonstrate their effectiveness. Second, effective altruism inspires critical thinking by applying evidence and reason to determine the most effective ways to improve the world. It requires, then, that we consider all possible causes and consequences (or, at least, the most that we can) and then act in a way that produces the greatest positive impact (Friedman, 2013). Third, effective altruism broadens our knowledge about the possibilities of living less selfishly. At the same time, it allows reason, rather than emotion, to determine how we should live. In this way, it fosters a kind of global empathy by forcing us to look beyond our own interests and value all sensitive lives, no matter what nationality, creed, ancestry, religion or species. In other words, to be an effective altruist, we should take "the point of view of the universe" (De Lazari-Radek & Singer, 2016; Sidgwick, 1981). Fourth, effective altruism is a philosophical approach that encourages the use of available time and money (usually in amounts that are not entirely meaningful to us) in a more effective way to reduce suffering, extend life and improve the quality of life of many others. Fifth, there is important evidence that effective altruism movement has significantly contributed to reduce global catastrophic risk, as well as to improve global health and farm animal welfare (MacAskill, 2019: 11). Sixth, effective altruism can engender some social structures to enable permanent and systemic change in the world. Gabriel and McElwee (2019: 99–114) ask themselves whether or not effective altruism can drive institutional action and structural policy for combating global poverty. They argue, against objectors who say that effective altruism fails in addressing issues of systemic changes, that effective altruists aimed at doing the best are and have been able to impact and support large-scale systemic change initiatives. In this fashion, regarding global poverty, effective altruism can impulse and power interjurisdictional initiatives to secure obtaining systemic outcomes, especially establishing alliances with more political movements that share the goal of improving the lives of poorest people in the world (Gabriel & McElwee, 2019: 112).

Therefore, while the world waits for competent governmental policies to be developed and implemented in order to fight global suffering, improve health systems and break the pandemic down, we think that effective altruism gathers merits enough to be considered as an alternative and complementary option to achieve sustainability from a cosmopolitan and collaborative point of view.

10.3 Why animal sustainability is human sustainability too

In his best seller, *Animal Liberation*, Peter Singer (2015: xxi) finishes his preface to the 1975 edition by stating that "Animal Liberation is Human Liberation too." He means that as in affluent nations rearing animals for food wastes as much food as it produces, stopping eating meat and killing animals are the best ways to make a lot of extra food available, which, correctly distributed, could eliminate starvation and malnutrition from the earth. In this way, liberating animals from death and suffering means to liberate humans from hunger. We can paraphrase his statement to argue that animal sustainability is human sustainability too. Two types of reasons to defend animal sustainability can be found: Instrumental and essential. *Instrumental* refers to respecting animals because by doing so, we can take care of the ecosystem and ourselves. This implies to justify upon evidence why to rear large livestock impacts environment for worse. *Essential* implies compelling enough reasons to demonstrate why animals deserve moral and juridical consideration for what they are and mean in themselves. This entails to raise moral reasons.

10.3.1 Instrumental reasons: Animals and environment

According to the UK Climate Change Agency, if we want to save the planet, we need to reduce the amount of meat we eat. The point is that meat and milk companies have become one of the biggest contributors to climate change by polluting more than the entire oil industry. The five corporations that process animal products are responsible for more greenhouse gases than the oil companies ExxonMobil, Shell or BP together.

Animals kept on farms, especially cows, emit a significant amount of methane, a flammable gas that can be used for fuel if captured and harnessed, but it is also a strong pollutant. It is well known that the increase in the concentration of carbon dioxide (CO_2) in the planet's atmosphere is causing global warming, which is accelerating the poles' melting and radically changing the climate, which increasingly impacts our lives.

Methane is a pollutant 25 times more potent than carbon dioxide, so it is critical to mitigate and minimize emissions of this harmful gas for the environment and ultimately for people. Each cow emits between 70 and 120 kg of methane per year, so each of these animals is responsible for more than 2,000 kg equivalent of CO_2 per year. Worldwide, it is estimated that there are around 1.5 billion cows and bulls, which together with other ruminant animals emit the equivalent of 2 billion tons of CO_2 per year.

One might think that this is insignificant compared to the greenhouse gas emissions caused by eruptions and volcanic activity in the world. Yet, it is not. If we take into account all the emanations from active volcanoes in the world, and we add emissions in volcanic and subaquatic lakes, we obtain an approximate of 645 million tons of CO_2 per year according to the specialized journals, *Nature* and *Forbes*. Thus, livestock activity emits three times the amount of volcanic activity on the planet.

These numbers do not include the slash and burn of grasslands and rainforests to create areas for livestock to graze, which account for another 2.8 billion tons of CO_2. According to the U.S. Environmental Protection Agency (EPA), livestock is the direct cause of 24% of greenhouse gases. Livestock currently occupy 30% of the total land surface of our planet, being an important cause of deforestation and being responsible for the destruction of almost 70% of the Amazon rainforest.

Since the beginning of the industrial age, the increase in CO_2 in the atmosphere to date has been nothing short of impressive, but even in an era of accelerated emission of greenhouse gas, it was not until after 1950 that it accelerated further the annual emission and concentration of CO_2 in our environment. This trend supports the idea that modern human activity, and not nature, is changing the chemistry of the air, and therefore, the climate of the entire planet.

However, despite these evidence, people think that decelerating climate change passes for other sorts of actions. For instance, many people think that they can positively impact climate change by switching from a conventional car to a hybrid one. In fact, they do, as that can dwindle about a ton of carbon emissions per year, which is significant. However, you can also switch your diet, for example, from a carnivorous one into a vegan one. If only one person in the United States made that change, he or she reduced 1.5 tons of carbon emissions per year. Hence, changing the diet is much more significant than switching the car. However, most people are not aware of that. Also, the United Nations has said that livestock produces more greenhouse gas emissions than the whole transportation sector. If we consider all cars, trucks, ships, planes and trains, they all together produce fewer greenhouse gases than the meat industry.

On the other hand, Peter Singer (2016b: 281) has demonstrated that feeding cows with grass is not better than doing it with grains. Many people think that feeding livestock with grass is better for climate change, but it is not. In fact, it is worse. When meat producers feed cows with grain at the very last months of their lives, they do it because the cows get fat quicker that way. So, they are producing more meat than feeding cows with grass. However, as livestock eats, it produces methane as well. Therefore, producing 1 kg of meat from a livestock fed with grass requires more days of feeding and digestion in comparison to livestock fed with grain. In other words, that kilogram of meat is responsible for more methane emissions due to the digestive process of animals. Feeding animals with grass is not friendly with the environment. There is no such thing as a friendly meat with the environment.

In December 2015, a report published in the context of the agreements reached at the Summit of Climate Change in Paris, better known as "The Paris Agreement," said that even doing great efforts to reduce livestock's emissions footprint, the meat industry will consume a growing proportion of the remaining carbon budget. This will make extremely difficult to limit the increase of 2°C of average global temperature over preindustrial levels. Therefore, even switching from solar energy to a wind one (being something good), dwindling global warming will be really hard.

Many people affirm that an intensive meat industry is necessary to feed a growing world population, expected to reach 10,000 million in 2050. However, this is not correct. We produce a lot of grains to feed livestock. Almost 35% of the total of grains we produce is to feed animals. Could not we use that to feed humans? As a matter of fact, feeding one cow to produce 1 kg of meat implies to use 6 kg of protein. Animals use proteins only to live, keep their bodies warm and develop their bones, among others. Thus, we are clearly wasting proteins.

Do we really need animal protein to live? Not at all. According to the U.S. Department of Agriculture (2015), soy is by far the most effective way of producing proteins, however; even rice and corn crops, as well as other legumes and wheat, produce more proteins per hectare than any animal product. Moreover, animal products vary in their efficiency. Milk is more efficient than eggs, which are more efficient than meat. In fact, cow meat is the less efficient among all of them.

Now, is eating fish better than eating meat? Not really. There is not such a thing as a compassionate slaughter of fish. They usually die suffocated. Also, slaughter itself deserves more reflection as it seems to be difficult to justify killing free animals when it is not necessary. Finally, is fishing sustainable? Fishing industry is depleting fishery resources, which certainly leads to an unsustainable situation. Already in the 1950s, cod fishing collapsed in the North Atlantic. At the beginning there were a lot of fish that fed Europe and North America for centuries. However, the indiscriminate fishing fractured the cod reproduction chain, which, despite the efforts implemented by some policies and regulations, never recovered. In fact, in terms of commercial purposes, the Atlantic cod has disappeared. Therefore, fishing does not represent a sustainable way of producing food whatsoever.

A study by the Oxford Martin School concluded that the massive adoption of a vegetarian diet around the world would reduce CO_2 emissions linked to food by two-thirds, which in turn represent one-third of CO_2 emissions. The livestock sector is responsible for 9% of carbon dioxide from human activities and other much more harmful gases such as methane (37%) and nitrous oxide (65%).

Likewise, 70% of the world's fertile land is used for agricultural crops intended to feed animals, which, in turn, use 30% of the planet's fertile surface, according to UN data. World livestock production uses about 77 million tons of plant protein annually to produce 58 million protein of animal origin for human consumption.

Yet, livestock contributes to soil degradation, land and water pollution and climate change. In addition, it has a great impact on water resources: Livestock consumes water in an amount of five to ten times greater than the cultivation of plants. About 1,500 liters of water are required to generate a kilo of grains and ten times that amount, 15,000 liters, to produce a kilo of beef.

Even if greenhouse gas emissions from industry and transport are totally suppressed, the climate crisis cannot be stopped or food security guaranteed if land uses and dietary habits are not changed. To achieve these objectives, it is necessary to increase the forest mass, end food waste and reduce the space dedicated to livestock, which implies minimizing the consumption of meat, according to the Intergovernmental Panel on Climate Change (IPCC), the group of scientists that advises the United Nations on global warming.

The report, commissioned by the United Nations in 2016, was presented in 2019 in Geneva after the draft prepared by 103 scientists from 52 countries. The final version highlights that the exponential growth of the world population and changes in consumption patterns have caused unprecedented rates of land and water use. About 70% of freshwater consumption is used for agriculture, and a similar percentage of the ice-free land surface is affected by human use. Since the middle of the last century, the per capita consumption of vegetable fats, meats and calories has skyrocketed, the report recalls.

These types of activities accounted for 23% of greenhouse gas emissions in the 2007–2016 period. If activities before and after the food system are included, the percentage shoots up to 37%. Fertilizers in agriculture and methane and nitrogen oxide associated with livestock are the main sources of contamination.

In addition, the document implicitly calls for consuming less meat when it recommends promoting plant-based nutrition, such as large grains, legumes, fruits, vegetables and "foods of animal origin" but associated with "resilient, sustainable and low production systems in greenhouse gas emissions." This change in consumption patterns could free several million square kilometers of land by 2050, reducing up to 8 million gigatons of carbon dioxide annually. We can represent that in the following graphic (Figure 10.1):

Delaying action could lead to some irreversible impacts on some ecosystems, which, in turn, would generate greenhouse gases that would further warm the planet. Rapid climate adaptation and mitigation actions, aligned with sustainable land management and sustainable development, could reduce the risk for millions of people exposed to extreme weather events, desertification, land degradation and food insecurity. And in this endeavor, stopping eating meat plays a crucial role.

10.3.2 Essential reasons: Animals and morality

We feel that providing moral arguments to stop killing animals may be an unnecessary task. Specialized literature is plenty of good and compelling reasons for people to make the decision to turn into vegetarianism or veganism. However, the indiscriminate slaughter of animals all over the world continues. In this order of ideas, dedicating some pages to insist on the importance of respecting animal lives is not a trivial or tautological idea. Human

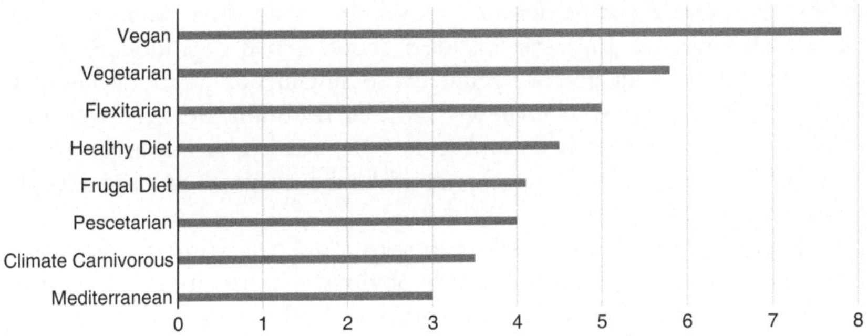

Figure 10.1 Potential mitigation of CO_2 emissions if we change our diet. Note: In billions of tons of CO_2 per year. Scenario in 2050. Source: United Nations Intergovernmental Panel on Climate Change (2019).

contempt for animal life seems not to have limits. In 2020, 100 billion cows were killed to supply the meat industry. More than 100 million animals died in scientific laboratories, and at least, other 80 million died at fur farms. On the other hand, back in November, the government of Denmark decided to cull 17 million minks in response to COVID-19 outbreaks. The measure is not proved to have been correct thus far. Also, we have to consider that minks are only reared to be killed at some point of their lives because of their coveted fur. Well, this does not seem to be so morally justifiable.

Being concerned about animal welfare means to be worried about the use of animals for food, because this is by far the biggest area in which humans exploit and abuse animals. If we simply look at the numbers, this area of using animals for food shadows all the other areas put together. So, the abuse of companion animals, of cats and dogs or horses; the abuse of animals in laboratories; and the abuse of animals for fur are really small settings compared to the use of animals for food.

Many people are concerned about the use of animals in research, for example, but we just mentioned about a hundred million animals used in research worldwide approximately. However, we also said that there are 100 billion animals used for food, and that is only talking about land animals and not about fish. Therefore, we have ten hundred times more animals used in food production than in research or experimentation, even without including fish. If we are concerned about this scenario, then we need to reduce animal suffering.

If we add fish, the numbers get larger still. If we look at fish caught in the wild for human consumption, we have about at least 1 trillion, 1,000 billion animals, and possibly even more. And although wild caught fish are unaffected during their lives, there is no humane slaughter for wild caught fish. They do suffer when they are killed. There is strong evidence that fish do feel pain, so we ought to be concerned about the catching and killing of fish as well.

As we are aimed at giving simple and understandable arguments to justify why humans should not participate in modern intense meat production, we will not elaborate on sophisticated ideas about animal cognition. We will expose two simple but precise arguments to sustain our position. The first argument comes from Rachels (2004), whose reasoning fits very well into what we want to express here, and it does not involve any complicated or controversial premises. We think that his ideas about animals and morality are almost self-evident.

Rachels' first premise is that it is wrong to cause pain without a good enough reason. And that seems to be fairly obvious. The second premise is that animals suffer in modern meat production. The third premise is that we could nourish ourselves in other ways, without using animals. And, in one sense, that is obvious, because there are many people who do not eat meat. Maybe, this is an indisputable premise. The next proposition is an ethical point, but it is not really a very controversial one. It says that our enjoyment of the meat tastes is not a good enough reason to justify the amount of suffering that animals have to endure. We should not make animals suffer just for our pleasure, so just because someone enjoys watching an animal suffer is not a good enough reason to make that animal suffer. Likely, if the pleasure obtained by eating meat does not justify the great amount of suffering inflicted on animals, we should stop slaughtering them.

The second argument comes from the principle of equal consideration of interests (Singer, 2015), which is fundamental to extend legal protection to animals, insofar as interests do matter, regardless of who owns them. In fact, it is likely that we all agree in the interest of living a life with as little suffering as possible. In this sense, pleasure and pain are important to all who can experience them. This situation implies the obligation to consider, at least, the interests of all those capable of feeling pleasure or pain, that is, all sentient entities. From this argument, it is possible to affirm, then, that sentience is a sufficient condition to (i) have interests and (ii) consider everyone's interests equally relevant.

Some contemporary philosophers argue that sentience is not a sufficient and necessary condition for their moral and legal consideration (Frey, 1980; Nussbaum, 2007; Steinbock, 1978). The common denominator of their arguments is the notion that moral and legal protection should be extended only to those individuals who also possess certain levels of rationality, intelligence or language, or those capable of moral reciprocity, which also implies a certain level of intelligence or rational language. It is not clear how such claims could be successful. First, why would animals' eventual lack of rationality, intelligence or language enable us to ignore or disregard their pain as morally and legally relevant? Second, if intelligence, rationality and language are necessary conditions for moral consideration, what happens to all those human beings who do not possess any of these faculties, such as babies or people in a persistent vegetative state, for example? Are they not worthy of moral concern? Third, many adult mammals and birds exhibit more rationality and intelligence than human infants. Some animals, such as apes or dolphins, are clearly capable of communicating with one another, while some humans are not. Should some human beings, such as those with brain palsy, be excluded from the moral and legal community while we should include apes and dolphins? Certainly, efforts to limit moral and legal consideration to human beings only, based on the possession of certain features, are unsuccessful either in including all humans or in excluding all animals from some moral and legal attention.

Therefore, the principle of equal consideration of interests requires us to consider interests and preferences of one individual as equally equivalent to those of any other. In other words, the equal consideration of interests requires that we adopt, as we have mentioned before, "the point of view of the universe" (De Lazari-Radek & Singer, 2014; Sidgwick, 1981), which we could translate into a cosmopolitan point of view.

If an animal is sentient and if its sentience is a sufficient condition for having interests, we must consider it on an equal basis with ours to make decisions whose consequences can cause great levels of pain and suffering. Indeed, the historical human tyranny that has oppressed animals for centuries and centuries continues to be perpetrated in many ways: Agriculture, livestock, cosmetic experimentation, scientific experimentation, entertainment, hunting and fishing, clothing and accompaniment, among others. In most of these activities, the human being treats animals as mere instruments, without thinking, even for a moment, about their interests, pain and suffering.

A cosmopolitan biolaw can generate normative force that, quickly, translates into changes in behaviors and habits, only because of the value contained in its biocentric and antispeciesist nature. Indeed, from this conception, it is possible to challenge the human being not only to reflect on the importance of morally and legally respecting animals and stop causing them unnecessary suffering but also, and very especially, to modify eating habits and, thus, stop institutionalizing the cruel slaughter and unjustifiable suffering of animals on the planet.

10.4 Biotechnology, pandemic and existential risk

The latent possibility of the global debacle caused by technological actions has haunted human consciousness for some time. Bostrom and Cirkovic (2008) inaugurated the concept of "global catastrophic risks," and although some of their epistemological approaches seemed to meet science fiction, all the threatening dangers preluded in their book had a powerful foundation in reality. We will use their concepts of global risk and existential risk to present, synoptically, our vision of the matter.

Planetary risk looms over contemporary life, and thinking about devastating corollaries to our existence does not seem like a futile task. The possibility of global catastrophe is not mere literature, so believing that humanity faces no threat in this age is not tenable in light of the evidence. Conjecturing about our future is not a trivial endeavor, as biotechnological developments unfold a whole constellation of new dangerous ups and downs faced never before in the history of our species.

Many say that talking about the risks involved in current biotechnologies is an exaggeration that lacks objectivity, because bioscience has not yet reached its perfection, and thinking about its potential threats only begets a hypothetical scenario. However, how sure can we be that there is no fatality lurking in new technologies, waiting its time to colonize and, at worst, annihilate our existence? Furthermore, even if we are not able to prove that there is an objective hazard in biotechnology, just taking such a possibility seriously involves at least a subjective risk. Either way, being objective or subjective, the possibility of disaster deserves special consideration, because even accepting that trying to distinguish between objective and subjective risk is an indecisive task, biotechnological practices tolerate its degradation, and although its consequences may not occur in our time, they can impact the near future. Thus, affirming that biotechnology only contains apocryphal threats does not represent a compelling perspective.

The exponential growth of the contemporary technological device seemed, at first, to herald the arrival of a promised dawn. However, that innocent conjecture was the prelude of disturbing events. All the super powerful biotechnological tools originally intended to improve life and fight disease hide the underlying risk of misuse. This scenario demands, now more than ever, positive actions from different regions of human thought. Ultimately, it is we humans who have caused the emergence of this impressive catalog of new global risks. For the same reason, we are called to rethink our existence. And thinking means doing. Suspension of thought and action when facing technological risks is not an acceptable attitude at the present time. Looking away, pretending that nothing is happening is the most cynical attitude that we could assume.

However, global risk does not imply existential risk. Rather, it happens the other way around. Global risk has the potential to inflict serious harm on human life and well-being at a global scale. Climate change and the current coronavirus pandemic are examples of global risks. All of them share at least three characteristics: (i) They imply destruction of human life (and extra human life in many cases), (ii) their scope is planetary and (iii) they cause social disruption. Therefore, addressing global risk, from a holistic perspective, tending to generate regulation and policies for its management is a complex task that contains several pragmatic difficulties. First, they require a homogeneous interjurisdictional will. Second, its mitigation is very expensive. Third, making decisions to face these risks in a transversal and consensual way that requires value judgments, always crossed by subjective and, many times, stubborn morals. Fourth, the evaluation of these risks requires a correct understanding of reality, which requires relevant levels of intelligence. Fifth, dealing with global risks implies being able to predict, with a significant degree of certainty, possible consequences of such risks and the actions taken to combat them, which is why, once again, important intellectual capacity is required. Sixth, if there is determination, but not much intelligence, policies implemented to mitigate threats usually cause other collateral damage and even create new risks, increasing the total risk coefficient. And seventh, as humanity has already been dealing with global risks for a long time, it has somehow naturalized them, so a serious consideration of them is only intense when the risk is evident to people's perception. This is clear in the current pandemic, where the vast majority comply with regulations implemented to avoid getting infected. However, not everyone in the world lives worried about climate change or the ozone layer's deterioration.

On the other hand, existential risk implies greater scale and danger. Every existential risk has a global reach, but its threat is not reduced to that single factor. In fact, its most notable characteristic is that it threatens to cause the extinction of intelligent life on the planet, at best drastically and at worst permanently. Other essential features of existential risk are the following: (i) It is irreversible, (ii) it is inexorable, (iii) i is completely devastating in terms of annihilation of life, (iv) it is transtemporal and (v) it does not grant the opportunity to learn from the experience, because it depletes it not only as a concept or idea (in a Platonic sense) but also as a circumstance and event.

When we refer to the transtemporal status of existential risk, we mean that the assessment of how devastating and threatening an existential catastrophe is regarding global risk depends on how much importance we give to future lives. If the content of our calculation is immediate, both risks assume an equidistant value with respect to the maximum danger contained in both catastrophic scenarios. On the other hand, if the equation includes a futuristic factor, clearly existential risk should concern us much more than global risk.

Bostrom (2002) distinguishes six qualitatively different types of risks according to their scope and intensity. The third dimension, probability, can be superimposed on the previous two dimensions. In equal conditions, a risk is more serious if it has a substantial probability to happen and if our actions can make that probability significantly higher or lower. In the following figure, we give content to these risks according to Bostrom (2002) taxonomy. However, we add three more, which we include in the concept of universal risks, whose dimension is imposed over all the previous ones (Table 10.1):

"Personal," "local," "global," "transgenerational" or "cosmic" refers to how large is the population (and entities) directly affected; a global risk is one that affects all humanity and offspring; and a universal risk impacts the entire cast of entities in the ontological space. "Tolerable" versus "terminal" indicates the intensity of damage. A bearable risk can cause great destruction, but we can recover from it or find ways to cope with its consequences. In contrast, a terminal risk entails that targets are irreversibly annihilated in ways that radically reduce their potential to live the kind of life they aspire to. In the case of personal risks, for example, a terminal outcome could be death, a permanent brain injury or a life sentence. An example of a local terminal risk would be genocide that leads to the annihilation of a people or an ethnic group. And a terminal universal risk would clearly be the extinction of the universe.

Now, creating a model to predict existential risks is certainly complex, because many of them are only hypothetical. However, many are also real and

Table 10.1 Types or risks

Scope					
Cosmic	Extinction of a star	Extinction of a very far galaxy	Extinction of the universe	**Universal risks**	
Transgenerational	Extinction of an insect species	Drastic loss of biodiversity/ Modification of genetic identity	Extinction of humanity	**Existential risks**	
Global	Global warming	Coronavirus	Aging of generations of humans	**Global catastrophic risks**	
Local	Congestion in the bank line for a person who takes so long in cashing a check	Unemployment in a country	Genocide		
Personal	Hair loss	Theft of my car	Fatal crash of two trains		
	Imperceptible	Bearable	Terminal	Type of risk	***Intensity***

very possible. The question is to know how much data and information we have to model this risk. The collision of an asteroid with the earth is an existential risk already modeled, because there is enough information about that scenario. And this data is quite accurate, because the impact of a galactic body with our planet indicates a catastrophe whose only factor of calculation is the imminent, inevitable and total destruction of the earth. However, other existential risks, such as a nuclear war, for example, involve many other factors that depend on a prediction exercise that must contain various elements of judgment, which ultimately are upon human decisions, always volatile. Therefore, modeling existential risk and then establishing public policies for its eventual management require a deeper calculation that must be supported by a holistic methodology, which seeks to capture and represent the essence of various characteristics and attributes inherent to a system exposed to risk, as well as its facets, dimensions and hierarchies.

While ontologically inverting the way of inhabiting the world, as well as reversing the actions that have already eroded the environment and the biosphere seems to be an implausible task, at least, we can avoid the occurrence of future damage and the emergence of new threats at a large scale. In this way, the probability of existential risk would express a downward curve. Controlling biotechnological practices' dangerous aftermaths implies to rule them efficiently, where biolaw comes into play in a very crucial role, because it has the ability to build binding regulatory frameworks to govern these new inventions, as well as it can promote the production of public policies to predict and manage potentially dangerous consequences of bioscientific action.

Conclusions: Toward a cosmopolitan biolaw in post-pandemic times

1 Toward a cosmopolitan biolaw

In this book we have proposed a cosmopolitan biolaw as an integrated vision for sustainable governance. On this basis, it is important to deal with the challenges of biolaw in the post-pandemic world. We argue that biolaw can contribute to engender more efficient and workable policy for organizational health care economics, global governance and sustainability in the context of a global society after the COVID-19 crisis. As biolaw historically has exhibited diverse conceptions, since its first relevant theoretical version appeared, four theories emerged in the past 20 years. We have seen that such biolaw's conceptions differ from one another, by getting biolaw's meaning from divergent ideologies. No version of those heterogeneous approaches has been able to get enough epistemological density to colonize the other ones. Thus, biolaw's traditional conceptions had peacefully coexisted until now.

However, configuring a cosmopolitan biolaw for governance and global sustainability has implied to make visible the legitimacy crisis of biolaw profession. In other words, we have demonstrated that cosmopolitan biolaw has jurisdiction over making biojuridical claims and judgments about bioscientific practices and global scenarios involving risks for humanity and life as a whole. While reviewing traditional epistemologies of biolaw, this problem seemed to be trivial, but it is not. While the conceptual lightness of biolaw's traditional conceptions comes from the fact that their theoretical and procedural bases are ethical rather than juridical, deepening into this historical mistake was not a minor task whatsoever. Claiming that biolaw cannot be understood without bioethics is reductionist and hides the real scope of this new field, as well as it reveals an oblique intellection that simply understands biolaw as parasitical upon bioethics.

This has engendered an overlapping of normative universes, preventing biolaw from being understood as a discipline different from bioethics. As traditional conceptions fossilized biolaw as a field at bioethics' command, biolaw slowed down its epistemological development. Indeed, there has been conceptual laxity to analyze this promiscuous relationship. Certainly, the

DOI: 10.4324/9781003147848-102

stubborn conviction that bioethics and biolaw were alike made the true meaning and, therefore, the true legal nature of biolaw invisible.

Consequently, we have explored biolaw's four different conceptions, closely linked to bioethics by deepening different types of wrong relationships between both fields, called juridification, complementation, subjection, overlap, substitution, colonization and intersection. The analysis's outcome was to offer a cosmopolitan conception of biolaw, which distinguishes itself from bioethics and traditional law, especially in its interjurisdictional scope. Cosmopolitan biolaw is then a new legal epistemology encompassing new hermeneutical and deliberative models to understand and peruse contemporary societal challenges raised by new paradigms of health care organizations and sustainable governance.

Therefore, cosmopolitan biolaw is able to achieve an interjurisdictional regulatory scope becoming the basis for international governance and sustainability in a post-COVID-19 world. In this way, cosmopolitan biolaw is a relevant instrument for the realization of the United Nation's Sustainable Development Goals (SDGs), by enabling a better equilibrium among a balanced environment, an ecological and organic animal care and the social and cultural development of society toward sustainability.

2 Ethical foundations of biolaw in the ethics of the body

In order to go deeper into the ethical foundations of biolaw in the phenomenological and hermeneutical philosophy of the body, we have looked more deeply into the philosophical foundations of the ethics of biolaw. It is characteristic that it is democratic politics that functions as the foundation of the development of legal decision-making on biolaw. The participatory public debate shapes and characterizes how a society deals with biolaw, even in terms of crisis like the COVID-19, where democratic governance takes form of a strong interventionist and authoritarian state. In complex societies there is always the risk of biopolitics and biopower as control and surveillance society that takes over the power of the body and defines its role in society as well as its legal status. However, it is the vision of the good life in ethics, law and politics that lies behind the conception of cosmopolitan biolaw in a given society. But such a vision of the good life needs to be measured and related to the categorical imperative of universal norms and rules in society. In this context, it is characteristic for biolaw that it forms a new relation to the living world implying a new kind of natural law based upon a nonanthropocentric respect for the whole living world with focus on the rights of human person to life and body. Here, we have seen how biolaw is closely related to a global and biocentric bioethics. In this context, it is the creative function of judgment to find the right balance between the different concerns of care in the decision-making of judgment of biolaw.

Nevertheless, the legal history of biolaw is taking place in the tension among biopower, biopolitics and the bioethical concern to find the right balance of the body between person and thing in society. If we consider the body in a phenomenological perspective, the body emerges as both lived experience and biological matter as part of a physical world. The double position of the body in relation to the human person influences our concepts of disease and functions as the basis for medical judgment. In history, there has been a cultural and social struggle about the human body, and this has defined the legal status of the body. Biopolitics, biopower and bioethics have shaped the different conceptions and discourses about the human body in theology, medicine and other different approaches to ethics and law of the body. In modern society this situation also influences that idea, as it is the case of our conceptions of the body in risk society, where the reception and understanding of disease in COVID-19 are influenced by this cultural and legal history of the body.

On this basis, we have discussed the ethical basis of biolaw in relation to some of the recent bioethical challenges to biolaw in the twenty-first century. Here, biolaw is related to the debate about the fundamental purpose of biomedicine, which confronts the question of the naturalness of disease and the dream of the long and immortal life, as a core dimension of the search for cure and a healthy life as proposed by biomedicine and biotechnology. Behind the use of science and technology to heal the human body, we find the dream of the use of reproductive and genetic technologies to create better people and to enhance humanity. There is the dream of creating a more perfect kind of human being behind the fantasies of the technocosmos. Nevertheless, this has also defined our concern for an ethics of vulnerability as fundamental for biolaw in the twenty-first century.

3 Health care, corporate social responsibility, values-driven management and organizational ethics

Indeed, we have in this book placed the discussion of bioethics and biolaw in the framework of corporate governance, business ethics and sustainability for public and private organizations. From presenting the ethical foundations of biolaw in contemporary health care systems, we have proposed to situate it in the perspective of corporate governance, social responsibility and stakeholder management. With sustainable development as a key concern in business ethics and bioethics, we can integrate biolaw with concerns for organizational governance. Stakeholder management is an essential instrument for corporate governance and social responsibility in health care organizations. When it comes to prioritization of different stakeholders, it is important to mention fairness as a basic principle of justice that can also be applied to health care economics, organization ethics and hospital management.

We have proposed an ethical framework for values-driven management and organizational ethics for management of hospitals and health care institutions, by presenting the challenge of realizing ethical principles in organization ethics and values-driven management in hospital organizations and health care institutions and organizations. As it is important to consider the governance challenges in health care organizations and hospitals in the tension between private and public organizations, we have integrated research perspectives from bioethics, biolaw, corporate social responsibility and business ethics in the conceptualization of sustainability in hospital organizations and health care institutions.

In this fashion, organization theory and concepts of corporate social responsibility need to be based on ethics in the context of governance in health care institutions. Recent changes and problems of organization in modern hospitals, for example, COVID-19, have increased the need for ethical principles in governance and management and health care. Concern for clinical ethics can further be situated at the level of management and leadership of hospital organizations. Values-driven management as essential for governance of sustainability has been proposed for improving the ethical culture of hospital organizations. It is possible to situate concerns for ethics at the level of quality management and values-driven management in the health care sector. Health professionals at many different levels are taking part in the management of the hospital. This has been important not only at the level of professional activities of health care personnel in relation to patients but also at the level of administration and other organizational activities. Many ethical issues are discussed at the level of management of health care organizations. In several cases it takes places in an interdisciplinary framework, but we also experience that different groups of professionals, for example, nurses and physicians, among others, are formulating their particular guidelines for management activities.

In this way, it has been possible to integrate principles of bioethics and biolaw with values-driven-management for sustainable governance in hospitals and health care organizations. Within such economic models for management and governance of clinical ethics in hospitals, biolaw is considered in a wider reflective space than the unspoken relation of protective responsibility between physicians and patients. We think this is a major step toward increased scientific, judgmental and ethical legitimacy of clinical decision-making at both the individual and the organizational levels in hospitals.

4 Universal principles for governance in the post-pandemic world

We have integrated bioethics and biolaw in relation to organization and governance ethics in health care organizations and hospitals. The current global situation points out the pressing need to rethink the way in which economic, social and environmental decisions are made. Multilateralism has resurfaced strongly, and emerging countries are demanding a greater presence in the international debate. This aims at the creation of a new form of global governance and the design of new cooperation mechanisms with developing countries.

Global governance in the twenty-first century aims to ensure the provision of global public goods, such as mitigation and adaptation to climate change, and the fulfillment of the social and environmental goals that the United Nations has set in the course of the past decades. However, global health seems to be a critical issue that must be urgently considered. We need ideas to develop a new international agenda adapted to a multifactorial and interdependent world, permanently exposed to catastrophe and disease. At this point, we can identify some categories to foster, from cosmopolitan biolaw categories that contribute to public policies construction, a more efficient cooperation system, constantly tending to be joint with that of global public goods, due to the growing global interdependence.

Traditionally, any approach to the culture of legality's issues is carried out from a local perspective, that is, understanding it as a constellation of social customs, norms, informal rules and expectations on how to behave in it. In this sense, culture of legality cannot be understood or justified without another legal device, namely, the rule of law, which also refers to a system in which the authorities and members of society adhere to a set of legal norms that guarantee the protection of rights and the compliance of obligations, through the application of law by impartial and objective institutions. In other words, the rule of law makes possible the participation, equity and protection of citizens, guaranteeing the free exercise of their rights and monitoring the fulfillment of their obligations.

We think there is a possibility of establishing a culture of global legality, contrasting biolaw principles with other general standards coming from other epistemological constructs, such as responsibility and solidarity. Given the global pandemic's current scenario, it seems plausible to reflect on a possible reconfiguration of global governance for an ever-changing world. Our analysis has been carried out by deepening into the relationships between some universal principles (with biojuridical content) and controversial contemporary scenarios such as dignity and interspecies policy, autonomy and public responsibility, integrity and the rise of bioscientific empowerment, vulnerability and the future of Life and justice and resource allocation in pandemics.

We have argued that cosmopolitan biolaw's universal principles for governance in an ever-changing world can build a framework for the protection of human and nonhuman beings from biomedical and biotechnological perils as well as from risky environments raised by current pandemics and other global threats. We have also justified how and why such principles are significant in constructing agendas for global governance in pandemic and post-pandemic times. This implies to be aware of that the principles are interdependent as they reciprocally presuppose one another as guides for the ethical and legal protection of persons and extra-human entities. However, as universal principles can fall into tensions, dilemmas and even contradictions, we have epistemologically configured them within a tacit framework of social solidarity and responsibility as meta-principles that shape legal systems aimed at protecting the weak and vulnerable.

5 Global responsibility, sustainability and cosmopolitan biolaw

As traditional law does not clearly understand its relationship with contemporary technology and sustainability, it has not been able to generate hermeneutical models that can efficiently regulate the systematic technological interventions on the natural environment. From this premise we have sought to demonstrate how contemporary technology raises a new problem for biolaw. Because of its novelty, this problem was not included, until now, in the traditional legal reflection. It could be stated like this: The scope of human beings' action has been modified in time and space and, therefore, has no comparison in the past.

We have shown that this new scope requires a new legal comprehension, namely, new hermeneutical keys tuned to the unprecedented implications and consequences emanating from such scope. On this basis, we postulate that contemporary technology is not only a means but mainly an end of human life, by relegating nature to a second level of ethical and legal consideration. This, which seems a constant of Western culture, made us examine different scenarios that pose ethical and biojuridical questions about economy and sustainability; effective altruism as individual and cosmopolitan action for sustainability; animal sustainability; and the relations between biotechnology, pandemic and existential risks. We think that a sustainable ecosystem encompasses a qualitative evolution toward holistic stability and harmony between several components of multifactorial nature, such as people, technology, policy, nature, governments and international regulations, among others. While economic growth is getting bigger by products, market transactions and accumulation of wealth, an important part of natural environment is intervened, and billions of animals are produced and slaughtered to maintain a highly polluting meat industry. Therefore, while sustainability and economics should be convergent, reciprocal and collaborative, they are oblique to each other, a scenario that deserved special consideration in this book.

In this way, we have shown and justified how cosmopolitan biolaw can engender policy for sustainability by understanding the economy-sustainability dichotomy from a holistic perspective. Sustainability is not only human sustainability but natural and animal ones as well, and the possibility of subsisting in a technologized world where existential risk comes into play is more feasible and viable if we understand sustainability from a nonanthropocentric point of view.

We have also shown how biolaw can contribute to engender policy and regulation for a whole-life sustainability. Indeed, in the context of the current reception of technology as an objectifying device of reality, especially built to dominate entities, animals are reified to the extreme. This translates not only into a completely instrumental treatment of them but also in the almost total absence of legal norms or regulations to protect them as subjects of rights or, at least, as subjects worthy of ethical and legal consideration. This undisputed fact deserved by itself some analysis indicating how a nonanthropocentric biolaw could and should contribute to the protection of animals and maybe further to the construction of a special protection regime, which recognizes them as subjects of moral and legal protection. The subject is sensitive and complex; in the same way, it has so many edges that we did not analyze comprehensively in this book. However, we displayed some reasons to demonstrate why animal sustainability is human sustainability too.

Therefore, biolaw encompasses normative force that can be quickly translated into respectful behaviors and habits toward nature and animals. Indeed, from a cosmopolitan understanding of biolaw, it is possible to challenge human beings not only to reflect on the importance of morally and legally respecting animals and stop causing them unnecessary suffering but also, and especially, to modify our feed customs and, thus, stop approving, supporting and institutionalizing the absurd slaughter and unjustifiable suffering of animals in the world, which, from several reasons that we have already discussed, impact negatively the possibility of a sustainable world.

In sum, we can emphasize that we have developed a universal and cosmopolitan biolaw as an important framework for sustainable development integrating basic ethical principles into sustainable development. Our vision of cosmopolitan biolaw in times of COVID-19 can be proposed as the basis for the United Nation's SDGs. Thus, this development of ethical principles and legal instruments for international global governance can be seen as a contribution to understanding the legal framework of the United Nation's SDGs in the perspective of bioethics and biolaw.

References

Abbot, A. (1988). *The system of professions: An essay on the division of expert labor*. Chicago, IL: The University of Chicago Press.

Andorno, R. (2013). *Principles of international biolaw: Seeking common ground at the intersection of bioethics and human rights*. Brussels: Bruylant.

Arendt, H. (1964). *Eichman in Jerusalem: A study of the banality of evil*. London: Penguin Books.

Arendt, H. (1982). In R. Beiner (Ed.), *Lectures on Kant's political philosophy*. Chicago: The University of Chicago Press.

Argandona, A. (1998). The stakeholder theory and the common good. *Journal of Business Ethics*, *17*, 1093–1102.

Arnoux, I. (1994). *Les droits de l'être humain sur son corps*. Bordeaux: Presses universitaires de Bordeaux.

Bataille, G. (1943). *L'Experience intérieure*. Paris: Gallimard.

Baud, J. P. (1993). *L'affaire de la main volée, Une histoire juridique du corps*. Paris: Éd. du Seuil (Coll. « Des Travaux »).

Baudrillard, J. (1990). *La transparence du mal*. Paris: Gallilée.

Bauman, Z. (1989). *Modernity and the Holocaust*. Cambridge: Polity Press.

Bayertz, K. (1992). *Rasse, blut und gene*. Frankfurt/M: Suhrkamp Verlag.

Beauchamp, T. L. (2019). A defense of universal principles in biomedical ethics. In E. Valdés, & J. A. Lecaros (Eds.), *Biolaw and policy in the twenty-first century: Building answers for new questions* (pp. 3–17). Switzerland: Springer.

Beauchamp, T. L., & Childress, J. F. (2019). *Principles of biomedical ethics* (8th ed.). Cambridge, MA: Oxford University Press.

Beauvoir, S. (1949). *Le deuxième sexe I-III*. Paris: Gallimard.

Beck, U. (1986). *Risikogesellschaft: auf dem Weg in eine andere Moderne*. Frankfurt/M: Suhrkamp.

Bernardo, J. M., & Smith, A. F. M. (2000). *Bayesian theory*. West Sussex: John Wiley & Sons.

Beyleveld, D., & Brownsword, R. (2000a). Legal argumentation in biolaw. In P. Kemp, J. D. Rendtorff, & N. M. Johansen (Eds.), *Bioethics and biolaw* (pp. 179–217). V. 1 Judgement of Life. Copenhagen: Rhodos.

Beyleveld, D., & Brownsword, R. (2000b). Human dignity, human rights, and the human genome. In J. D. Rendtorff, & P. Kemp (Eds.), *Basic ethical principles in European bioethics and biolaw* (pp. 15–44). II. Copenhagen-Barcelona: Centre for Ethics and Law-Institut Borja de Bioética.

Bompiani, A. (1992). *Bioetica in Italia, lineamenti e tendenze*. Bologna: Dehoniane.

Bonnafous-Boucher, M., & Rendtorff, J. D. (2016a). *Stakeholder theory: A model for strategic management* (pp. 1–83). Cham: SpringerBriefs in Ethics.

Bonnafous-Boucher, M., & Rendtorff, J. D. (2016b). From "the stakeholder" to stakeholder theory. In *Stakeholder theory: A model for strategic management* (pp. 1–20). Cham: SpringerBriefs in Ethics.

Bonnafous-Boucher, M., & Rendtorff, J. D. (2016c). Stakeholder theory in strategic management. In *Stakeholder theory: A model for strategic management* (pp. 21–39). SpringerBriefs in Ethics, 2016.

Bonnafous-Boucher, M., & Rendtorff, J. D. (2016d). Stakeholder theory as a theory of organizations. In *Stakeholder theory: A model for strategic management* (pp. 45–51). SpringerBriefs in Ethics.

Bonnafous-Boucher, M., & Rendtorff, J. D. (2016e). Political philosophy interpellated by stakeholder theory. In *Stakeholder theory: A model for strategic management* (pp. 53–65). SpringerBriefs in Ethics.

Bonnafous-Boucher, M., & Rendtorff, J. D. (2016f). Stakeholder theory and ethics. In *Stakeholder theory: A model for strategic management* (pp. 67–78). SpringerBriefs in Ethics.

Bostrom, N. (2002). Existential risks: Analyzing human extinction scenarios and related hazards. *Journal of Evolution and Technology*, *9*(1), 1–37.

Bostrom, N., & Cirkovic, M. (Eds.). (2008). *Global catastrophic risks*. Oxford: Oxford University Press.

Buchholz, R. A., & Rosenthal, S. B. (1999) [2002]. Social responsibility and business ethics. In R. E. Frederick (Ed.), *A companion to business ethics*. Oxford: Blackwell Publishing.

Butler, J. (1999) [1987]. *Subjects of desire: Hegelian reflections in twentieth-century France*. New York: Columbia University Press.

Butler, J. (2006) [1990]. *Gender trouble: Feminism and the subversion of identity*. New York: Routledge.

Canguilhem, G. (1999). *Le Normal et le Pathologique*. Paris: PUF.

Capron, M., & Quairel-Lanoizeelée, F. (2004). *Mythes et réalités de l'entreprise responsable. Acteurs, Enjeux, Stratégies*. Paris: La Decouverte.

Carrol, A. B., & Buchholtz, A. K. (2000). *Business and society: Ethics and stakeholder management* (4th edn.). Cincinnati: South Western College.

Carroll, A. B. (1979). A three-dimensional model of corporate social performance. *Academy of Management Review*, *4*, 497–505.

Casonato, C. (2019). The essential features of 21st century biolaw. In E. Valdés, & J. A. Lecaros (Eds.), *Biolaw and policy in the twenty-first century: Building answers for new questions* (pp. 77–91). Switzerland: Springer.

Clarkson, B. E. (Ed.). (1998). *The corporation and its stakeholders: Classic and contemporary readings*. Toronto: University of Toronto Press.

Clouser, D., & Gert, B. (1990). A critique of principlism. *The Journal of Medicine and Philosophy*, *15*, 219–236.

Comte-Sponville, A. (2004). *Le Capitalisme est-il moral? Sur Quelques ridicules et tyrannies de notre temps*. Paris: Albin Michel.

Cook, J. A. (1962). *Law and life of ancient Rome*. Ithaca, NY: Cornell University Press.

Crane, A., & Matten, D. (2004). *Business ethics: A European perspective: Managing corporate citizenship and sustainability in the age of globalization*. Oxford: Oxford University Press.

Daly, H. E. (1996). Sustainable growth? No thank you. In J. Mander, & E. Goldsmith (Eds.), *The case against the global economy* (pp. 192–196). San Francisco: Sierra Club Books.

De Lazari-Radek K., & Singer, P. (2014). *The point of view of the universe: Sidgwick and contemporary ethics*. Oxford: Oxford University Press.

Delmas, M. (1994). *Pour un droit common*. Paris: Le Seuil 1994.

Di Maggio, J. P., & Powell, W. W. (1983). The iron cage revisited: Functional isomorphism and collective rationality in organizational fields. *American Journal of Sociology, 48*, 147–160.

Dijon, X. (1991). *Condition juridique du corps humain avant la naissance et après la mort*. Lille: Presses Universitaires de Lille.

Dolgin, J. L., & Shepherd, L. L. (2005). *Bioethics and the law*. New York: Aspen Publishers.

Donaldson, T., & Preston, L. E. (1995). The stakeholder theory of the corporation: Concepts, evidence and implications. *Academy of Management Review, 20*, 92–117.

Doudna, J. A., & Charpentier, E. (2012). A programmable dual-RNA-guided DNA endonuclease in adaptive bacterial immunity. *Science, 337*, 816–821.

Dworkin, R. (1994). *Life's dominion: An argument about abortion, euthanasia, and individual freedom*. New York: Random House.

Easterby-Smith, R., & Gherardi, S. (1998). Organizational learning: Diverging communities of practice? *Management Learning 29*(3), 259–272.

Eliade, M. (1988). *Le sacré et le profane*. Paris: Gallimard (Folio Essais).

Elias, N. (1968). *Über den Prozess der Zivilisation I-II: Soziogenetische und psychogenetische Untersuchungen*. Frankfurt/M: Suhrkamp Verlag.

Elkington, J. (1999) [1997]. *Cannibals with forks: The triple bottom line of 21st century business*. Oxford: Capstone.

Enderle, G. (1999). *International business ethics, challenges and approaches*. Notre Dame: University of Notre Dame Press.

Engelhardt, T. (1986). *The foundations of bioethics*. New York: Oxford University Press.

Etzioni, A. (1988). *The moral dimension: Towards a new economics*. New York: The Free Press.

European Commission (2001). *Corporate Social Responsibility, Meeting of High Level Group of National Representatives*, March 2001: *Draft Discussion and Issues Paper on CSR.*, Brussels. European Commission (2001), Directorate-General for Employment and Social Affairs, Industrial Relations and Industrial Change, Unit EMPL/D.1 (2001): *Promoting a European Framework for Corporate Social Responsibility, Green Paper*, July 2001. Office for Official Publication of the European Communities, Luxembourg. European Commission (2001): *Livre vert: promouvoir un cadre européen pour la repsonsabilité sociale des entreprises*, Juillet 2001.

European Commission. (2002). *La responsabilité sociale de l'entreprise: Une contribution au développement durable*. Bruxelles: European Commission.

Evans, J. H. (2012). *The history and future of bioethics: A sociological view*. New York: Oxford University Press.

Ewald, F. (1984). *L'Etat providence*. Paris: Gallimard.

Fagot-Largeault, A. (2000). Evaluating and judging: Bionorms vs. human judgment. In P. Kemp, J. D. Rendtorff, & N. M. Johansen (Eds.), *Bioethics and biolaw* (pp. 27–39). V. 1 Judgement of Life. Copenhagen: Rhodos.

Ferry, L. (1992). *Le nouvel Ordre ecologique à l'âge classique, L'arbre, l'animal et l'homme*. Paris: Grasset.

Foucault, M. (1964). *Histoire de la Folie à l'âge classique*. Paris: Gallimard.

Foucault, M. (1973). *Surveiller et punir, Naissance de la prison*. Paris: Gallimard.

Frederick, W. C. (1994, August). From CSR1 to CSR2: The maturing of business and society thought. *Business and Society*, p. 33.

Frederick, W. C. (1995). *Values, nature and culture in the American corporation.* Oxford: Oxford University Press.

Freeman, R. E. (1984). *Strategic management: A stakeholder approach.* Boston: Pitman Publishing.

Freeman, R. E. (1994). A stakeholder theory of the modern corporation. In T. L.,Beauchamp, & N. E. Bowie (Eds.), *Ethical theory and business.* Englewood Cliff, NJ: Prentice Hall.

Freeman, R. E. (1998). The stakeholder corporation. In L. P. Hartman (Ed.), *Business ethics.* Chicago: McGraw-Hill.

Freeman, R. E. (2004, November). *Managing for stakeholders: An argument.* Ten Principles and Eight Techniques, Lecture, p. 1. Copenhagen Business School.

Freeman, R. E., & Ramakrishna Velamuri, S. (2006). *Company stakeholder responsibility: A new approach to CSR.* Charlottesville: Business Roundtable Institute for Corporate Ethics.

Freeman, R. E., & Reed D. (1983). Stockholders and stakeholders: A new perspective on corporate governance. In C. Huizinga (Ed.), *Corporate governance: A definitive exploration of the issues.* Los Angeles: UCLA Extension Press.

French, P. (1984). *Collective and corporate responsibility.* New York: Columbia University Press.

Frey, R. G. (1980). *Interests and rights: The case against animals.* Oxford: Clarendon Press.

Friedman, M. (1970). *The social responsibility of business is to increase its profits.* New York: New York Times Magazine.

Friedman, E. (2013). *Reinventing philanthropy: A framework for more effective giving.* Nebraska: Potomac Books.

Gabriel, I., & McElwee, B. (2019). Effective altruism, global poverty, and systemic change. In H. Greaves, & T. Pummer (Eds.), *Effective altruism: Philosophical issues* (pp. 99–114). Oxford: Oxford University Press.

Gadamer, H. G. (1995). *Die Verborgenheit der Gesundheit, Aufsätze und Vorträge.* Frankfurt/M: Suhrkamp Verlag.

Gaylin, W., & Jennings, B. (2003). *The perversion of autonomy:Coercion and constraint in a liberal society.* Washington, DC: Georgetown University Press.

Glover, J. (1984). *What sort of people should there be?* London: Penguin Books.

Goodpaster, K. E. (1991). Business ethics and stakeholder analysis. *Business Ethics Quarterly, 1*, 53–73.

Grunig, J., & Hunt, T. (1984). *Managing public relations.* New York: Holt, Reinhart, & Winston.

Habermas, J. (1981). *Theorie des kommunikativen Handelns I-II.* Frankfurt/M: Suhrkamp.

Habermas, J. (1992). *Faktizität und Geltung, Beiträge zur Diskurstheorie des Rechts und des demokratischen Rechtsstaats.* Frankfurt/M: Suhrkamp Verlag.

Haraway, D. (1989). A cyborg manifest: Science, technology and feminist socialism in the 1980s. In *Simians, cyborgs and women.* London: Routledge.

Heidegger, M. (1927). *Sein und Zeit.* Tübingen: Max Niemeyer Verlag, 15 Auflage, 1984.

Hildebrandt, S., & Schultz, M. (1997). *Fokus på sygehusledelse* [Focus on Hospital Management]. Copenhagen: Munksgaard.

Honnefelder, L., & Rager, G. (Eds.). (1994). *Ärztliches Urteilen und Handeln. Zur Grundlegung einer medizinischen Ethik.* Frankfurt: Insel Verlag.

Hounsgaard, l., & Eriksen J. J. (Eds.). (2000). *Læring i Sundhedsvæsenet* [*Learning in Health Care*]. Copenhagen: Gyldendal Uddannelse.

Husserl, E. (1973). *Cartesianische meditationen und pariser vorträge*. Husserliana, Den Haag: Martinius Nijhoff.

Huxley, A. (1932). *Brave new world*. London: Harper Collins Publishers.

International Labour Organization. (2002). *A guide to tripartite declaration of principles concerning multinational entreprises programme*. Geneva: ILO.

Irigaray, L. (1984). *L'Ethique de la différence sexuelle*. Paris: Editions de Minuit.

Jahr, F. (1927). Bio-ethics. Reviewing the ethical relations of humans towards animals and plants. In *Selected essays in bioethics* 1927-1934 Fritz Jahr, Zentrum fur Medizinische Ethik, Bochum, November 2010, Issue 186. Translation, Postcript and References by Hans-Martin Sass. "Bio-Ethik. Eine Umschau über die ethischen Beziehungen des Menschen zu Tier und Pflanze," in *Kosmos. Handweiser für Naturfreunde und Zentralblatt für das naturwissen-schaftliche Bildungs und Sammelwesen,* Stuttgart.

Jahr, F. (1934). Three studies on the Fifth Commandment, 1934. In *Selected essays in bioethics 1927-1934* Fritz Jahr, Zentrum für Medizinische Ethik, Bochum, November 2010, Issue 186. Translation, Postcript and References by Hans-Martin Sass. "Drei Studien zum 5. Gebot'" in *Kosmos. Handweiser für Naturfreunde und Zentralblatt für das naturwissen-schaftliche Bildungs und Sammelwesen*, Stuttgart.

Jamrozik, E., & Selgelid, M. J. (2020). COVID-19 human challenges studies: Ethical issues. *Lancet Infectious Diseases*, *20*(8), 198–203.

Jensen, O. B., & Schultz N. (Eds.). (2020). *Det epidemiske samfund* [*The epidemic society*]. Copenhagen: Hans Retizels forlag.

Johnson, S. H., Iltis, A. S., & Hinze, B. A. (2008). Law and bioethics. In A. S. Iltis, S. H. Johnson, & B. A. Hinze (Eds.), *Legal perspectives in bioethics* (pp. 1–9). New York: Routledge.

Jonas, H. (1979). *Das Prinzip Verantwortung*. Frankfurt/M: Insel Verlag.

Jonas, H. (2003). *Das Prinzip Verantwortung: Versuch einer Ethik für die technologische Zivilisation*. Frankfurt: Suhrkamp.

Jones, T. M. (1995). Instrumental stakeholder theory: A synthesis of ethics and economics. *Academy of Management Review*, *20*(2), 404–437.

Jørgensen, K., & Rendtorff, J. D. (2018). Patient participation in mental health care – perspectives of healthcare professionals: An integrative review. *Scandinavian Journal of Caring Sciences*, *32*(2), 490–501.

Jørgensen K., Rendtorff, J. D., & Holen, M. (2018). How patient participation is constructed in mental health care: A grounded theory study. *Scandinavian Journal of Caring Sciences*, *32*(4), 1359–1370.

Kaplan, R.S. & Norton, D.P. (1998). *The balanced scorecard*. Cambridge, MA: Harvard Business Publishing.

Kaplan, R. S., Robert, S., & Norton, D. P. (1996). *The balanced scorecard: Translating strategy into action*. Cambridge, MA: Harvard Business Press.

Kass, L. R. (1988). *Toward a more natural science: Biology and human affairs*. New York: Free Press.

Kaufmann, A. (1994). *Grundprobleme der Rechtsphilosophie*. München: Beck Verlag.

Kemp, P. (2019). The idea of European biolaw: Basic principles. In E. Valdés, & J. A. Lecaros (Eds.), *Biolaw and policy in the twenty-first century: Building answers for new questions* (pp. 19–32). Switzerland: Springer.

Kemp, P. (2000). Bioethics in law and biolaw in bioethics. In P. Kemp, J.D. Rendtorff, & N.M. Johansen (Eds.), *Bioethics and biolaw* (pp. 63–78), V.1. Judgement of Life. Copenhagen: Rhodos.

Leenen, H. J. J. (1994). *Handbook Gezondheidsrecht, Deel 1, Rechten van mensen in de gezondheidszorg*. Samsom: Alphen aan den Rijn.

Lenoir, N. (2000). Legal argumentation in biolaw. In P. Kemp, J. D. Rendtorff, & N. M. Johansen (Eds.), *Bioethics and biolaw* (pp. 219–227). V. 1 Judgement of Life. Copenhagen: Rhodos.

Lévinas, E. (1961). *Totalité et Infini, Essai sur l'extériorité*. La Haye: Martinus Nijhoff.

Locke, J. (1993). In M. Goldie (Ed.), *Two treatises on government* (1698). London: J. M. Dent.

MacAskill, W. (2019). The definition of effective altruism. In H. Greaves, & T. Pummer (Eds.), *Effective altruism: Philosophical issues* (pp. 10–28). Oxford: Oxford University Press.

Maccio, C. (2001). *Exercer une responsabilité*. Lyon: Savoir Communiquer, Editions Chronique sociale.

MacIntosh, M. (2003). *Living corporate citizenship: Strategic routes to socially responsible business*. London: Prentice Hall.

Mattsson, J., & Rendtorff, J. D. (2006). E-marketing ethics: A theory of value priorities. *International Journal of Internet Marketing and Advertising*, *3*(1), 35–47.

McIntosh, M. (1998). *Corporate citizenship: Successful companies for responsible strategies*. London: Financial Times, Pitman Publishing.

Mekinoff, J. (2001). *Law and bioethics: An introduction*. Washington, DC: Georgetown University Press.

Merleau-Ponty, M. (1945). *Phénoménologie de la perception*. Paris: Gallimard.

Meyer, J. W., & Rowan B. (1977). Institutionalized organizations: Formal structure as myth and ceremony. *American Journal of Sociology*, *83*(2), 40–363.

Mittchell, R. K., Agle B. R., & Wood, D. S. (1997). Toward a theory of stakeholder identification and salience: Defining the principle of who and what really counts. *Academy of Management Review*, *22*(4), 853–886.

Monks, R. A. G., & Minow, N. (2004). *Corporate governance* (4th edn.). Oxford: Blackwell Publishing.

Moon, J., Slager, R., Anastasiadis, S., Brunn, C., Hardi, P., & Knudsen, J. S. (2012). *Analysis of national and EU policies supporting CSR and Impact* (IMPACT Working Paper No. 2). European Commission. http://csr-impact.eu/documents/documents-detail.html?documentid=5

Müller-Hill, B. (1984). *Tödliche Wissenschaft, Die Aussonderung von Juden, Zigeunern und. Geisteskranken 1933–1945*. Reinbek bei Hamburg: Rowohlt.

National Academy of Science. (2017). *Human genome editing: Science, ethics and governance*. Washington, DC: The National Academies Press.

National Commission for the Protection of Human Subjects of Biomedical and Behavioral Research. (2009). Reprint from the collection of the University of Michigan Library, 2009, Appendix Volume I, 78-0012. *Belmont report: Ethical principles and guidelines for the protection of human subjects of research*. Washington, DC: US Government Printing Office.

Nerheim, H. (1995). *Vitenskap og kommunikasjon, Paradigmer, modeller og kommunikative strategier i helsefagenes viteskapsteori*. Oslo: Universitetsforlaget.

Nonaka, I. (1994). A dynamic theory of organizational knowledge creation. *Organization Science*, *5*(1), 14–37.

Nussbaum, M. (2007). *Frontiers of justice: Disability, nationality, species membership*. Cambridge, MA: Harvard University Press.

OECD. (2002). *Principes Directeurs des entreprises multinationales*. Paris: OECD.

Oliver, C. (1991). Strategic response to institutional processes. *Academy of Management Review, 16*(1), 145–179.

Orwell, G. (1947). *1984.* London: Penguin Books.

Ost, F. (1995). *La nature hors la loi.* Paris: La Découverte.

Paine, L. S. (1994). Managing for organizational integrity. *Harvard Business Review, 72*(2), 106–117.

Paine, L. S. (2003). *Valueshift: Why companies must merge social and financial imperative to achieve superior performance.* New York: McGraw-Hill.

Pedersen, J. S., & Rendtorff, J. D. (2004). Value-based management in local public organizations: A Danish experience. *Cross Cultural Management, 11*(2), 71–94.

Philips, R. (2003). *Stakeholder theory and organizational ethics.* San Francisco: Berrett-Koehler, Inc.

Porter, M. E., & Kramer M. R. (2002). The competitive advantage of corporate philanthropy. *Harvard Business Review, 80*(12), 56–68.

Potter, V. R. (1971). *Bioethics: Bridge to the future.* New Jersey: Prentice-Hall, Inc.

Powell, W. M., & DiMaggio, P. J. (Eds.). (1991). *The new institutionalism in organizational analysis.* Chicago: The University of Chicago Press.

Rachels, J. (1975). Active and passive euthanasia. *The New England Journal of Medicine, 292*, 78–80.

Rachels, J. (2004). The basic argument for vegetarianism. In S. Sapontzis (Ed.), *Food for thought* (pp. 70–80). New York: Prometheus.

Rawls, J. (1971). *A theory of Justice.* Cambridge, MA: Harvard University Press.

Rawls, J. (1992). *Political liberalism.* Cambridge, MA: Harvard University Press.

Rawls, J. (1999). *A theory of justice* (Rev. ed.). Cambridge, MA: Belknap, Imprint Harvard University Press.

Rawls, J. (2001). *Justice as fairness: A restatement.* Cambridge, MA: Harvard University Press.

Rendtorff, J. D. (1998). The second international conference about bioethics and biolaw: European principles in bioethics and biolaw. *Medicine Health Care and Philosophy, 1–4*(3), 271–274.

Rendtorff, J. D. (1999). *Bioetik og ret, Kroppen mellem person og ting.* København: Gyldendal.

Rendtorff, J. D. (2001). Emergence of clinical ethics in hospitals in Denmark: Some thoughts on ethics, education and hospital management. In G. Lebeer, & M. Moulin (Eds.), *Ethical function in hospital ethics committees: working papers, workshop 2.* (pp. 47–61). Bruxelles: Centre de Sociologie de la Santé, Institut de Sociologie, Université libre de Bruxelles.

Rendtorff, J. D. (2002a). Basic ethical principles in European bioethics and biolaw: Autonomy, dignity, integrity and vulnerability. Towards a foundation of bioethics and biolaw. *Medicine Health Care and Philosophy, 5*, 235–244.

Rendtorff, J. D. (2002b), Ethics committees, organization ethics and hospital management. In G. Leeber (Ed.), *Ethical function in hospital ethics committees, biomedical and health research* (pp. 173–185). Amsterdam: ISO Press, European Commission, Directorate-General, Science Research, Development.

Rendtorff, J. D. (2002c). Hospital ethics committees in Denmark. In G. Lebeer (Ed.), *Ethical function in hospital ethics committees* (pp. 9–8). Amsterdam: IOS Press.

Rendtorff, J. D. (2002d). Krop, menneskesyn og maskine. In G. Balling (Ed.), *Homo sapiens 2,0: Når teknologien kryber ind under huden* (pp. 157–195). Copenhagen: Gad.

Rendtorff, J. D. (2003). Bioethics in Denmark. In I. J. F. Peppin, & M. J. Cherry (Eds.), *The annals of bioethics: Regional perspectives in bioethics* (pp. 209–224). Lisse, The Netherlands: Swets & Zeitlinger.

Rendtorff, J. D. (2008). The limitations and accomplishments of autonomy as a basic principle in bioethics and biolaw. In I. D. N. Weisstub, & G. D. P. Pintos (Eds.), *Autonomy and human rights in health care: An international perspective: Bind 36. International library of ethics, law, and the new medicine* (pp. 75–87). The Netherlands: Springer.

Rendtorff, J. D. (2009a). *Responsibility, ethics and legitimacy of corporations.* Copenhagen: Copenhagen Business School Press.

Rendtorff, J. D. (2009b). Basic ethical principles applied to service industries. *Service Industries Journal, 29*(1), 9–19.

Rendtorff, J. D. (2010a). Philosophy of management: Concepts of management from the perspectives of systems theory, phenomenological hermeneutics, corporate religion and existentialism. In I. P. Koslowski (Ed.), *Elements of a philosophy of management and organization* (pp. 19–47). Heidelberg: Springer Studies in Economic Ethics and Philosophy.

Rendtorff, J. D. (2010b). *Power and principle in the market place: On ethics and economics.* London: Ashgate.

Rendtorff, J. D. (2011a). Business ethics, strategy and organizational integrity: The importance of integrity as a basic principle of business ethics that contributes to better economic performance. In I. C. Wankel, & A. Stachowicz-Stanusch (Eds.), *Handbook of research on teaching ethics in business and management education* (pp. 274–288). New York: IGI global.

Rendtorff, J. D. (2011b). Institutionalization of corporate ethics and social responsibility programs in firms. In I. K. Buhmann, L. Roseberry, & M. Morsing (Eds.), *Corporate social and human rights responsibilities: Global, legal and management perspectives* (pp. 244–266). London: Palgrave Macmillan.

Rendtorff, J. D. (2011c). Corporate citizenship as organizational integrity. In I. I. Pies, & P. Koslowski (Eds.), *Corporate citizenship and new governance: The political role of corporations* (pp. 59–91). Dordrecht, Heidelberg, London, New York: Springer. Studies in Economic Ethics and Philosophy.

Rendtorff, J. D. (2012). *Business ethics.* In I. R. Chadwick (Ed.), *Encyclopedia of applied ethics* (pp.365–372). San Diego: Academic Press.

Rendtorff, J. D. (2013a). Basic concepts of philosophy of management and corporations. In I. C. Luetge (Ed.), *Handbook of the philosophical foundations of business ethics* (pp. 1361–1386). Dordrecht, Heidelberg, New York, London: Springer Science +Business Media.

Rendtorff, J. D. (2013b). Philosophical theories of management and corporations. In I. C. Luetge (Ed.), *Handbook of the philosophical foundations of business ethics* (pp. 1409–1432). Dordrecht, Heidelberg, New York, London: Springer Science+Business Media.

Rendtorff, J. D. (2013c). Recent debates in philosophy of management. In I. C. Luetge (Ed.), *Handbook of the philosophical foundations of business ethics* (pp. 1433–1457). Dordrecht, Heidelberg, New York, London: Springer Science+Business Media.

Rendtorff, J. D. (2013d). The history of the philosophy of management and corporations. In I. C. Luetge (Ed.), *Handbook of the philosophical foundations of business ethics* (pp. 1387–1408). Dordrecht, Heidelberg, New York, London: Springer Science+Business Media.

Rendtorff, J. D. (2014a). European perspectives. In A. M. J. Have, & B. Gordijn (Eds.), *Handbook of global bioethics* (pp. 293–310). Dordrecht, Heidelberg, New York, London: Springer Science+Business Media.

Rendtorff, J. D. (2014b). *French philosophy and social theory: A perspective for ethics and philosophy of management.* Netherlands: Springer Science+Business Media. Ethical Economy, No. 49.

Rendtorff, J. D. (2014c). Risk management, banality of evil and moral blindness in organizations and corporations. In I. C. Luetge, & J. Jauernig (Eds.), *Business ethics and risk management* (pp. 45–71). Dordrecht: Springer Science+Business Media. Ethical Economy, No. 43.

Rendtorff, J. D. (2015a). Case studies, ethics, philosophy and liberal learning for the management profession. *Journal of Management Education, 39*(1), 36–55.

Rendtorff, J. D. (2015b). The need for a theoretical reexamination of sustainability in economics and business. In I. G. Aras (Ed.), *Sustainable markets for sustainable business: A global perspective for business and financial markets* (pp. 41–58). Farnham: Gower Publishing. Finance, governance and sustainability: challenges to theory and practice.

Rendtorff, J. D. (2015c). Integrity, concept of. In(Ed.), *Encyclopedia of global bioethics* (pp. 1–7). Cham: Springer Science+Business Media.

Rendtorff, J. D. (2016a). Basic ethical principles as symbolic foundations and core values of European biolaw. *Ethics, Medicine and Public Health, 2*(2), 205–212.

Rendtorff, J. D. (2016b). Review of Le tournant de la théorie critique, collection Solidarité et société, Éditions Desclée de Brouwer, Paris, 2015. *Journal of Classical Sociology, 16*(3), 305–309.

Rendtorff, J. D. (2017a). *Cosmopolitan business ethics: Towards a global ethos of management.* Abingdon: Routledge. Finance, Governance and Sustainability: Challenges to Theory and Practice Series.

Rendtorff, J. D. (2017b). Creating shared value as institutionalization of ethical responsibilities of the business corporation as a good corporate citizen in society. In I. J. Wieland (Ed.), *Creating shared value: Concepts, experience, criticism* (pp. 119–139). Cham: Springer. Ethical Economy, No. 52.

Rendtorff, J. D. (2017c). *Perspectives on philosophy of management and business ethics: including a special section on business and human rights.* Cham: Springer. Ethical Economy , No. 51.

Rendtorff, J. D. (2017d). The Danish model of corporate citizenship: The novo group. In'Higgins, & L. Zsolnai (Eds.), *Progressive business models: Creating sustainable and pro-social enterprise* (pp. 221–240). London & New York: Palgrave Macmillan. Palgrave Studies in Sustainable Business In Association with Future Earth

Rendtorff, J. D. (2019a). Sustainable development goals and progressive business models for economic transformation. *Local Economy, 34*(6), 510–524.

Rendtorff, J. D. (2019b). The concept of business legitimacy: Corporate social responsibility, corporate citizenship, corporate governance as essential elements of ethical business legitimacy. In I. D. Crowther, S. Seifi, & T. Wond (Eds.), *Responsibility and governance: The twin pillars of sustainability* (pp. 45–60). Switzerland: Springer VS. Approaches to Global Sustainability, Markets, and Governance.

Rendtorff, J. D. (2019c). The honest businessperson: Cosmopolitan theory and cultural praxis (The example of Denmark and Scandinavia). In I. C. Lütge, & C. Strosetzki (Eds.), *The honorable merchant – Between modesty and risk-taking: Intercultural and literary aspects* (pp. 41–53). Cham: Springer. Ethical Economy, No. 56.

Rendtorff, J. D. (2019d). *Philosophy of management and sustainability: Rethinking business ethics and social responsibility in sustainable development.* Bingley: Emerald Group Publishing.

Rendtorff, J. D. (2020a). The concept of business legitimacy: Learnings from Suchman. In J. Rendtorff (Ed.), *Handbook of business legitimacy: Responsibility, ethics and society* (pp. 3–30). Cham: Springer.

Rendtorff, J. D. (2020b). Capitalism, religion, business legitimacy, and the ethical economy. In J. Rendtorff (Ed.), *Handbook of business legitimacy: Responsibility, ethics and society* (pp. 217–242). Cham: Springer.

Rendtorff, J. D. (2020c). Philosophical theory of business legitimacy: The political corporation. In J. Rendtorff (Ed.), *Handbook of business legitimacy: Responsibility, ethics and society* (pp. 763–781). Cham: Springer.

Rendtorff, J. D. (2020d). Principles of business ethics and business legitimacy. In J. Rendtorff (Ed.), *Handbook of business legitimacy: Responsibility, ethics and society* (pp. 783–798). Cham: Springer.

Rendtorff, J. D. (2020e). Sustainability, basic ethical principles, and innovation. In J. Rendtorff (Ed.), *Handbook of business legitimacy: Responsibility, ethics and society* (pp. 1631–1658). Cham: Springer.

Rendtorff, J. D. (2020f). Paul Ricœur and Danish philosophy: Dissemination of Ricœur's philosophy in the philosophical debate in Denmark, Ricœur's influence on particular Danish Philosophers and themes of discussion in Denmark. *Danish Yearbook of Philosophy, 53*(1), 84–107.

Rendtorff, J. D. (2020g). *Moral blindness in business: A social theory of evil in organizations and institutions*. London: Palgrave Macmillan.

Rendtorff, J. D., & Kemp, P. (2000a). *Basic ethical principles in European bioethics and biolaw (Vols. 1–2)*. Copenhagen and Barcelona: Centre for Ethics and Law & Institut Borja de Bioetica.

Rendtorff, J. D., & Kemp, P. (2000b). *Basic ethical principles in European bioethics and biolaw, I-II*. Barcelona & Copenhagen: Centre for Ethics and Law & Institut Borja di bioetica.

Rendtorff, J. D., & Kemp, P. (2009). The Barcelona declaration: Towards an integrated approach to basic ethical principles. *Synthesis Philosophica, 23*(2), 239–251.

Rendtorff, J. D., & Kemp, P. (2019). Four ethical principles in European bioethics and biolaw: Autonomy, dignity, integrity, vulnerability. In E. Valdés, & J. A. Lecaros (Eds.), *Biolaw and policy in the twenty-first century: Building answers for new questions* (pp. 33–40). Switzerland: Springer.

Rendtorff, J. D., & Mattsson, J. (2012). Ethics in the bank internet encounter: An explorative study. *Journal of Information, Communication and Ethics in Society, 10*(1), 36–51.

Ricœur, P. (1990). *Soi-même comme un autre*. Paris: Le Seuil.

Ricœur, P. (1994). *Lectures 1*. Paris: Le Seuil.

Ricœur, P. (1995). *Le Juste I*. Paris: Éditions Esprit.

Romeo Casabona, C., & Romeo Malanda, S. (2019). Approach to biolaw as an autonomous juridical discipline. In E. Valdés, & J. A. Lecaros (Eds.), *Biolaw and policy in the twenty-first century: Building answers for new questions* (pp. 59–76). Switzerland: Springer.

Ryan, J., & Glarum, J. (2008). *Biosecurity and bioterrorism: Containing and preventing biological threats*. Burlington: Butterworth-Heinemann.

Sartre, J. P. (1943). *L'Etre et le néant, Essai d'ontologie phénoménologique*. Paris: Gallimard.

Savulescu, J. (2001). Procreative beneficence: Why we should select the best children. *Bioethics, 15*(5–6), 413–426.

Savulescu, J., Vergano, M., Craxi, L., & Wilkinson, D. (2020). An ethical algorithm for rationing life-sustaining treatment during the COVID-19 pandemic. *The British Journal of Anaesthesia 125*(3), 253–258.

Scott, R. W. (1998). *Organizations, rational, natural and open systems*. New Jersey: Prentice Hall.

Sedel, F. (Ed.). (1995). *Guide pratique et théorique de l'éthique des affaires et de l'entreprise*. Paris: Editions Eska.

Serres, M. (1992). *Du Contrat naturel.* Paris: Flammarion (Collection Champs).

Sexty, R. W. (2001). Corporate philanthropy: Donations, voluntarism, and sponsorship. *Canadian Business and Society: Understanding Social and Ethical Challenges.* Ontario, Scarborough: Prentice Hall.

Sidgwick, H. (1981). *The methods of ethics* (7th edn.). Indianapolis: Hackett.

Singer, P. (2011). *Practical ethics.* (3rd edn.). Cambridge, MA: Cambridge University Press.

Singer, P. (2015). *Animal liberation.* London: Penguin Random House.

Singer, P. (2016a). *Famine, affluence and morality.* Oxford-New York: Oxford University Press.

Singer, P. (2016b). La ética de lo que comemos. In B. Aguilera, J. A. Lecaros, & E. Valdés (Eds.), *Ética animal: Fundamentos empíricos, teóricos y dimensión práctica* (pp. 271–284). Madrid: Comillas.

Singer, P. (2019). Foreword. In E. Valdés, & J. A. Lecaros (Eds.), *Biolaw and policy in the twenty-first century: Building answers for new questions* (pp. vii–ix). Switzerland: Springer.

Skelton, A. (2016). The ethical principles of effective altruism. *Journal of Global Ethics, 12*(2): 137–146.

Spencer, E. M. A. E., Mills, M. V., & Werhane, P. H. (2000). *Organization ethics in health care.* Oxford: Oxford University Press.

Steinbock, B. (1978). Speciesism and the idea of equality. *Philosophy, 53*, 247–256.

Strauss, L. (1953). *Natural right and history.* Chicago: The University of Chicago Press.

Strauss, L. (1964). *The city and man.* Chicago: The University of Chicago Press.

Thombs, K. (1993). *The meaning of Illness, a phenomenological account of the different perspectives of physician and patient* (Philosophy and Medicine, 42), Den Haag: Kluwer Academic Publishers.

Titmuss, R. M. (1970). *The gift relationship: From human blood to social policy.* London: Allen & Unwin.

Trappenburg, M. (1993). *Soorten van gelijk: Medisch-ethische discussies in Nederland.* Zwolle: Tjeenk Willink.

Tribe, L. H. (2000). *American constitutional law* (3rd edn.). New York: Foundation Press.

United Nations. (1958). *ILO Convention 111: Convention Concerning Discrimination in Respect of Employment and Occupation.* UN International Labour Organization (ILO). Date of Adaption: 25 June 1958. Date of Coming into force: 15 June 1960

United Nations. (2000). *Cartagena protocol on biosafety.* Montreal: Cartagena.

United States Sentencing Commission. (1995). *Corporate crime in America: Strengthening the "good citizen" corporation.* Proceedings of the Second Symposium on Crime and Punishment in the United States (September 7–8). Washington DC, United States Federal Sentencing Commission.

Valdés, E. (2019). Towards a new conception of biolaw. In E. Valdés, & J. A. Lecaros (Eds.), *Biolaw and policy in the twenty-first century: Building answers for new questions* (pp. 41–58). Switzerland: Springer.

Valdés, E. (2021). *Biolaw: Origins, doctrine and juridical applications on the biosciences.* Switzerland: Springer.

Valdés, E., & Lecaros, J. A. (Eds.). (2019). *Biolaw and policy in the twenty-first century: Building answers for new questions.* Switzerland: Springer.

Villey, M. (1972). *Le droit romain, son actualité.* Paris: Presses univ. de France.

Walther-Busch, E. (1996). *Organisationstheorien von Weber bis Weich.* Amsterdam: GIB Verlag Fakultas.

Walzer, M. (1984). *Spheres of justice: A defense of pluralism and equality*. New York: Basic books.

Wheeler, D., & Sillanpää, M. (1997). *The stakeholder corporation: The body shop blue print for maximizing stakeholder value*. London: Pitman Publishing.

WHO. (2010). *Biosecurity: An integrated approach to manage risk to human: Animal and plant life and health*. Washington, DC: INFOSAN.

World Commission on the Environment and Development. (1987). *Our common future*. New York: Oxford University Press.

Zaner, R. (1965). *Problem of embodiment: Some contributions to a phenomenology of the body*. Den Haag: M. Nijhoff.

Zaner, R. (1981). *The context of the self: A phenomenological enquiry, using medicine as a clue*. Ohio: Ohio University Press.

Zaner, R. (1988). *Ethics and the clinical encounter*. Chicago: The University of Chicago Press.

Index

administration xi, 4, 154, 155, 156, 167
autonomy xi, 6, 9, 19, 21, 24–28, 30, 32, 41, 52, 55, 64–65, 68–69, 74, 76

Baudrillard, Jean 100–101, 103–104
Beauchamp, Tom 21–23, 26, 44, 56
Belmont Report 14, 17–21
beneficence 18–21, 27–28
bioethics x–xiv, xvi–xviii, 2, 5, 8–9, 13–27, 29–39, 44–47, 61–62
biolaw x–xviii, 1–3, 5–6, 8–10, 13, 17–19, 22–48, 61–62, 145–149, 169–172, 214–220
biomedicine xi–xiii, 9, 24, 28, 32, 35, 38, 41–42, 47, 64, 67, 104–105
biopower 62–64, 66–67, 94, 106
biorights x, 39–41, 45, 47, 65, 68, 71–72, 93–94
biosciences xii, 13, 21, 23–24, 33, 46
biosecurity 6, 53–54
biotechnology xiii, 10, 22, 54, 106, 185, 187
Bostrom, Nick 209, 211
business xi, xiv, xvi, 9, 119–122, 124–131, 134–136

Childress, James 21–23, 26, 44, 56
climate change 169, 197, 204–207, 210–211
COVID-19 xiv, xv, 1–5, 7–10, 20, 36, 48, 55, 207, 214–217, 220

dignity x–xi, 19, 27–30, 32, 35–36, 62, 65, 68, 69, 71–74, 78–79, 171–174
disease 2–5, 50–51, 53–55, 80–83, 216, 218

economics xiv, xviii, 1, 14, 122, 157, 196, 198
economy xiv, 2, 9, 54, 63, 104, 107, 120–121, 131, 141, 196–199
education 14, 67, 146–147, 149–153, 161, 177, 186, 188
effective altruism 199–202, 219
existential risk 173, 197, 210–213, 219

finance x, xiv–xviii, 1
freedom 63–71, 74–75, 96–97, 99
Foucault, Michel 3–4, 62–63, 82, 87–88
future 2, 9, 16, 69, 71–72, 81, 95, 99, 109–113, 120–121

genome 29, 35, 40, 48–53
governance x–xviii, 1–3, 5, 8–10, 14, 16, 36–39, 41–43, 61–63, 119, 123–127, 129–133, 135–144, 153, 169–178

Habermas, Jürgen 61, 65, 130, 164
health care x–xi, xiv, 2–4, 7–9, 119, 145–161, 163–164
hospital 64, 119, 145–164
human beings 4, 15–19, 28–29, 31, 41, 61–63, 169–171, 174, 177, 183–186
human challenge trials 8, 20, 48, 55–58
human rights 7, 17–19, 23–24, 27, 30–32, 35–36, 88, 92–93, 125

integrity 27–30, 32, 39, 41, 62, 65, 77–79, 87–88, 90, 92–93, 109, 112, 115

Jahr, Fritz 13–17
Jonas, Hans 14–15, 71, 91, 129–121, 178, 186–187
judgment 9, 22–23, 74–79, 81, 83, 144, 149–153, 164
justice 1, 9, 15, 19, 21, 27, 30, 62, 66–70, 75–76, 109, 111–112

Kemp, Peter 17–18, 22–23, 25–27, 48, 62, 74, 92, 95, 175
knowledge x, 8, 14, 16–17, 20–21, 36, 43, 46–47, 54, 56, 69, 82–84, 109–110, 150–153

law ix–xiii, xvi–xvii, 3, 8–9, 13, 20–40, 42–47, 61–70, 72–78, 86–88, 90–94, 122–124, 215–216
legal x–xv, 6, 8–9, 19–21, 23–31, 33–47, 50–52, 61–62, 64–68, 70–79, 85–94, 120–123, 215–216
legislation x, xiii, 8, 9, 27–28, 39, 61–62, 72–73, 91–94, 131, 148
legitimacy 9, 46, 61, 123, 126–130, 135–139, 141, 143–144, 162–163
life 1–2, 5–6, 9, 13, 15–16, 27–30, 32–34, 61–74, 80–85, 93–101, 107–113, 173–180, 183–186, 197–202, 207–211, 214–216
livestock 186, 203–206, 209

management xi, xiv, xvii, 6, 9, 62–63, 119, 121–124, 128–140, 142–147, 150–151, 153–164
market 67, 106, 121–122, 128, 131–132, 140, 143, 154, 196–197
medicine 3, 9, 19, 34–35, 46, 51, 56, 63, 78, 81–85, 152, 216
morality 5, 21–23, 26–27, 29–30, 112, 169–170, 189–190

nature x, xvi, 8–9, 14–15, 17–18, 33–34, 42–43, 51–53, 70–72, 98–103, 105–107, 184–188, 219–220
nonmaleficence 15, 21, 56–57, 179, 182

obligations 14–15, 42, 47, 56, 71, 114, 120, 141–142, 175, 181–182, 188, 218
organization xii, xiv, 3, 9, 18, 29, 48, 66, 77, 79, 84, 119, 121, 124–125, 132–135, 138–143, 145–147, 149–151, 153–163, 216–217

pluralistic 8, 14, 29, 61–62, 68–69, 75
policy xi, xiv, xvii, 2, 39, 43, 46, 51–52, 61–63, 72–74, 89, 91–93, 119–120, 160–161, 187, 196–199
post-pandemic 1, 5, 38, 169–170, 214
privacy 21, 24, 27–28, 40, 52, 62, 78, 124, 128, 174

Rawls, John 69, 139–142, 192
Rendtorff, Jacob Dahl 17–18, 22–23, 25–27, 62, 74, 92, 95, 159, 163, 175
resources 7, 41, 48, 71, 120, 122, 124, 130, 132, 156–157, 162, 169, 187–194, 198, 200–201, 205
responsibility xi, xiv, xvi, 2, 4, 7, 9, 14–15, 17, 38–39, 52, 71–74, 76, 90–92, 119–127, 144–147, 153–155, 170–181, 216–219
risks 4–6, 9–10, 18–21, 37–39, 54–58, 179–180, 182–183, 209–214

science 14–17, 79–84, 88–91, 95–97, 182
Singer, Peter 14, 23, 181, 199–204
species 54, 71, 82, 95, 172–174, 184–185, 202, 209
stakeholders 119, 121–124, 126–144, 160–163
sustainability x–xii, xiv–xviii, 1–10, 36–39, 119–121, 123–131, 143–145, 170–174, 196–199, 203

technology 3, 16, 48, 61, 63–64, 95–96, 99–107, 148–149, 219

Valdés, Erick 22–27, 31–32, 34–36, 41–47, 51–52, 185–186
values-driven 146, 153–156, 159–163, 216–217
virus 1–4, 6–8, 48–49, 53, 58, 72, 104
vulnerability x–xi, xvi–xvii, 1, 4, 9, 27–30, 65–67, 70–71, 112–115, 183–187

world 1–9, 70–72, 74–75, 96–97, 99–110, 123–125